DOING BUSINESS IN LATIN AMERICA AND THE CARIBBEAN

Including Mexico
The U.S. Virgin Islands and Puerto Rico
Central America
South America

Lawrence W. Tuller

American Management Association

New York • Atlanta • Boston • Chicago • Kansas City • San Francisco • Washington, D.C.
Brussels • Toronto • Mexico City

*This book is available at a special
discount when ordered in bulk quantities.
For information, contact Special Sales Department,
AMACOM, a division of American Management Association,
135 West 50th Street, New York, NY 10020.*

Library of Congress Cataloging-in-Publication Data

Tuller, Lawrence W.
     Doing business in Latin America and the Caribbean / Lawrence W.
  Tuller.
          p.   cm.
     Includes index.
     ISBN 0-8144-5035-0
     1. Latin America—Commerce.   2. Caribbean Area—Commerce.
  3. Latin America—Economic conditions—1982-   4. Caribbean Area—
  Economic conditions—1945-   I. Title.
  HF3230.5.Z5T85   1993
  330.98—dc20   93-9247
                                                                  CIP

Printing number

10 9 8 7 6 5 4 3 2 1

To
Barbara, Susan, and **Charles**
for putting up with a wayward wayfarer all these years

Table of Contents

Part III
The Caribbean and Central America

Management, and Facilities * Quality-of-Life Considerations *
Foreign Sales Corporations

Preface

My love affair with Latin America began when I stepped across the Mexican border in the early 1950s. I sensed that this was a different world—a marvelous new world of untapped opportunity. My love affair with the Caribbean began shortly thereafter, and continued for thirty years, when I jumped at the chance to move there.

Over the last forty years, the politics, social structure, and economics of Latin America and the Caribbean have radically changed. Yet continued visits have convinced me that the enthusiasm of the region's people and the wealth of its opportunities remain unaltered. If anything, its potential improves with each passing year.

For decades, the people and business communities of Latin America and the Caribbean have taken a beating from corrupt politicians and abusive rulers—not to mention from the U.S. media, banking community, and government leaders. Much of what has been said about the region has been justified, but an equal amount has been undeserved. This book is designed to set the record straight. I also hope to provide companies from the United States, Canada, and around the world with the kind of solid information and encouragement they need to give this burgeoning economic frontier a second chance.

In one very important respect, U.S. and Canadian companies are missing the boat. While getting caught up in the much-touted business potential of Southeast Asia, Eastern Europe, and the former Soviet Union, they are ignoring opportunities in their own backyards. It appears certain that before the end of the 1990s, new, difficult trade barriers will be erected around Europe and East Asia, severely reducing the ability of companies in the Western

Hemisphere to penetrate new markets or even compete in the old. As a consequence, like it or not, we may find that our own hemisphere offers the best, and possibly the only, reasonable opportunities for substantial new trade and investment.

The U.S. Government acknowledged this likelihood when, on the heels of the U.S.–Canada Free Trade Accord, it pushed ahead to bring Mexico into a North American Free Trade Agreement and invited the rest of Latin America and the Caribbean to join an Enterprise for the Americas Initiative.

Hemispheric free trade agreements offer more than opportunities for business exploitation. They also establish a mechanism for turning environmental cleanup and protection into viable business markets while simultaneously forming new political structures to sustain ecologically safe industrial development. By providing a framework for shifting the Latin American/Caribbean development burden to the private sector, free trade agreements offer the means to avoid a repeat of always inept and frequently corrupt government meddling in social programs. And finally, the integration of hemispheric trade provides a far more solid buffer to militant aggressors than the ships, planes, and guns that are becoming too expensive to develop and maintain.

This book reflects not only a favorable personal bias toward our Latin American and Caribbean neighbors but also the firm conviction that by not taking advantage of the many doors being opened, North American companies will, in the not too distant future, find themselves playing second fiddle to strong competitors from across both oceans.

Fifty-one political entities call this region home: thirteen in South America; five in Central America; thirty-two in the Caribbean; and Mexico. English, Spanish, French, Portuguese, Dutch, Chinese, and numerous patois dialects are spoken. Economic variation is just as great, ranging from a per capita GDP low of US$350 to a high of US$23,000 (the United States averages approximately US$21,000).

I have tried to treat all countries fairly, although unavailable data, a few obstreperous government officials, and the wide diversity in political institutions, social structures, and economic conditions make it impossible to be inclusive. The limits of space have necessitated a somewhat condensed treatment of business opportunities and obstacles in certain countries and the complete exclusion of such analyses in others. Those countries or regions that *have* been included are those offering the most promise in the foreseeable future. I extend my apologies to all interested parties—citizens, residents, foreign traders, and investors—whose areas I have been unable to cover in greater detail.

Extensive research has gone into marshalling the background material for this book. The interpretation of that material is based on insights I have gained over forty years of experience in the region. Current and historical data were compiled from hundreds of sources. Where statistical data about a country's demographics and trade are relevant, relatively current, and reliable, they have been included. Unfortunately, data from some countries have not met all three criteria and, in those cases, have been omitted.

Reading this book from cover to cover will give those unfamiliar with Latin America and the Caribbean a broad understanding and insight into the entire region. A cover-to-cover reading is not, however, a prerequisite to gaining valuable information about specific countries. Three easily identifiable sections—Mexico; the Caribbean and Central America; and South America—and chapters devoted to the individual countries offering the greatest opportunities should provide ready access for readers needing definitive information.

Every effort has been made to report completely and accurately, but in as dynamic an environment as Latin America and the Caribbean, inaccuracies inevitably creep in. I take full responsibility for the analyses, comments, and recommendations; they do not reflect the opinions of the publisher or of any other person or entity, except as noted.

The opportunities for building corporate and personal wealth in Latin America and the Caribbean are vast, though there are many roadblocks to overcome. Conducting business in some of the countries in South America can be substantially more difficult and risky than it is in Europe or North America. On the other hand, small U.S. and Canadian companies frequently find friendlier surroundings in the Caribbean or Mexico's maquiladora free trade zones than they do elsewhere. And regardless of the country, the rewards of doing business in the Latin American/Caribbean region are usually far greater and the experience far more invigorating than they are at home. Godspeed!

Lawrence W. Tuller
Berwyn, Pennsylvania

January 1993

Acknowledgments

Without the enthusiastic support of many individuals, private organizations, and government agencies throughout Latin America and the Caribbean, the United States, Canada, and the United Kingdom, as well as those within the United Nations, this book would fall far short of being comprehensive. Several good friends and business associates whose contributions cannot be measured in mere words have passed on. Others have either retired or left the Latin American/Caribbean region. Still others have moved from public-sector organizations to the private sector and vice versa.

I owe much to all these people and their organizations. A mere listing of acknowledgments is insufficient. Yet so many have brought ideas, information, and interpretations to this book that I would be remiss not to acknowledge at least those to whom I am especially indebted for data and insight into specific situations. I list them alphabetically to avoid slighting any one of them.

Bahamas Agricultural and Industrial Corporation; Brazilian Ministry of the Economy; Brazilian-American Chamber of Commerce (Clelia de Toledo Leite Moraes, General Manager); Business Advisory Service, International Finance Corporation; Canadian-Caribbean Business Corporation Office; Caribbean Development Program, Commonwealth of Puerto Rico/Department of State; Caribbean/Latin America Action; Cayman Islands Government Information Services; Central Bank of Nicaragua; Chilean-American Chamber of Commerce in Santiago; Citibank and Chase Manhattan offices throughout the region.

Commission of the European Communities, Directorate-General for Information; Commonwealth Development Corporation; Conference Board of Canada; Costa Rica National Tourist Bureau; Nancy Comache Churnoa; Division of International Trade and Development, Department of Commerce, State of Florida; the Honorable Dante B. Fascell, Chairman of the Committee on Foreign Affairs, U.S. House of Representatives, and Trustee of Caribbean/

Latin America Action; Guatemalan-American Chamber of Commerce; Inter-American Investment Corporation; Jamaica Promotion; Latin America/Caribbean Business Development Center, International Trade Administration.

Ministry of Commerce and Industrial Development, Government of Mexico; Ministry of Development and Commerce, Turks and Caicos Islands: Multilateral Investment Guarantee Agency (Stine Andresen); North American-Chilean Chamber of Commerce (Lester Ziffren, executive director); Overseas Private Investment Corporation; Puerto Rico Economic Development Administration; Howard Thomas Roberts; Hector Rodriguez; Jack Smyth; U.S. Agency for International Development, Bureau for Latin America and the Caribbean; United States Virgin Islands Industrial Development Corporation.

Washington International; Washington Report on Latin America & the Caribbean; Peter Whitney, senior advisor on the Enterprise for the Americas Initiative, U.S. Department of State; the World Bank; and the American Chamber of Commerce offices in Bogotá, Buenos Aires, Caracas, La Paz, Mexico City, Panama, Santo Domingo, and São Paulo.

Nonbank organizations stand in the forefront of innovative financing schemes when traditional sources are reluctant to move forward. Although several have contributed to this book, one stands out as the most specialized in Latin America and the Caribbean: Midland International Trade Services, USA (Bill Fowler, vice-president, and Barbara A. Meyer, assistant treasurer), Midland Montagu.

Personnel from Ernst & Young, one of the world's largest professional organizations, and especially Celia Berenz of the Miami executive office, Latin America, have been very helpful in providing information about tax and related matters throughout the region. I strongly recommend the use of their facilities in Buenos Aires, La Paz, Rio de Janeiro, Santiago, Bogotá, Asunción, Lima, Montevideo, Caracas, and Quito, in South America; San José, San Salvador, Guatemala City, San Pedro Sula, and Panama City, in Central America; Santo Domingo, Nassau, Bridgetown, Grand Cayman, Kingston, Port of Spain, Curaçao, and San Juan in the Caribbean; and Mexico City in Mexico.

A final thank-you must go to a few of my many friends

throughout the region who, over the years, have taught me so much about living, investing, and doing business in their countries: Frank Ailwyn, Marjorie Lopez Brown, Jack James, Jorge Carlos Menucho, Juan Porcio, and Robert H. V. Reisenberg.

I am sorry that space prevents the inclusion of an even more comprehensive list of contributors.

PART I

Regional Overview

Chapter 1

Emerging From the Lost Decade

According to President George Bush at the June 1992 Forum of the Americas conference held in Washington, D.C., the Americas have launched an era of far-reaching and hopeful change. As the President explained, "Barriers to trade and investment are coming down. Go to the financial centers of the world and you'll get the same message: One of the most exciting regions for investment is Latin America." Mr. Bush elaborated, stating that the Americas are on the verge of creating something that humankind has never seen: "a hemisphere wholly free and democratic, with prosperity flowing from open trade."

If that is true, and it certainly seems to be, such an era represents quite a change for Latin America—especially when compared to the decade of the 1980s.

The Lost Decade

Many historians have labeled the 1980s Latin America's "lost decade." A more accurate description might be the "lost quarter-century," referring to the period from 1965 through 1989.

As the 1970s and 1980s saw the United States, Europe, and East Asia enjoy sweeping gains in technology and economic growth, Latin America, and to a lesser extent the Caribbean, sank deeper into the quagmire of political isolationism.

While the United States used foreign capital to fuel the fires of growth, many Latin American countries did the same to support unworkable protectionist policies, only to find by 1982 that isolationism had failed to rejuvenate their economies. Industrial disintegration accelerated. Fiscal irresponsibility ensued. Repayment of enormous debt burdens became impossible. In 1982, Mexico's default on its external debt obligations set off a chain reaction. Financial panic followed throughout the region.

Startled by this unexpected but certainly foreseeable turn of events, the U.S. Government and American banks jointly retreated. Together, they effected a regional quarantine on all but a handful of unobtrusive Caribbean Basin states.

Instead of reversing ineffective internal policies and embarking on the road to economic integration as was the case with President de la Madrid in Mexico, most Latin American leaders, content to blame their woes on the "Yankee imperialists," increased the repression of their populations and continued protectionist trade policies.

As the 1980s wore on, the financial plight of these countries worsened. Currency reserves dried up. World market prices for oil, indigenous produce, minerals, and other traditional exports plummeted. Rapidly growing populations demanded more housing, food, energy, and transport. Environmental degradation eroded rich forests and farmland, forcing increasing numbers of people into urban areas and exacerbating already serious public health problems.

With inflation running rampant (approaching 20,000 percent per year in Argentina and Brazil!), daily currency devaluations, soaring unemployment, and, for all practical purposes, an embargo against foreign imports, Latinos had had enough. In late 1988, democratically elected governments began replacing civilian and military dictatorships. Newly elected leaders embarked on a path toward market economies. With the conflicts of the 1980s resolved or at least muted, a new era of mutual cooperation developed between the United States and Latin America. The lost decade ended.

The Beginning of a New Era

Since 1989, this era of good feeling has driven a series of events that would have been unthinkable in earlier times:

- A restructuring of concessional, nonconcessional, and private external debt for most Latin American and Caribbean countries and a concomitant willingness on the part of the International Monetary Fund (IMF) and World Bank to grant new financial aid
- A free trade agreement between the United States, Canada, and Mexico, leading to an accelerated economic integration of North America
- A call by the President of the United States for the eventual development of a free trade area that would incorporate every country in the Western Hemisphere, from Canada in the north to Argentina and Chile in the south
- A response from Latin American nations expressing their enthusiastic willingness to move rapidly toward free trade with the United States
- Close cooperation between the United States and the Organization of American States (OAS) to restore to power the Haitian populist president Jean-Bertrand Aristide by enforcing a stringent economic embargo against Haiti
- A United States–mediated peace accord in El Salvador
- A resolution by 21 Latin American and Spanish-speaking Caribbean nations to seek economic integration and eventual union

The days of Latin American leaders openly confronting Washington or seeking political advantage at home by denouncing U.S. interventionism, hegemonic whimsies, or economic exploitation are over. On the contrary, most now openly advocate stronger political and economic ties with their northern neighbor.

Concurrently, Washington has shown increased interest in the well-being of Latin American and Caribbean nations. As if by magic, decades of hostility have given way to genuine rapport. Although it is difficult to pinpoint the exact timing or reasons for this turn of events, five closely intertwined factors seem to offer the best explanation:

1. With very few exceptions, the region's nations have made a dramatic switch from military and civilian dictatorships to democratically elected administrations.

2. Virtually all administrations have consciously moved toward conversion from state-controlled to free-market economies.
3. The 1988 Presidential election caused a major shift in Washington's policies toward Latin America. Unilateral, ideologically driven policies have given way to more multilateral, pragmatic responses.
4. The end of the Cold War and the collapse of Communism have nullified the United States' forty-five-year policy of military intervention in Latin America.
5. The globalization of money and trade and the concomitant specter of European and East Asian trading blocs have replaced military aggression with economic aggression, thus forcing a new direction in regional monetary and trade policies.

If the decade of the 1980s was a lost decade for Latin America and the Caribbean, it was also a lost decade for U.S. exports. Official estimates place the total U.S. loss in exports to the region from 1982 to 1988 at a whopping US$100 billion. It wasn't until 1988 that U.S. companies saw the volume of their regional exports climb back to the 1981 level. In other words, the benefits to the United States of having more prosperous southern neighbors can be measured in practical as well as political terms.

Why Latin America and the Caribbean?

Political and economic changes, coupled with a new era of cooperation with the United States, are rapidly changing the complexion of Latin American and Caribbean business opportunities. Massive new consumer and industrial markets, abundant natural resources, and expanded capital markets are now within easy reach of American and Canadian companies. For many, the opening of Latin America and the Caribbean has come as a surprise. For the first time ever, Western Hemisphere markets rival and in many cases surpass those in Europe and East Asia.

The rapidly changing economic climate in our own hemisphere went unnoticed as the American business community remained focused on its strenuous competition with Japanese and Western European firms on their home turf and abroad. Even today, nearly midway through the 1990s, many Americans remain unaware of the enormous potential in their own backyard.

With the barrage of publicity centered on the new European Community and potential openings in Japan, one might ask, "Why bother with Latin American and the Caribbean?" Clearly this region is still in the developing stages when compared to Europe, Japan, and much of East Asia, and is still suffering a hangover from the "lost decade." So why does it merit our attention at this point? The answer, say thousands of U.S. and Canadian companies, lies in the region's enormous and growing potential. Companies of every size and industry are not only opening new export markets but finding enormous direct investment opportunities. The reasons for tapping Latin American and Caribbean markets and resources are as varied as the countries themselves. However, ten primary factors account for the ever-increasing number of companies that are now looking at the region as a serious alternative to Europe, Japan, and East Asia:

1. In the years ahead, hemispheric solidarity will be necessary to compete with the large trade blocs now forming in Europe and East Asia. A strong presence in Latin America and the Caribbean will give American and Canadian companies added clout for negotiating terms and conditions for export sales to Europe and Asia. At the same time it will forestall usurpation of hemispheric trade by European or Asian competitors.

2. Market demand is escalating rapidly for basic and high-tech products, professional and financial services, tourism, health care, environmental products and services, and infrastructure-development equipment and services.

3. The size of consumer markets will exceed those of either Europe or Japan by the year 2000.

4. Both the World Bank and the Organisation for Economic Cooperation and Development (OECD) project a 1993 and 1994 growth in gross domestic product (GDP) for several Latin countries that will equal that of East Asia's most booming economies. And this growth will be taking place against a projected background of

merely stable or modest growth in the twenty-four industrialized members of the OECD.

5. Political and commercial risk is substantially less in the Western Hemisphere than it is in Eastern Europe or the Commonwealth of Independent States (the former Soviet Union).

6. Labor is much less expensive and far more accessible in Latin America than it is in East Asia or Europe.

7. An abundance of natural resources, including oil and hydroelectric power, makes sourcing materials or energy elsewhere unnecessary.

8. Financial aid pouring in from the United States and multilateral agencies gives most countries in the region more than sufficient hard currency reserves to develop their market economies and engage in international trade, making it easier and less costly for small and midsize companies to arrange trade and investment financing.

9. For more adventurous companies, privatization, debt/equity swaps, and emerging stock markets offer creative ways to finance new or expanded facilities.

10. Proximity, plentiful air and sea transport, and a strong pro-American attitude in most countries facilitate easy access to new markets.

Europe and Japan are erecting more stringent external trade barriers. The financing of expansion and trade in these markets and in the United States is becoming more difficult and costly. The competition from European, Japanese, and American multinationals is intensifying. Given these developments, the wisdom and the benefits of looking to our own backyard for new market and growth opportunities could not be clearer.

New Business Opportunities

As economic liberalization takes effect to stamp out abject poverty, narrow the gap between the haves and the have-nots, and resurrect

Table 1-1. GDP Growth in the Six Largest Latin American Markets.

	Increase, 1991	Change, 1981–1991	1991 Exports*	1991 Imports*	Surplus/ Deficit*
Mexico	4.0%	21.9%	$27.17	$37.53	−$10.4
Argentina	4.5	−7.7	11.70	7.40	4.3
Brazil	1.0	18.1	32.00	21.00	11.0
Venezuela	8.5	12.0	15.70	10.50	5.2
Chile	5.0	39.3	8.90	7.30	1.6
Colombia	2.0	46.8	7.54	4.86	2.7

*U.S. billion.
Source: UN Economic Commission for Latin America and the Caribbean.

environmental protection as a social necessity, vast markets are opening for new products as well as for traditional U.S. exports. Untapped natural resources—energy, minerals, raw foodstuffs, aquatic life, and timber—beckon foreign development. Huge pools of low-cost skilled and unskilled labor, hungry for jobs, await foreign factories. And eager trained and trainable management talent thirsts for the opportunity to learn from foreign investors.

The largest markets in the region are Mexico, Argentina, Brazil, Venezuela, Chile, and Colombia. Table 1-1 demonstrates the remarkable resurgence of these economies.

Although the Dominican Republic, Costa Rica, Jamaica, and Panama are much smaller markets, they also hold substantial promise for trade and investment, especially for small companies inexperienced in international trade.

Latin America and the Caribbean truly offer something for everyone. For small companies lacking financial resources or international experience, Puerto Rico, the U.S. Virgin Islands, the eastern Caribbean island states, and Mexico's *maquiladora* free trade zones offer an excellent training ground. Companies in need of minerals, agricultural commodities, aquatic life, low-cost and skilled labor, or access to European Community markets can reap benefits from a direct investment in the Dominican Republic, Jamaica, and several countries in Central America. The offshore financial services and tax-haven benefits of the Cayman Islands, the Turks and Caicos

Islands, and Panama appeal to many businesses. More experienced, perhaps larger companies find extensive resources and burgeoning markets in South America.

With the wide range of opportunities in Latin America and the Caribbean, no company, regardless of industry, size, or resources, should miss out on what could become the opportunity of a lifetime over the next ten years.

The best prospects for exports across the board to virtually all Latin American and Caribbean markets can be loosely grouped by product and service as follows:

- Pollution control and waste-management services and equipment
- Automobiles, trucks, buses, spare parts, and service equipment
- Medical diagnostic and treatment equipment
- Pharmaceuticals and medical supplies
- Telecommunications products and services
- Industrial chemicals
- Computers, peripherals, and software
- Food products and packaging equipment
- Hotel and restaurant supplies and equipment
- Chemical production equipment
- Machine tools and metalworking machinery
- Construction engineering
- Oil and gas field equipment (for oil-producing states only)
- Fashion apparel and accessories

Don't be misled, however. The primary benefits of the Caribbean Basin, Mexico, and several countries in South America to modest-size Canadian and American firms do not come from exporting to these countries. Nor do the greatest benefits accrue from supplying domestic markets with goods and services produced locally, except for companies in the tourist industry.

With the exception of a few of the larger South American countries where good export markets do exist—Argentina, Brazil, Venezuela—the region's major attraction derives from establishing local facilities to exploit plentiful, low-cost labor and natural resources for making components or products to be shipped back to the United States or overseas—in much the same manner that East Asian locations have been used for twenty years.

Despite the region's remarkable recovery and the opening of good relations with the American business community, two thorny issues continue to frustrate unified efforts toward regional development: the failure of government efforts to stem the flow of illegal drugs; and the concurrent failure to topple the Castro regime after thirty years of economic boycotts. Both bear consideration when developing long-term strategic plans for the region. Neither, however, should deter companies from going ahead.

The War on Drugs

It's difficult to assess what impact the U.S. government's war on drugs has had in delaying the development of several South and Central American market economies. Few would argue the necessity of finding a solution to drug trafficking and the ongoing guerrilla warfare and street crime it breeds. Unfortunately, the United States and the countries experiencing the greatest drug-related problems—Colombia, Peru, and Bolivia—take markedly different approaches to solving the problem.

For ten years Washington blamed Latin America for U.S. drug abuse. In their turn, Latin American leaders saw U.S. drug abusers as the root problem. Eventually, it became clear that both sides were being hurt and that solutions had to come from producer as well as user nations. But the acceptance of responsibility has not abated the continuing friction between the United States and the three drug-producing Andean nations.

Accusations have been levied against U.S. policy as being too confrontational, narrow, and confusing to be effective. Public chastisement and threats of withholding foreign aid at one time, and promises of increased financial assistance at another, appear to have done little to change the production or trafficking of illicit drugs. Accusations of economic blackmail only magnify U.S.–Latin American differences.

Basically, the two sides view the solution from different perspectives. Colombian officials see their first objective as one of containment: to harness the violence that drug cartels inflict on government officials and citizens. For the Colombians, a second but equally important goal is to battle the many guerrilla gangs roaming the nation's mountains and valleys. Peru and Bolivia have tried in vain to find alternative means of sustenance for millions of coca-growing peasants. In conflict with these goals, the United States has pushed military intervention as the solution.

The clear lack of U.S. success in stemming the tide of illicit drugs confounds many Latin American leaders. Why continue to pour millions of dollars into overseas projects that reap so little return? Worse, some perceive these apparently inept policies as clouding a hidden agenda. The age-old distrust of Yankee imperialism has not disappeared. Suspicion about what the U.S. Government's real but undeclared objectives in the Andes might be still hampers U.S. efforts and hardens the resolve of local leaders to go their own way.

By 1992, the United States had begun to reassess its war-on-drugs policies. It stopped insisting on crop eradication programs that were costly, ineffective, and damaging to the national interests of Andean nations. The United States also began to finance rural development programs in an effort to lure farmers away from coca production. Nevertheless, U.S. military advisers continue their desultory tactics in the mountains of Peru and Bolivia, much to the chagrin of local leaders.

Regardless of the policies employed by either Andean governments or the United States, drug trafficking continues unabated. Its effect on free-market development in Colombia, Peru, and Bolivia remains pervasive. Foreign direct investment cannot increase in proportion to potential market demand until this problem is brought under control—or at least contained to specific areas. In terms of competing for direct investment dollars and, to a large extent, for export markets, these three countries remain at a severe disadvantage.

The Cuban Dilemma

The second thorn in the side of U.S. regional policy is the apparent indestructibility of Fidel Castro. In 1993 it's hard to visualize how Cuba poses any threat to the United States or anyone else. Nevertheless, even though little has been gained over thirty years, Washington's boycott remains in effect. Several critics from academia charge that the sole reason for administration obstinacy is to boost the ego of a small number of Washington bureaucrats who refuse to acknowledge the end of the Cold War. On the other hand, powerful Cuban émigrés in Florida applaud such steadfast policies.

Nearly every Latin American and Caribbean leader shares the view that political and economic change in Cuba is desirable. However, most consider the position of the United States untenable, dangerous, and probably self-defeating.

Informally, most of these leaders also agree that eventually Castro will either topple or change, and that when that happens, the worst impact on the region would be the presence of another Rumania. All regional political leaders, including most of those in Washington, agree that a Cuban soft landing after Castro is imperative in order to maintain stability in the Caribbean Basin. The main difference of opinion is how to effect that soft landing.

The U.S. Government is steadfast in its policy of remaining politically and economically isolated from Cuba until Castro is deposed—regardless of how long that takes. While this posture may have had validity at one time, thirty years without concrete results seem to make it a bit unrealistic in the mid-1990s.

To add fuel to the fire, the large Cuban population in Miami and southern Florida remains fairly evenly split over the issue. According to a recent *Miami Herald* survey, a large minority favors the regional approach of gradually reintegrating the Cuban economy into the hemispheric community. A slight majority, however, favors the stance taken by Washington, and with a strong lobby going for it, that majority has been successful in rejecting any formal policy change.

Latin American and Caribbean leaders are generally unanimous in their belief that the only safe way to avoid a catastrophic Cuban collapse and a potential replacement who might take a harder line than the aging Castro is to begin opening the Cuban economy to regional trade. They argue that with the demise of the Soviet Union and Communist Eastern Europe—the main suppliers of Cuban oil, food, consumer goods, and industrial products—the time is ripe to open trade doors and gradually ease Cuba back into the global mainstream.

Regardless of the precise timing, it seems evident that the date of Cuba's reentrance into the world community is rapidly approaching. When it does occur, a large, long-suppressed consumer and industrial market will blossom. Foreign companies would be well-advised to begin planning now for eventual competition in this major Caribbean market.

Drug trafficking and Cuba are not the hemisphere's only unresolved issues, but they are certainly the most persistent and resistant to a satisfactory resolution. Issues such as environmental protection, immigration practices, armaments, human rights abuses, political and labor union corruption, and various other matters must eventually be addressed and resolved.

None of these obstacles, however, including the war on drugs and the Cuban issue, are sufficiently serious to deter the tying of the economic knot between the United States, Canada, Latin America, and the Caribbean.

The Permanence Issue

Looking to the future, as any reasonable businessperson must do, several logical questions arise:

- Is the welcome reversal of political fortunes in Latin America and the Caribbean permanent, or is the struggle toward democracy and free markets merely a coincident fallout of the demise of the Cold War and other global events?
- Will the tentative political coalitions in many South and Central American countries be fortified by popular support, or will governments revert to traditional dictatorships as soon as economic reforms begin to pinch?
- Can American, Canadian, and other foreign companies risk investing huge sums in factories, distribution centers, and management organizations without running headlong into a return to the national expropriation policies prevalent in the 1960s and 1970s?
- In other words, is the Latin American and Caribbean shift toward friendly, cooperative relations based on long-term

mutual advantage, or is the current dialogue between Washington, Mexico City, Buenos Aires, Caracas, Brasilia, Bogotá, and Santiago only the short-lived posturing of political expediency?

While answers will be partially based on the determination of current Latin American and Caribbean leaders to fulfill their personal ambitions, the fundamental initiative probably rests with the U.S. Government.

Traditionally, the United States has been a curious bystander to developments in Latin America, keeping its attention and resources focused on more politically expedient areas of the world—Europe, Saudi Arabia, Israel, Russia, Japan, and China. Latin America has taken a backseat primarily because more voters have been interested in events occurring overseas than in those taking place in the lands of their southern neighbors.

But the voter mix is changing. Powerful Mexican voter blocs are forming in Texas, southern California, and Arizona. Central American and Caribbean immigrants to southern Florida have already mustered political clout in Washington. Voters from the northern states have as much to gain from economic integration with Mexico as do Texans or Californians. Whether these voter shifts carry enough weight to influence congressional and administration foreign policy, only time will tell.

It does seem clear, however, that if the United States begins retreating from previously announced hemispheric free trade objectives, if Washington reneges on Latin American debt relief measures, or if the United States becomes more protectionist and unilateral in its economic relations with the region, recent regional recovery gains could be thwarted.

While only U.S. citizens can direct the affairs of their government, Latin American countries also have responsibilities to fulfill. For example, if either Brazil or Argentina were to relinquish its hard-earned gains toward market reform, American voters could easily turn a deaf ear to further trade or financial assistance.

If Mexico, Venezuela, or Chile slipped back to political dictatorships and escalated the level of human abuse, it seems doubtful that U.S. companies would be very eager to rush in. If Colombia, Peru, or Bolivia gave up its struggle against cocaine production and drug trafficking, the United States could easily sever its economic and diplomatic ties to the offending nation.

The rise of military dictatorships in Central America, replete with death squads and marauding guerrilla bands, would surely stifle any additional U.S. support. After all, the reasons for U.S. involvement in Central America in the mid-1990s are far different from what they were a decade earlier.

Clearly, the risk involved in making direct investments in or establishing trading ties with these countries is real. But risk is also present in Europe, Japan, and any other international market. At least in Latin America and the Caribbean, Americans and Canadians are close to home.

New Economic Identities

During the Cold War, 101 nations counted themselves part of the nonaligned movement. The end of U.S.–Soviet rivalry left nothing for these nations to be nonaligned against. The failure of apartheid in South Africa removed the one unifying cry that fractious African nations could rally around. The Persian Gulf conflict rent the Arab League asunder. The collapse of the Warsaw Pact left Eastern European countries without an identifying banner. One Warsaw Pact member, Yugoslavia, fell apart completely. The Czech and Slovak Federal Republic has split in half. The twelve republics of the former Soviet Union are now grappling with the basics of self-definition. Throughout the world, as political and military alliances have come apart, countries have been left with the difficult problem of determining their own national missions.

The outcome has been a transfer of emphasis from ideological and military homogeneity to economic self-interest alliances as the means for shaping global events. Since 1990, the trend has gained such momentum that countries on every continent are scrambling to form new economic alliances, expand existing trading blocs, or revive long-dead cross-border economic agreements. And this is having a major impact on the strategic plans of globally minded companies.

Describing this phenomenon, a Harvard professor of international trade, Robert Z. Lawrence, says, "The new economic alliances taking form and the new economic linkages between countries are changing the very way we look at the world." In a similar vein, Alexander Yeats of the World Bank states, "There's a mentality now that a country has to be a member of a bloc to survive." One might add that a company must position itself to take advantage of these blocs in order to thrive.

Virtually dozens of new economic blocs—alliances, common markets, and free trade areas—address specific aspects of international trade and cooperation aimed at advancing the economic interests of members. Even as this book goes to press, new blocs are coming on line.

In addition to the well-known European Community and the East Asian Economic Group common markets, non–Western Hemisphere alliances include:

European Free Trade Association (EFTA):	Iceland, Norway, Sweden, Finland, Switzerland, Liechtenstein, and Austria
Black Sea Economic Cooperation Accord:	Turkey, Russia, and seven former Soviet republics
Hexagonal Accord:	Italy, Austria, Hungary, the Czech and Slovak Federal Republic, Poland, and Yugoslavia (before its breakup)
Economic Cooperation Organization (nicknamed the "Islamic Common Market"):	Iran, Turkey, Pakistan, five former Soviet Asian republics, and Afghanistan
Caspian Sea Pact:	The five states bordering the world's largest inland lake
Preferential Trade Area of Africa:	An eighteen-member African alliance
Magreb Union:	Algeria, Libya, Mauritania, Morocco, and Tunisia

Not to be outgunned in the alliance game, the nations of the Western Hemisphere have formed or revived no fewer than eleven intraregional alliances, common markets, and free trade areas since 1989. These include:

Northern American Free Trade Agreement (NAFTA): United States, Mexico, and Canada

Enterprise for the Americas Initiative (EAI)

United States-Canada Free Trade Accord (FTA)

Caribbean Basin Initiative (CBI)

Caribbean Common Market (CARICOM)

Caribbean-Canada Free Trade Agreement (CARIBCAN)

Eastern Caribbean Common Market

Central American Common Market (CACM)

Group of Three (G3): Mexico, Venezuela, and Colombia

Southern Cone Common Market (MERCOSUR): Argentina, Brazil, Uruguay, and Paraguay

Andean Pact: Bolivia, Colombia, Ecuador, Peru, and Venezuela

Although economic blocs come in all sizes and shapes, they tend to be grouped under three headings:

1. *Common markets*, such as the European Community, with tariff-free trade between members but common trade barriers for the outside world
2. *Free-trade areas*, such as NAFTA, with duty-free trade between members but with latitude allowing for each member to set its own barriers/incentives with the outside world

3. *Economic alliances,* such as the Caspian Sea Pact, that encourage common projects and planning among member states on issues such as development, the environment, and information links, but with some trade barriers remaining between members

The Impact of Regionalism

Political analysts claim that this forty-year trend toward regionalization reflects a fundamental shift in the perception of the mission of the state. For centuries, nations concentrated on geographic or territorial space as the highest calling of statecraft. After World War II, Japan, Hong Kong, and Singapore proved to the world that a country does not need territorial space to become powerful—that economic space can serve that end even better.

In this new world that values economic power above military might, the number and size of corporations are becoming more important than the size of armies. More government funding will eventually be going into the support of foreign trade than into military budgets.

Such a shifting of worldwide emphasis has as profound an effect on private-sector strategies as on national governments. The strategic importance of positioning a company to take advantage of regional trading blocs cannot be overemphasized. Although it is becoming increasingly difficult to establish new footholds in Europe or Japan, much of the Western Hemisphere—Mexico, Central America, the Caribbean, and South America—is still wide open.

As the economic power of the Western Hemisphere grows, companies firmly positioned within the region's major trading blocs can use that power to negotiate preferential trade with suppliers and customers in the European Community and East Asian groups.

What Are the Risks?

Opening new trade and investment in Latin America is not without risk. As earlier described, the future of democracy and hence of economic reform remains questionable in several countries.

In 1992, Peru's President Alberto Fujimori gave up on a fractious legislature and opted for the army's support as he overthrew the constitution and dismissed congress. Bolivia's President Jaime Paz Zamora still rails against his country's democratic strictures. Venezuelan President Carlos Andres Perez faced first the anger of a Caracas mob disenchanted with hardships brought on by economic reforms, and then a military uprising, but survived both. Brazil continues to languish like a sleepy giant, dispirited and cantankerous, even though significant progress has been made to lower trade barriers and privatize businesses.

If history repeats itself, it is not unlikely that one or more of these countries will fall once again to military or civilian dictators, abandoning any pretense of democratic reform. Obviously, this would have a demoralizing effect on private investment and trade. Critics of the Latin American free-market miracle point to these dangers as reason enough to stay away from the region.

On the other hand, the European Community has its problems as well. By admitting such weak Mediterranean partners as Greece, Portugal, Spain, and (to a lesser extent) Italy, the risk of economic nonconvergence, which could potentially kill the European Monetary Union (the foundation of a Fortress Europe), looms even after several years of experimenting with trade-based market economies. Voter consensus is still lacking for several Treaty of Maastricht provisions.

A blunted Japanese economic steamroller, the floundering economies in Indonesia, the Philippines, and South Korea, and the uncertainties of a post-1997 China—all these cast a long shadow over economic opportunities for foreign traders in East Asia.

When all is said and done, no trading region, regardless of its stage of development, can be considered free of risk. It is hard to argue how the twenty-first century in Latin America and the Caribbean looks any more risky than it does in other regions.

Critics and supporters agree, however, that if companies in the Western Hemisphere are to assume a competitive posture in world trade, it can only come through economic integration of at least the region's major trading partners: the United States, Canada, Mexico, Argentina, Brazil, Venezuela, and Chile, and, to a lesser extent, the Caribbean Basin nations of Jamaica, Trinidad and Tobago, Barbados, the Dominican Republic, Costa Rica, and Panama.

Difficulties Facing Newcomers to Latin America and the Caribbean

In nations as culturally, politically, and economically diverse as those in the Caribbean and Latin America, there are numerous opportunities to be exploited and hurdles to be overcome. Although similarities exist, no two countries are exactly alike. Furthermore, many are experiencing dynamic changes, racing to escape Third World stagnation. Others slumber in the sun, seemingly untouched by twentieth-century dramas.

The fifty-one political entities comprising the region can be loosely grouped into four categories reflecting the level of difficulty newcomers will encounter there, starting with the least difficult: Mexico.

Mexico

A vital neighbor, Mexico plays a unique role as the Latin American member of the North American tripartite trade zone. Business leaders in southern Texas and Monterrey, Mexico, for example, are already functioning as if it were an open-border, homogeneous region. Mexico also presents the fewest cultural and business protocol problems for Americans.

Mexico is rapidly moving to shed the status of developing or Third World nation. Economic development in many industries outshines the rest of the region. The country's legal system and regulatory bodies are being revamped. The Mexican banking system and capital markets have advanced well beyond the less-developed country stage. And the Mexican business climate is more conducive to foreign trade and direct investment than in any other Latin American nation.

The only real negative is that smaller foreign companies will find it difficult to compete and vie for resources with much larger Mexican and multinational firms. On the other hand, the Mexican maquiladora free trade zones offer one of the least difficult entries in the entire region for smaller companies.

The Caribbean Islands

Although very diverse, the Caribbean's thirty-two political entities have many similarities and are home to either a West Indian or Hispanic culture (interspersed, of course, with a variety of European, East Indian, and North American cultural elements).

With the exception of the Mexican maquiladora zones, the Caribbean islands—especially the U.S. Virgin Islands and Puerto Rico—offer small companies, or those unfamiliar with international trade, the least expensive, most easily accessible entrée. Plentiful low-cost labor and a plethora of U.S.-sponsored financing programs provide an excellent base for newcomers.

Central America

Much of Central America is still reeling from the lost decade. Nevertheless, several countries offer both resources and markets that are more difficult to access than the Caribbean islands but certainly less expensive and easier than South America. Political stability, capable skilled labor, and extensive use of free trade zones make Costa Rica an ideal environment for midsize companies with a modicum of experience in international trade. Panama offers a well-oiled offshore financial center, tax-haven status, and one of the largest free trade zones in the region. The five Central American countries have a common Hispanic heritage (mixed with indigenous groups), with Spanish as the common language.

South America

The countries of South America—especially Argentina, Brazil, Chile, Venezuela, and eventually Colombia—offer the largest sophisticated markets for foreign goods in the region. Virtually all types of natural resources as well as abundant labor and management talent are available.

This is a vast continent of thirteen countries with a common Spanish or Portuguese (Brazil) heritage and language. South American markets are by far the most difficult to penetrate for Americans or Canadians and provide the greatest personal challenge. Competition from relatively sophisticated local firms and multinationals is fierce. Although several countries offer abundant opportunities for experienced companies, smaller firms or those with less experience will probably do better elsewhere.

The relevance of these benchmarks is changing rapidly. The growth in regional trade and a commitment by the United States government to a Western Hemisphere free trade zone will, during the next ten years, exert significant influence over the global trading strategies of companies of all sizes and in practically all industries. The next chapter sets the stage for developing meaningful trade and investment programs to compete effectively in a new paradigm of international trade.

Chapter 2

Rearranging the World Economy

Throughout recorded history, national economic pendulums have swung between self-sufficient protectionism and cross-border integration. During much of the twentieth century, protectionism was in favor in the Western Hemisphere. Argentina, Mexico, and several other Latin American countries carried it to extremes, stoically structuring trade barriers through import substitution policies that effectively kept foreign "imperialists" at bay.

The United States also fashioned protectionist tariffs, quotas, and anti-dumping laws as a safety net to shore up inefficient domestic industries. Abroad, Germany, France, Italy, Portugal, Spain, and several other Western European nations protected their trade borders with fierce nationalism zeal. For years, the Communist Soviet bloc and Maoist China used excessive protectionism to virtually wall themselves off from the rest of the world.

Then as the millennium approached, the pendulum swung back. Once again protectionism had proved incapable of keeping bread on the table. Economic revolts led to the collapse of Soviet communism. Even with old-guard Maoists in power, China succumbed to international trade as the only way to feed its huge and growing population. European nations began strenuous efforts to overcome centuries of intraregional antagonism to form an economic union. Latin American dictators gave way to democratically elected administrations intent on converting their countries to market economies. And the United States enhanced its status as the world's leading economic power by opening its borders to foreign investment.

So, in changes felt all over the globe, the pendulum has swung away from protectionism and back to cross-border trade. This time, however, something new has been added. Modern technology has replaced conquering armies and adventurous seafarers. For the first time in recorded history, nations around the world are banding together in economic coalitions in an effort to present a stronger presence in world trade than any one nation could achieve by itself. These economic coalitions, or "fortresses" as some would have it, are forcefully driving the world toward clearly defined trade zones.

It is clear that, to compete in this new world of regional interests, companies must develop strategies to obtain natural resources, labor, and management talent where they are most easily accessible at the lowest cost. They must develop sales tactics to reach burgeoning markets where they have a definitive edge over European and East Asian competitors. That means the Western Hemisphere—Mexico, the Caribbean Basin, and South America—rich in resources, plentiful low-cost labor, and, in some countries, rapidly growing domestic markets.

Furthermore, strategic planning must utilize footholds in those Western Hemisphere nations that already have established trading ties with Europe and Japan, either through intraregional trade pacts or through cultural relationships. Establishing facilities in these locations will cement access to markets across both oceans.

This chapter examines the forces leading to increased regionalism in the Western Hemisphere. It also summarizes the efforts of the U.S. Government and of other governments throughout the hemisphere to develop regional trade policies that will help their businesses compete with European and Japanese companies without destroying the achievements eventually reached in multilateral trade agreements.

The Inexorable Tide of Regionalism

The paradox of protectionist trade zones promoting global interdependence can be partly explained by the steady reduction of trade barriers *within* regions at the same time that import restrictions are raised against the outside world.

By the mid-1980s, 70 percent of all Western European trade was conducted among nations within the region. In East Asia, the proportion hit 31 percent and increased dramatically during the early 1990s. Some estimates place East Asian regional trade at nearly 60 percent by 1993. In North America, more than 41 percent of all foreign trade was regional: United States trade officials estimate that by the end of the 1990s, intrahemispheric trade will be close to 70 percent of its total.

This trend toward trade concentration in a tripolar world has been apparent for some time and seems set to continue for the foreseeable future. It will probably have a greater impact on the competitive strategies of private enterprise than has any other single event in this century.

Regional trade zones permit companies in one member nation to trade in markets of another, unencumbered by stringent tariffs or strict quotas. Restrictive external trade barriers bar companies in nonmember countries from competing at the same price level as trade-zone firms.

Instead of three national powers—the United States, Germany, and Japan—dictating trade policy to less-well-endowed nations, trade accords such as the General Agreement on Tariffs and Trade (GATT)—or its successor—will be negotiated between the three major trade zones: Europe, the Western Hemisphere, and East Asia. Each such coalition will strive for the arrangement that most substantially benefits private enterprise within its member nations.

With common external barriers, companies from nonmember nations that want to export to the zone will be faced with special inspection requirements, costly labeling laws, and other nontariff rules, making it difficult and costly to sell foreign-made products in local markets. International "black markets" will be supported by companies from nonmember nations to circumvent trade-zone barriers.

Farfetched? A fantasy scenario straight out of a futuristic novel? Hardly. These conditions already exist, cloaked in bilateral trade arrangements, voluntary export restraints (VERs), stringent import licensing, and complex anti-dumping laws. Other external barriers are being hotly debated in Europe, North America, and Japan, with ultimate enactment in all three trading blocs a high probability.

Japan started the ball rolling in the 1970s when it captured one American market after another. Granted, subsidies from the

Japanese government, combined with lethal alliances among Japanese trading companies, financial institutions, and manufacturing companies, provided an unbeatable competitive edge. However, without Japan's ability to keep its own borders closed to foreign competition, it seems doubtful that the country's economic expansion could have moved so rapidly and been so successful.

Fortress Europe?

The fear of Japanese competition added impetus to the implementation of European Community (EC) trade practices in 1993. "Europe 1992" opened the borders of the twelve member nations to duty-free movement of goods and services, cross-border personnel travel without visas, export incentives, uniform product standards, a new European currency unit (the ecu), and the possibility of eventual monetary union.

Simultaneously, frightened by visions of American and Japanese superiority in several critical industries, Europe's business tycoons convinced EC bureaucrats to implement a set of external trade barriers, drawing on the most stringent tariffs, quotas, and licensing procedures previously employed by each of the twelve member nations.

It might be a few years before these barriers come to full fruition, but many non-European companies already incorporate retaliatory plans in their business strategies. With 70 percent of exports going to European buyers and the obstinacy of negotiators during the Uruguay round of the GATT talks, evidence abounds that European governments and the business community are determined to protect their turf by any means available.

The eventual merger of the seven-member European Free Trade Association (EFTA)—Austria, Finland, Iceland, Liechtenstein, Norway, Sweden, and Switzerland—with the EC, and the incorporation of Poland, the Czech and Slovak republics, and Hungary, will broaden Fortress Europe to compete on an equal footing with the best that the Japanese or Americans can offer.

With some form of European union looking more promising day by day, Europe's ability to compete in the international arena against the likes of Japan, Inc. and U.S. multinational powerhouses

Table 2-1. Comparative Statistics of Three Trade Giants in 1990 ($US).

	United States	European Community	Japan
Population	251 million	328 million	124 million
GNP at mid-1991 exchange rates	$5,391 billion	$6,010 billion	$2,942 billion
Exports excluding intra-EC trade	$393 billion	$526 billion	$287 billion
Percentage of total foreign exchange reserves	51%	37%	9%
Stock market capitalization as of 8/31/91	$3,350 billion	$2,040 billion	$2,841 billion
Number of companies in Fortune 500	164	129	111
Government debt	$1,796 billion	$2,022 billion	$874 billion
IMF voting power	19.6%	28.9%	6.1%
World Bank voting power	15.1%	29.7%	8.7%

Source: OECD, World Bank, *Fortune, The Economist.*

such as IBM, Ford, and Boeing is beginning to look like a reality to the European business community. Disdaining charges of a Fortress Europe, industrial leaders in Germany, France, Britain, and the rest of the EC are moving toward shoring up their respective international competitive positions.

Multinational corporations from Germany, France, Britain, the Netherlands, and Italy have been formidable international competitors in specific industries for decades. In a unified trade bloc (the EC or the EC and EFTA), European megacompanies could overshadow those from both the United States and Japan as world trade superpowers. Table 2-1 shows some interesting comparisons between the three adversaries.

Fortress East Asia?

On the other side of the world, regional protectionism started later than it did in Europe. Nevertheless, East Asian nations did finally catch the fever. In 1992, the six countries comprising the Association of South East Asian Nations (ASEAN)—Singapore, Indonesia, Brunei, Malaysia, the Philippines, and Thailand—signed an agreement to create a single-market, free-trade area of 320 million consumers by the year 2008. Trade officials announced the decision in response to concerns about the development of trading blocs in Europe and North America.

As a first step, the ASEAN nations agreed to begin phasing in tariff cuts for goods produced in the six member states. On January 1, 1993, tariffs on fifteen items were cut, including pharmaceuticals, rubber products, and vegetable oil—all major exports for the region.

Japanese investment also began shifting from the United States to East Asia. The drop in direct investment of more than 40 percent in 1990 and another 79 percent in 1991 indicates the declining interest of Japanese firms in buying U.S. office towers, hotels, factories, and other businesses. With Japan leading the charge, Taiwan, South Korea, and Hong Kong were soon exporting more to intraregional markets than to the United States.

Although hesitant to discuss the possibility in public, several Japanese and Taiwanese business leaders have privately acknowledged that when Japan, a unified Korea, Taiwan, Hong Kong, and most likely China join forces with ASEAN to form a unified East Asia trading bloc, the same degree of protectionist trade barriers practiced by the European Community and the United States should be expected from East Asia.

Fortress Americas?

The year 1991 will go down in history as the date the President of the United States gave full recognition to the long-term benefits of consolidating strategic trade policies in the Western Hemisphere. It was during that year that President George Bush changed the focus of the United States from that of Cold War antagonist of the Soviet Union to beneficent leader of North and South America.

Although Mr. Bush has said he wants history to identify him as the environmental and the education President, it seems far more likely that twenty years from now school children will be taught that George Bush was the foreign trade President.

The current wave of North American regionalism began under Ronald Reagan with the signing of the U.S.–Canada Free Trade Accord (FTA). Mr. Bush's contribution began with his mid-1990 whistle-stop tour of South America and subsequent meetings with regional leaders in Cartegena, San Antonio, and Washington.

As one Latin country after another threw out outmoded dictators in exchange for democratically elected administrations intent on converting state-controlled economic and banking systems to market economies, U.S. companies were granted a unique opportunity. As if presented on a silver platter, the chance arose to substitute Latin American and Caribbean resources and markets for those being lost in Europe, Japan, and the Middle East.

President Bush seized the moment. In short order Washington executed framework trade agreements with countries throughout the region that would ultimately lead to a trade bloc stretching from the Yukon to Tierra del Fuego. The Enterprise for the Americas Initiative (EAI) was born, followed by the North American Free Trade Agreement (NAFTA) with Mexico and Canada.

The Enterprise for the Americas Initiative (EAI)

Administration trade officials called the EAI a "partnership for economic liberalization and growth" throughout the hemisphere. The idea was to "support policy reforms which either are taking place or which are being called for in various countries and to build a stronger trade and investment relationship in the Western Hemisphere."

Formally, the Enterprise for the Americas Initiative consists of three segments: one for increasing regional trade; one for encouraging regional direct investment; and one for reducing Latin American and Caribbean external debt burdens. Informally, a fourth—protection of the environment—was added but it is really part of the segment for restructuring government debt obligations.

The official position of the Bush administration was presented at the Conference of the Fourth Congress of Economists of Latin America and the Caribbean on November 27, 1991, in Quito, Ecuador, by Peter D. Whitney of the Bureau of Inter-American Affairs, Department of State. It defined four EAI objectives as an extension of U.S. policy.

1. *Expand trade.* "We propose that we begin the process of creating a hemisphere-wide free-trade zone." To achieve this the United States government is committed to four courses of action:

- To continue to work toward a multilateral trading system exemplified by the GATT talks. The EAI is not viewed as a contingency plan in the event GATT or successive multilateral trade negotiations fail to reach satisfactory conclusions. On the contrary, it is designed to complement such agreements.
- To use the North American Free Trade Agreement (NAFTA) as a model for a broader, regional free-trade accord.
- To conclude framework agreements with all regional common markets and individual countries. These agreements specify that the two parties will work toward mutually acceptable accords on certain key issues, including quotas, health and sanitary regulations affecting trade, and intellectual property rights. They do not, however, provide for the immediate reduction of trade barriers.
- To encourage the formation of minicommon markets among groups of Latin American and Caribbean countries that would remove trade barriers among member nations.

2. *Expand investment.* "We suggest measures to create a new flow of capital into the region and to encourage capital which has fled to return." Holdover regulations from protectionist days make starting or acquiring a business in many Latin American and Caribbean countries inordinately complex and present a major stumbling block to building a country's infrastructure and industrial base with private-sector investment. The EAI proposes two new approaches to deal with such impediments:

- An Investment Sector Loan Program from the Inter-American Development Bank (IDB), in conjunction with the

World Bank, to provide technical advice and financial
support for privatization efforts and for the liberalization
of investment laws and rules.
* A Multilateral Investment Fund (MIF) to grant loans directly to the private sector for financing direct investment projects.

3. *Further reduce the debt burden.* "We offer a new approach to
ameliorating the debt situation in the region for countries which
are undertaking economic reform." At the outset, the U.S. Government will forgive a substantial amount of concessional debt owed
the Agency for International Development (AID), the PL-480 food
financing program, the Export-Import Bank of the United States,
and the Commodity Credit Corporation, and then restructure the
remaining amounts over a much longer payback period.

4. *Provide aid for the environment.* "We offer the use of debt
reduction mechanisms to provide funds for the environment." Lo-
cal-currency interest payments on concessional debt will be deposited in local Environmental Funds, administered by a committee
comprised of representatives from the host country, members of
local nongovernmental organizations, and the U.S. Government.

In addition, an Environment for the Americas Board has been
established to review the administration of the program. It consists
of members from the U.S. Treasury, the Department of State, the
Environmental Protection Agency, the Agency for International
Development, the Inter-American Foundation, and representatives
of four private, nongovernmental organizations: the Natural History Museum of Los Angeles, the IWC Resources Corporation, the
World Wildlife Fund, and the Nature Conservancy.

A quick call to the Office of Latin America, U.S. Department
of Commerce, at (202) 377-8475, will provide any information you
need about the current status and projected modifications of the
Enterprise for the Americas Initiative.

The EAI as a Private-Sector Business Incentive

At the August 12, 1991, U.S.–Central American Conference on
Trade and Investment, U.S. Trade Representative Carla Hill clearly

pointed out that the final version of NAFTA sets the tone for structuring other agreements in the region under the Enterprise for the Americas Initiative.

Although Ms. Hill's comments would seem to indicate a long, drawn-out process for the full integration of hemispheric trade, such is not necessarily the case. The U.S.–Canada Free Trade Accord (FTA) was the foundation for NAFTA, yet NAFTA negotiations began a scant three years after the signing of the FTA (which will not be fully implemented until 1996).

The points made by Ms. Hill, however, are worthy of consideration by companies contemplating strategic plans to exploit regional free trade agreements. Here is a summation of her six criteria for free trade pacts with the United States:

1. Any agreement must be compatible with the General Agreement on Tariffs and Trade and therefore must provide a schedule for the elimination of all tariffs on trade that originates in the customs territories of the parties.
2. There must be an analogous phase-out of nontariff barriers such as quotas and anti-dumping laws. (Presumably this includes those enforced by the United States.)
3. Since services are becoming an increasingly important part of international trade, they must be afforded broad-scale market access, the same as goods.
4. Procedures must be in place to guarantee that both the physical property and the intellectual property of foreign investors are protected from expropriation and piracy.
5. Operational and technical arrangements must be amenable to both parties and in place. Such arrangements include rules of origin, public health and safety conditions, environmental safeguards, dispute settlement provisions, and mechanisms for adding future free trade agreements.
6. Provisions must be operative to restrain government action that could undermine the agreement, such as subsidies, state trading, restraints justified on balance-of-payment grounds, and the imposition of foreign exchange restrictions and controls.

No one should expect free trade agreements to remove all

trade barriers. Every country has legitimate reasons for protecting specific industries, natural resources, and social classes. Every country must take responsibility for protecting its borders against aggressors, and therefore ensure that its defense industry is secure and functional. Every country has different cultures to preserve as well as public health and safety priorities. And every country has unique political pressures that must be satisfied.

It is rare indeed to find a group of countries that are so homogenous that cross-border agreements do away with national interests. The European Community is trying to achieve just that with its monetary union and uniform standards. Time may prove that such goals are useless and in fact do more harm than good between nations.

Certainly the U.S. Government has no intention of pressing for homogeneity in the Western Hemisphere. Free trade agreements will not encompass the free movement of people. They will not entail uniform product standards. And it will be a long time before monetary union is achieved, if ever.

The primary objectives in executing free trade agreements between the United States and its Latin American and Caribbean neighbors are: first, to bolster neighboring economies as the best protection of U.S. borders against aggressive foreign actions; and second, to provide increased markets and resources for U.S. companies that will stimulate the U.S. economy. Many corollary benefits follow, but those are the primary goals.

A number of questions inevitably arise that will probably not be answerable for many years:

- Does this hemispheric effort to reduce trade barriers indicate a potential Fortress Americas on a scale commensurate with the European Community and the East Asian Economic Group?
- When the EAI becomes fully implemented, is it likely that stringent external barriers will spring up to make it difficult for East Asian and European countries to trade in the Western Hemisphere?
- Have communications technology and cross-border financial markets negated the advantages sought through GATT as viable international trade objectives?

- Is the world, in fact, running headlong toward a situation in which three economic superpowers control trade in a tripolar world?

There are some who answer an unqualified yes. Such results are certainly possible when one considers the sheer size and economic strength of the major free trade zones, as shown in the following figure.

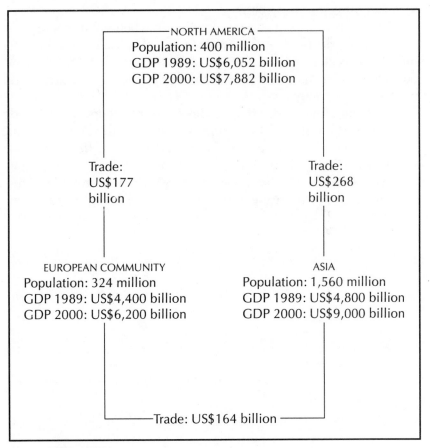

NORTH AMERICA
Population: 400 million
GDP 1989: US$6,052 billion
GDP 2000: US$7,882 billion

Trade:
US$177
billion

Trade:
US$268
billion

EUROPEAN COMMUNITY
Population: 324 million
GDP 1989: US$4,400 billion
GDP 2000: US$6,200 billion

ASIA
Population: 1,560 million
GDP 1989: US$4,800 billion
GDP 2000: US$9,000 billion

Trade: US$164 billion

Source: INTERMATRIX.

On the other hand, the trend of world trade does have a way of swinging like a pendulum, first to cross-border trade, then to protectionism, then back to cross-border trade. Perhaps what we are experiencing in the 1990s is merely one swing toward cross-border trade, with a confusing aberration that looks like protectionism.

Regardless of the direction in which world trade may be heading, companies in the Western Hemisphere need markets and resources from each other's turf more now than ever before. Natural resources are being consumed at an ever-increasing rate. Environmental degradation continues at an alarming pace. Poverty and social injustice are not abating.

The world may be at peace for the time being, but history has shown that worldwide peace tends to be a fleeting luxury. Borders must be protected against aggressive nations and dictators. Defense policies must ensure access to technology, energy resources, and production capacity.

If for no other reason than to defend our borders against trade aggressors and military thugs, it makes sense to develop economic and political ties with our neighbors. That's what the Enterprise for the Americas Initiative is all about. That's what trade agreements achieve. And that's why Western Hemisphere companies must nurture cross-border trade and investment with one another.

PART II
Mexico

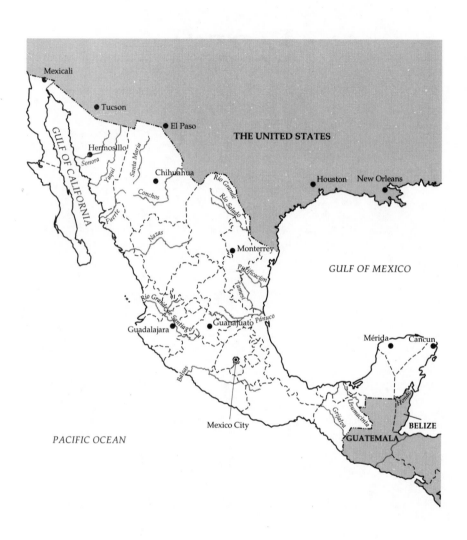

Chapter 3

Trade and Direct Investment

In fact, if not in principle, the United States and Mexico have enjoyed virtual free trade for many years—certainly since long before anyone dreamed of a free trade agreement. More than 85 percent of Mexico's exports entered the United States virtually duty-free—mostly from maquiladora free-trade zones.

Beginning in 1965, 3,000 American-owned factories in maquiladora zones have produced everything from screws to soap, and from electronic assemblies to automobile spare parts. Finished products are shipped to U.S. markets virtually duty free. (They also go to Mexican domestic markets, of course.) Furthermore, according to Glen L. Tilton, a vice-president of Mexico's fifth-largest bank, Banco Internacional SNC, "85 percent of the Fortune companies already have interests in Mexico."

Initially, NAFTA did little either to increase Mexican exports to the United States or to increase U.S. exports to Mexico. Shipments from both maquiladora and nonmaquiladora sites were already subjected to very low U.S. tariffs—a mere 9.5 percent for most items, with a maximum rate of 20 percent. Tariffs on U.S. exports to Mexico averaged 4 percent. These were the lowest average tariffs between two countries in the entire world.

To be sure, U.S. tariffs for certain industries exceeded these averages: a 13 percent tariff on imports of Mexican fruits and vegetables; a 20.5 percent tariff on imports of footwear; a 17 percent tariff on clothing; a 9.3 percent tariff on yarn. Voluntary export restraints (VERs) were also imposed on imports of textiles, a few steel products, and cement. Once the full impact of NAFTA is realized, these barriers will vanish.

The opening of the Mexican–U.S. border has had a major impact on competitive corporate strategies, however, particularly with regard to satellite plant locations. Many U.S. companies have moved branch facilities from East Asia to Mexico, where labor is less expensive, more skilled, and more plentiful (and growing at 4 percent per year).

The open border has also given U.S. companies potential access to Mexico's vast wealth of critical natural resources, not the least of which are oil, platinum, and gold. Concurrently, Mexican companies now enjoy a broader access to huge North American markets.

U.S. firms have enjoyed partial access to Mexico's low-cost labor and natural resources (except oil) for several years through joint ventures, maquiladora free trade zones, and (more recently) newly liberalized foreign ownership laws. At the same time, Mexican firms have benefited from relatively free access to U.S. markets. But the dissolution of remaining trade barriers is stimulating further cross-fertilization of competition. In the end, this will undoubtedly bring more economic benefits to consumers on both sides of the border.

The North American Free Trade Agreement

The primary goal of the North American Free Trade Agreement (NAFTA) is to ensure long-term trade cooperation among the United States, Canada, and Mexico. The NAFTA negotiations, concluded in August 1992 and scheduled to take effect January 1, 1994, will phase out all tariffs and other barriers to trade, services, and investment among the three countries over a fifteen-year period.

One of the most significant features of the agreement is that it will open Mexico's US$146 billion services market to U.S. and Canadian banks, telecommunications, insurance, accounting firms, trucking companies, and other businesses. The agreement will also improve access to Canada's US$285 billion services market.

In addition to setting up the fifteen-year phase-in period, the negotiators carefully incorporated safeguards that will provide sufficient time for import-sensitive industries to adjust to free trade. Among these safeguards are:

- Provisions that permit the temporary reimposition of higher, pre-NAFTA tariff rates, to offer protection against actual or threatened injury from increased imports
- Tough rules of origin and limits on duty drawbacks (rebates) that prohibit foreign encroachment on duty-free exports

The following list summarizes the major NAFTA provisions advocated by U.S. Department of Commerce officials as incentives to the opening of new markets for U.S. and Canadian firms:

- Approximately 65 percent of industrial and agricultural exports to Mexico will be duty free, either immediately or within five years.
- Banks and financial services firms will be permitted to open wholly owned subsidiaries in Mexico. By January 1, 2000, all restrictions, including limits on foreign market share, will be eliminated.
- Insurance firms with existing joint ventures will be able to obtain 100 percent ownership by 1996. New entrants can reach majority ownership by 1998. By the year 2000, all equity and market-share restrictions will be eliminated.
- Telecommunications firms will have nondiscriminatory access to Mexico's US$6 billion telecommunications services and equipment market by July 1995.
- Beginning in 1995, truckers will be able to carry international cargo to Mexican states contiguous to the United States; by the year 2000 they will have cross-border access to all of Mexico.
- Tariffs on vehicles and light trucks were halved immediately. Within five years, duties on 75 percent of parts exported to Mexico will be eliminated. "Trade balancing" and "local content requirements" will be phased out over ten years.
- Only automobiles that contain 62.5 percent North American content will benefit from tariff cuts. The agreement contains tracing requirements to determine the content of major components and subassemblies, such as engines.
- Tariffs on US$250 million worth of textile and apparel exports to Mexico were immediately eliminated; another US$700 mil-

lion will be freed up in six years; all duties will be gone in ten years.

- Import licenses that previously covered 25 percent of the US$3 billion of agricultural exports to Mexico will be phased out.
- Increased access to Mexico's electricity, petrochemical, gas, and energy services and equipment markets took effect immediately.
- There is now a much higher level of protection against the piracy of intellectual property, which is of special concern to companies in high-tech, entertainment, publishing, and consumer goods industries.
- Mexican domestic-content rules that apply to foreign direct investment will be eliminated; Mexican export requirements will be dropped; and U.S. companies operating in Mexico will receive the same treatment as Mexican businesses.

Further information about NAFTA provisions and the status of congressional approval by the three countries can be obtained from a U.S. Department of Commerce Flash Facts Hotline, at (202) 482-4464.

This chapter and Chapter 4 examine opportunities now and in the foreseeable future for foreign companies to export to Mexico's growing markets and to tap the country's vast natural resources and labor pool. With one of the fastest-growing economies in the region, Mexico can no longer be regarded as a poor country cousin knocking on America's door for assistance. The country's phenomenal economic growth over the last four years and the remarkable success of its government's economic reforms have transformed Mexico into a viable, competitive trading partner.

This chapter identifies growing markets for exports from foreign companies and the key elements for planning direct investment strategies to produce goods and services for domestic as well as export markets. In as large and complex an economy as Mexico's—and in the context of intense competition from Mexican, European, East Asian, U.S., and Canadian companies—strategies that focus on an either/or equation—either exports or direct investment—no longer make sense.

Mexican trade and investment opportunities must be viewed jointly, as a combination of marketing, financial, and production tactics. This chapter, therefore, treats trade and direct investment topics as inseparable—two basics that must be considered together in order to gain the competitive edge necessary to succeed in Mexico. Chapter 4 deals with special topics unique to Mexico—maquiladora free trade zone opportunities and the petroleum industry—and concludes with a discussion of the obstacles—infrastructure, labor unions, taxes, and so on—that foreign firms must deal with when doing business in Mexico.

Toward a New Mexico

In 1993, Mexico is nearing the conclusion of its economic success story, with one of the most open economies in the world. Manufactured products have replaced oil as the dominant export, soaring to 56 percent of total exports in 1991 (compared to 14 percent in 1982). The nation's fourfold growth in exports has even exceeded the phenomenal growth rates of Korea (2.8 percent) and Taiwan (2.9 percent) during a comparable period.

Six major economic reforms stimulated this very substantial improvement:

1. The privatization of nearly 1,200 businesses, large and small, from Mexicana and Aeromexico airlines to steel mills, banks, and the national telephone company
2. The revision of foreign investment regulations, permitting foreigners to own up to 100 percent of Mexican firms in a variety of industries
3. The opening of the Mexican stock market to foreign investors
4. A reduction in the average import duty to a level acceptable to foreign suppliers
5. The elimination of import licensing requirements
6. The removal of Mexico from the United States' "watch list" of countries without adequate protection for intellectual property

Despite such bold steps toward economic sanity, some serious financial, economic, environmental, and political issues remain that could restrict further progress. The Mexican government must resolve these issues before the country finally takes it place among the big winners of the 1990s.

On the financial side, more than 75 percent of the new capital flooding Mexico's financial institutions is devoted to portfolio investments, not new factories, and most of this represents repatriated Mexican capital. Portfolio capital has always been hot capital. If investors lose confidence in Mexico's economic reforms or in the stability of the Mexican political system, this capital could move out of the country as rapidly as it moved in.

Economic growth could be thwarted if inflation isn't quickly brought under control. A 17 percent inflation rate is still much too high compared to the 3- to 4-percent rate in the United States. Currency reserves are also threatened. If the 1992 trend that saw imports begin to exceed exports continues for several years, Mexico's hard-earned currency reserves will be drained.

Political reform has barely begun. Many unsavory characteristics of the past are still embedded in the system: corporatism, authoritarianism, corruption, and rigged elections, to mention a few. Human abuses by military and political cronies remain widespread.

Environmental degradation in several sections of the country is causing serious concern on the part of both the Mexican government and world leaders. Mexico City, for example, is so polluted that residents wear gas masks and breathing filters when moving about outside. And air, water, and ground pollution from maquiladora facilities are beginning to contaminate U.S. border cities.

Notwithstanding these unresolved issues, a great many foreign companies view the Mexican consumer base of 92 million as a substantial untapped market and Mexico's natural resources, especially oil, as a virtual gold mine of opportunity. Table 3-1 shows Mexico's key statistics.

Market Demand and Product Trends

Long-standing trading practices and neighborhood proximity give American companies a large competitive edge over European or East Asian firms as suppliers of Mexican import needs. In fact, the United States is far and away Mexico's largest source of both foreign

Table 3-1. Key Economic and Trade Statistics as of 1990 ($US).

GDP	$227.3 billion
GDP per capita	$2,566
Population	92.3 million
Literacy	87.3%
Land area (km)	1.9 million
Exports	$26.8 billion
Imports	$29.8 billion

Source: U.S. Department of Commerce, Ministry of Commerce and Industrial Development, Government of Mexico.

trade and direct investment. Mexico, in turn, is America's third-largest trading partner, behind Canada and Japan and ahead of Germany and the United Kingdom.

Motor vehicle parts and telecommunications equipment account for 85 percent of manufactured imports. Agricultural products—milk and cream, hydrocarbons, cereals, and so on—comprise approximately 16 percent of the total.

Mexican trade officials list the following products and services as the best markets for exports from U.S. companies:

	U.S. Share of Mexican Markets
Chemical production machinery	72%
Machine tools and metalworking equipment	67
Telecommunications equipment	52
Computers and peripherals	36
Industrial chemicals	35
Automotive parts, service, and equipment	27
Electrical power systems	24
Computer software and services	22
Apparel	20
Oil and gas field machinery and services	15

Despite the success of American multinationals in capturing significant market shares in these broad categories, several growing niche markets remain attractive to smaller firms. However, with each passing month the number of new entrants, and hence the amount of competition, increases. Some of the more interesting niche markets are arising from demographic shifts.

Mexican Demographics

The demographic shifts in Mexico's population probably give as much insight into future market size and product demand as any statistical projection. In 1990, out of a total population of 92.3 million, 79 percent, or nearly 73 million people, lived in urban areas. The most populous was Mexico City, with 9.8 million people—8.2 million of them living in the Federal District (similar to the District of Columbia in the United States) in the center of Mexico City.

The trend toward urbanization has been accelerating for thirty years. In 1960, 50 percent of Mexico's citizens lived in cities. This increased to 60 percent in 1975, to 79 percent in 1990, and is projected to grow to 85 percent soon after the year 2000. Mexico's ten most populous states as of the 1990 census were:

	Number of Inhabitants
Mexico	9,800,000
Federal District	8,200,000
Veracruz	6,200,000
Jalisco	5,300,000
Puebla	4,100,000
Guanajuato	4,000,000
Michoacán	3,500,000
Chiapas	3,200,000
Tamaulipas	2,200,000
San Luis Potosí	2,000,000

With nearly 90 percent of the population under 50 years of age, the trend toward urbanization is projected to continue well past the millennium. Since nearly half are under the age of 20 and have a projected life expectancy of 70.4 years, the nation will likely experience a large wave of older people by the year 2030—mostly centered in already overcrowded cities.

With such a high proportion in the under-20 age group, it's not surprising that less than half of the male population is economically active, nor that fewer than one in five women holds a job. However, in line with figures for the rest of the world, the percentage of working Mexican women has been increasing dramatically. In 1970 17.8 percent of the work force was women; in 1990, the figure was 27.1 percent.

A literacy rate of more than 90 percent bespeaks a sound educational system. All children are required to attend primary school. As in other countries, attendance drops for higher education: 44 percent have a secondary education and a mere 5.3 percent go on to higher levels.

Women and Youth

Increasing numbers of working women and young people have created many other new market opportunities. Products needed for these consumer groups include women's wear and accessories (especially for the workplace); toys; household goods (large and small appliances, furniture, wall and floor coverings); women's and children's footwear; athletic and leisure time goods and services; and automobiles and spare parts.

Not all of these goods will be imported. Many small and mid-size Mexican producers are gearing up for the increased demand. It appears doubtful, however, that local manufacturers will be able to meet rapidly growing consumer needs. Imports will, of necessity, fill the gap.

Construction and Peripheral Products

Such demographic trends point to a variety of market opportunities for services and products. Construction of living quarters, shopping centers, roadways, electric power generation and distribution, telecommunications, schools, and hospitals is mushrooming in urban areas. Although some foreign contractors are getting a piece of the primary action, the chief opportunities for foreign companies lie in subcontracting technical specialties.

Local manufacturing of peripheral, state-of-the-art products to equip and service these facilities is minimal. This opens the door to foreign imports of air conditioners and air conditioning systems;

medical supplies, medical diagnostic and treatment equipment; school buses; repair parts and components; paper products and office supplies; office equipment; elevators; and school supplies, furniture, and textbooks.

Tourism

With the stabilization of the economy and the outreach policies of the Salinas administration, tourism has become a flourishing industry. New hotels, resorts, and condominiums in Cancún and Puerto Vallarta supplement the thriving tourist attractions at Acapulco, Mazatlán, La Paz, Cozumel, Hualulco, Los Cabos, Ixtapa-Zihuatanejo, Manzanillo, and Guadalajara. Mexico City attracts more tourists than all the combined resort areas, with arrivals up from 4.2 million in 1985 to 6.4 million in 1990. Tourist expenditures experienced an even greater jump: from US$1.7 billion in 1985 to US$3.4 billion five years later.

Although Mexican firms supply much of the building materials required for new construction, import demand for modern hotel equipment and supplies continues to be substantial. Much of the tourist transport equipment, such as rental cars, taxis, public and hotel buses, railway cars, and short-haul aircraft, as well as corollary spare parts, must also be imported.

Other high-demand imported products include cash registers and hotel computer systems; pleasure boats and ferries; liquor, beer, and wine; dairy products; meat and produce that appeal to American and European tastes; East Asian foods; stand-alone electricity generators; water purification systems; and satellite telecommunications equipment.

Financial Services

The demand for a variety of financial services is just beginning to reach fever pitch as incomes rise and the number of entrepreneurial businesses increase. Quality insurance—both the underwriting of policies and brokerage services—is in very short supply. There is a high demand for all types of insurance common in developed countries: life, health, product liability, casualty, automobile, and business interruption. Although a few international insurance companies have made an entrance, there is plenty of room for competitive policies and aggressive marketing.

The dramatic growth in the Mexico City Stock Exchange has brought increased demand for investor services. Although investment choices in listed companies and the variety of investment instruments are still very narrow compared to developed exchanges, the public demand for investment advice and brokerage services is skyrocketing. Along with the increasing interest in investment opportunities, the public accounting and financial planning fields are beginning to open to foreign participation.

Environmental Products and Services

The environmental field, commonly referred to as envibusiness or ecobusiness, probably offers the greatest opportunity for foreign imports. The huge concentration of people and industry in greater Mexico City living and working without adequate environmental or public health safeguards has created one of the most polluted cities in the world. Vehicle fumes, combined with industrial smoke, render the air virtually unbreathable. Untreated sewage seeps into city water supplies. The city's noise level is deafening. Environmentally safe waste disposal—of both solid waste and hazardous waste—has been seriously neglected. Conditions in Mexico's other two industrial centers, Guadalajara and Monterrey, aren't much better.

The Mexican government is just beginning to recognize the need to clean up these environmental hazards and enforce ecologically safe policies as a prelude to sustained economic growth. As a start, it has stopped issuing business licenses in all three cities and is redirecting development toward regions that can better absorb the effects of industrialization.

In addition to redirecting new businesses away from polluted cities, current policy prohibits foreign corporations from owning 100 percent of companies established in Guadalajara and Monterrey without special permission—which is difficult to obtain. As an alternative, the government has set up industrial parks with sufficient water supplies and acreage to hold new industries. The most prominent ones are located in: Puebla, Puebla; Querétaro, Querétaro; Guanajuato, Guanajuato; Pachuca, Hildago; Hermosillo, Sonora; and Ciudad Acuña, Coahuila.

Vociferous objections from American activists, coupled with Mexico's desire to hasten full implementation of the free trade agreement, have combined to force the Salinas administration into actions aimed at shutting down environmentally dangerous facilities in the maquiladora areas. Enforcement efforts will inevitably focus on doing the same in Mexico City and elsewhere.

Such critical environmental and public health issues offer a vast untapped reservoir of demand for products and services, most of which must initially be furnished by foreign firms. Capital expenditure for pollution control equipment is expected to grow at 20 percent a year for at least the next ten years. The government plans to spend more than US$100 million in the next few years in Mexico City alone. U.S. firms already command the lion's share of this market. Smaller exporters should not be deterred, however; the market is large enough to accommodate many new entrants.

To date, prices have held at reasonably high levels. However, trade officials on both sides of the border predict that the market for larger types of equipment and systems will begin to mature by the end of the decade. If that happens, expect slimmer margins on new products but a concurrent burgeoning demand for replacement components and parts.

Among the types of equipment, products, and services currently in high demand are the following:

- *Air pollution control equipment:* Vehicle emission controls, lead-free gasoline and alternative fuels, air filtration systems for commercial and industrial facilities, residential air filters
- *Municipal waste water treatment:* Chemicals, filtration equipment, water storage facilities, sewer pipe and fixtures, pumps and valves
- *Water purification:* Commercial and residential filtration systems, pumps and valves, organic and inorganic water treatment processes, chemicals, water transport vehicles, pipe
- *Noise abatement:* Sound attenuation materials, industrial earmuffs, dampers, vehicle mufflers
- *Industrial waste treatment:* Detoxification chemicals and facili-

ties, hazardous waste transport, haulage of trash to steam
and other waste conversion plants, ash detoxification systems

In addition to pollution control equipment, good markets are
beginning to open for so-called second-tier envibusiness products,
such as environmentally safe packaging materials and equipment;
resource recovery and recycling equipment; private water utilities;
and sanitation equipment and supplies for hospitals, prisons, low-
income housing, and schools.

U.S. companies contemplating direct investments in virtually
any Mexican industry should be aware that new environmental
and safety regulations have become much stricter than in the past.
While lax enforcement tends to diminish the government's efforts
to clean up and safeguard both public health and the ecology,
foreign companies entering Mexican markets should develop strategies that recognize the likelihood of new enforcement measures
more stringent than those currently applied in the United States.
Although difficult to estimate, the added costs of compliance must
be weighed against market and resource advantages.

Shipping

Tampico and Veracruz, both on the Gulf of Mexico, serve as
the major ports of entry, although the government is building other
ports on the Gulf and the Pacific coasts. The nation has 36,000 miles
of railroad, providing relatively convenient inland transport. Well-
maintained highways connect major cities served by several private-sector trucking companies. Shipping to rural areas is still difficult, although most areas can be reached eventually by overland
freight carriers.

Distributors and Agents

Selling into Mexican markets, or any Latin American market
for that matter, is never easy. It can be especially treacherous for
American companies. Whether using in-house sales personnel or
manufacturer's representatives and sales agents, U.S. companies
will find that the business protocol, labor laws, and contractual
arrangements are entirely different from those they may be accus-

tomed to at home. Language, custom, and the absence of legally enforceable deterrents to under-the-table deals have sent more than one U.S. company scurrying for shelter.

Smaller companies and those new to international trade—whether exporting to Mexico or setting up a local facility to tap domestic markets—will usually do better with local agents (or partners) than with in-house sales personnel. There are two advantages to distributors or agents: the avoidance of unfathomable labor laws and the benefit of a knowledgeable local partner to pave the way with strange, frequently obstreperous customers and bureaucrats. These pluses usually outweigh the control advantages of using sales employees.

Going this route, however, poses another series of hurdles, some legal, some commercial. Take distributors and agents, for instance. In the United States, distributors are generally understood to be independent entities (corporation or partnership) or persons authorized to sell goods provided by the supplier within a designated territory. In Mexico, distributing functions are frequently intermingled with other business activities involving customers. Territories are ill-defined. Commercial and industrial customers tend to be fairly large, with facilities and market coverage throughout the country. This contrasts strongly with U.S. markets, which are more commonly characterized by many small, local businesses.

Furthermore, U.S. distributors sell to customers on their own account, earning income on their markup over the cost of purchasing the goods from a manufacturer. In Mexico, distributors may not only buy and stock imported goods for resale, but may also have retail outlets or sell consigned goods on commission.

Third, U.S. distributors generally have the authority to act on behalf of a manufacturer without special authorization, bear all commercial risks, and sell goods in original packaging. None of these conditions is a given in Mexico, or in any Latin American country for that matter. Almost without exception, exporters assume all commercial risk, distributors none. Packaging may be altered to comply with local laws or fit specialized niche markets. And few U.S. companies will grant carte blanche authority to act on their behalf in foreign markets.

The practices of sales agents are equally equivocal. Agents may sell on commission, stock goods and sell them for their own account, own or have an interest in retail outlets or industrial or commercial businesses that buy the goods, or even reexport a manufacturer's products to other Latin American, European, or Asian countries.

Agency and distributor contracts are helpful in defining relationships but are frequently unenforceable. Remedies are generally not provided for. In addition, not many U.S. companies, especially small companies, want to litigate in Mexico.

The best approach is a joint-venture agreement with a Mexican partner to handle sales and distribution. This should be arranged in person, in Mexico, with the assistance of Mexican legal counsel. Let the Mexican partner manage bureaucratic relationships. Let the Mexican partner be a party to advertising campaigns. And by all means, structure the arrangement to let the Mexican partner share in joint-venture profits. It's not a surefire solution for getting products to market, but it is usually satisfactory.

These same principles apply to selling and distribution channels in most other Latin American markets. Therefore, once established in Mexico, expansion to other countries becomes much easier.

Direct Investment Opportunities

Many foreign companies, especially those from the United States, now view a branch operation in Mexico as a viable alternative to facilities in Taiwan, South Korea, Hong Kong, and Southeast Asia, where costs are rising. From a consumer base of ninety-two million people they also see enormous pent-up demand ready to burst the floodgates for virtually any type of product or service. Furthermore, relaxed foreign investment laws make an abundance of scarce natural resources ripe for the picking.

Mexico's liberalized foreign-ownership rules are attracting the attention of companies around the world. In 1991, foreign companies made US$8.3 billion in direct investments and another US$5 billion in portfolio investments. U.S. companies accounted for more than one third of the total; German, Japanese, and British companies followed, in that order.

Although smaller companies are finding lucrative niche markets in tourism, infrastructure construction, financial services (especially consulting and insurance), and consumer products, the bulk of the direct investment to date, outside of the maquiladora area, has come from large multinationals. Needless to say, this creates fierce competition for market share, especially in high-value manufactured products such as machinery, equipment, and vehicles.

About two thirds of total foreign direct investment has been in manufacturing; approximately one fifth went to the service sector; the balance has been split among mining, agriculture, aquaculture, banking, and tourism.

Part of the government's program for attracting foreign capital was the formation of the Mexican Board of Investment. Its mandate—to implement a worldwide promotion program—was directed at encouraging foreign companies to take a second look at Mexico's potential. Its initial thrust was aimed at U.S. companies. Subsequent efforts focused on Canada, Germany, and Japan.

According to officials from Bancomext (Banco Nacional de Comercio Exterior), the government-owned national foreign trade bank, "Mexico has made a definitive, permanent invitation to foreign investors interested in ownership and control of Mexican-based operations."

Although more than two thirds of Mexico's industries are open to 100-percent foreign ownership, certain sectors remain restricted. Rules for specific companies continue to undergo revisions, but the current permissible foreign ownership percentages in restricted industries are as follows:

> *Carbon, phosphoric rock, minerals containing iron, and iron:*   34 percent
>
> *Banks:*   40 percent
>
> *Auto parts and accessories and secondary petrochemicals:*   40 percent
>
> *Telecommunications, fisheries, rental agencies, extraction of other minerals, firearms, explosives, and fireworks:*   49 percent

More than 3,000 American companies have already taken advantage of direct investment opportunities. Most are centered in maquiladora areas along the U.S. border (see Chapter 4). Others dot the Mexican landscape from the Caribbean to the Pacific and from Texas to Guatemala.

They run the gamut from such giants as Westinghouse, Johnson & Johnson, G.E. Aerospace, ALCOA, and Rohm & Haas to small, privately owned firms like JLC Electronics, Pennsylvania Diapers, and Red-Glow Lighting. Here is a sampling of the types of products Mexican subsidiaries of these firms produce, mostly for export back to the United States but also for domestic markets:

- Industrial textiles
- Electronic aerospace components
- Bedspreads
- Resistors
- Electric transformers
- Hospital gowns
- Auto parts
- Cable TV lines
- Medical supplies
- Electromagnetics

- Acrylic sheets
- Hydraulic springs
- Heating elements
- Cosmetic containers
- Lighting fixtures
- Dental products
- Wire harnesses
- Work clothes
- Electrical outlets
- Plastic toys

Japanese companies are also making inroads. Nissan Motor Company of Tokyo recently built a second Mexican automobile factory and expanded its Mexican engine facility to the tune of US$1 billion. Kyoto News Service reported that the company plans to build 50,000 cars and 50,000 vans a year in its new plants. In addition, the Japanese government committed nearly US$500 million for a water purification facility.

Major District Investment Benefits

Mexico has four major attractions for direct investment:

1. A potential consumer market of 92 million people
2. Abundant energy, mineral, and agricultural resources
3. Low-cost labor (about one half the cost of labor in Taiwan,

South Korea, Singapore, and Hong Kong; about one tenth
the average U.S. wage rate)
4. A 2,000-mile border with the United States

European and East Asian companies can add a fifth advantage:
Mexico provides them with a strategic position to qualify for coun-
try-of-origin products under free trade agreement rules with the
United States and other countries of the Western Hemisphere.

Other features of the Mexican economy also encourage foreign investment:

• *Deregulation and procedural simplification* opened a broad range
of direct investment forms: joint ventures, full business acquisitions,
trusts, "pyramided" share ownership, neutral stock options, and
venture capital funds, to mention a few.

• *Economic restructuring efforts* have returned the country to
real growth of 3 to 4 percent a year—a sure sign that domestic
markets are picking up. Nonpetroleum export trade is also burgeoning, principally in automotive assemblies and components,
electronics, computers, appliances, plastics and plastic products,
building materials (including PVC products), agriculture and aquaculture products, and precious and nonprecious metals. Mexican
exports have quadrupled over the last ten years, and now approach
US$20 billion a year. Large American manufacturers and engi-
neering contractors have played a vital role in this growth, investing
more than US$26 billion in Mexican facilities and infrastructure
projects.

• *An abundant supply of skilled labor,* which far outstrips that
available in many East Asian developing countries, provides a
broad base for manufacturing expansion. The quality and training
of the work force improves each year. Nearly one third of Mexico's
92 million people are enrolled in some form of educational program.
Worker-training programs have doubled over the last ten years.
Multinational companies such as Ford and Sony consistently acknowledge their Mexican plants with quality-of-workmanship
awards.

• *Labor productivity* continues to improve. While U.S. annual
gains in real productivity have leveled out at about 1 percent since

the mid-1970s, Mexican productivity has increased 2.5 times this rate. During the 1980s, accumulated productivity increases totaled 26 percent, a significant achievement by any count.

• *Professionals* are beefing up their expertise and knowledge of international trade. Law firms have become conversant with U.S. customs and tax laws. Local public accounting firms are expanding services to foreign firms. Even the Mexican offices of international consulting firms now project a professional air.

The Advertising Infrastructure

As developing countries go, Mexico boasts one of the most sophisticated advertising infrastructures in the Latin American/Caribbean region. Effective advertising focuses mainly on newspapers, magazines of all types, and radio. Television attracts a lesser audience.

Four major daily newspapers claim a circulation of 10.2 million readers. Although many rural areas and small towns have their own local papers, the four national dailies are: *Excelsior, El Universal, El Sol de Mexico,* and *La Prensa.* By American standards newspaper advertisements are inexpensive and, for financial services and consumer goods and services, reach the widest audience.

Although Mexico certainly doesn't have the sheer number of magazines that flood the U.S. and Canadian markets, a variety of publications address middle- and upper-income families. These provide an excellent means to reach consumers with disposable incomes, especially in the larger cities and resort areas.

Resort areas, of course, produce their own publications aimed at local consumers and tourists, just as other tourist regions do. Trade magazines in virtually every industry offer exposure to industrial and commercial markets. Many larger firms and banks advertise in American news and trade publications subscribed to by Mexican consumers and businesses.

Radio advertising also reaches a wide market, especially in rural states. The government has licensed more than 900 radio stations.

Television advertising doesn't come close to the saturation levels it reaches on U.S. channels, yet for certain highly competitive consumer products it can be effective. The government reports that

55 percent of Mexican households own TV sets. More than 30 percent of the nation's 8 million sets are located in Mexico City households. Of seven television channels, the two state-owned channels—Televisa and Imevision—broadcast over the widest area.

Mexico City, Guadalajara, and Monterrey each have many qualified advertising agencies to choose from. U.S. agencies represent most of the large firms. Market research firms proliferate in the larger cities. Anyone interested in a complete listing can get one free of charge from the Commerce Department's Mexico Division.

Obtaining Visas

The Mexican government has established several levels of entrance permits, depending on a person's reason for entering the country and the type of activity to be pursued there. Most business consultations not involving the execution of contracts or remuneration from a Mexican company can be conducted by foreign nationals carrying a simple *tourist card*.

This is the same permit granted tourists and other short-term visitors. It can be obtained either from a foreign office of the Mexican Consulate or from any major international airline serving Mexico. It can also be purchased for a small fee at any Mexican port of entry. Proof of citizenship is required and can be accomplished with a passport, birth certificate, voter's registration card, or official naturalization letter. Tourist cards remain valid for a maximum of 180 days.

Work permits are another matter entirely. Persons wishing to work in Mexico and to receive compensation must carry a *visitor visa*. It must be stamped upon entrance and remains valid for a designated time period, depending on the work to be performed. A visitor visa is also required in order to execute Mexican contracts.

A special *counselor visa* must be obtained by consultants or others whose intent is to sell advice to Mexican companies. This special visa must also be carried when conducting or attending Mexican shareholder meetings. Persons wishing to establish a permanent residence in Mexico must get a standard *immigration visa*.

Applications for all types of visas can be filed with any Mexican consulate office in the United States, Canada, and many other countries.

Financing Trade and Investment

A restructured financial system is now capable of handling trade finance and investment funding throughout the country, including the maquiladora zones. The banking industry has been materially strengthened through privatizations and closures. The total number of financial institutions declined from sixty to eighteen. Several Mexican banks are now better capitalized than their U.S. counterparts.

Capital is flowing in, both from Mexicans who invested abroad during the tumultuous years of the 1970s and 1980s and from foreigners investing in Mexican securities and in operating businesses. Brokerage houses, fund management, and leasing operations have all grown significantly. Many larger houses now offer full-service capabilities.

Mexico's banking and financial systems are far and away the most fully developed of any in the Latin America/Caribbean region. Although still lacking the sophistication and breadth characteristic of developed countries, the Mexican capital market and banks offer very real alternatives for financing both trade and direct investment.

Multilateral and Bilateral Financing Assistance

The nation's progress toward economic reform has opened the door to a variety of external financing sources. Subsequent to Mexico's external debt restructuring in line with the Brady Plan, the Inter-American Development Bank stepped forward with a substantial line of credit to help local companies increase exports.

Mexico also qualifies for assistance from the Inter-American Investment Corporation, or IIC. The IIC, in which Mexico holds a 7.5 percent equity interest, provides direct loans and guarantees to local development banks and commercial banks who then finance direct investments by small and midsize businesses, both domestic and foreign.

The Overseas Private Investment Corporation (OPIC), Eximbank, the European Investment Bank, and a variety of Japanese, Taiwanese, and South Korean government export agencies also actively participate in funding Mexican projects and trade. However, most companies seeking trade finance start with the banking system.

Mexican Banks

Since most of the larger U.S. banks are still reluctant to make loans in Latin America (including Mexico), newly privatized Mexican banks offer much better possibilities.

American companies that sink trade or investment roots either in Mexico or elsewhere in the Latin American/Caribbean region usually find that a Mexican bank tends to open more doors than any U.S. bank except Citibank and Chase Manhattan. Despite the many market-economy reforms throughout the region, pockets of hard-core nationalism and protectionism are still in evidence, and probably will be for several years.

As bank ownership has passed to the private sector, each has developed its own niche strategy for exploiting foreign trade markets, especially from U.S. companies. Banco Internacional, for instance—which operates a thriving branch in San Antonio and now has branches in Miami and Los Angeles—has decided to concentrate on U.S. exporting companies. Bank officials boast of financing instruments specifically designed to "take risk away from selling products into Mexico." They also claim that interest charges are competitive with those charged by U.S. banks for comparable transactions.

Banca Serfin adopted a different strategy. Its mission is to assist foreign companies finance direct investments in Mexican businesses, either in maquila zones or elsewhere. It recently set up a New York-based asset funding division to compete with major U.S. banks in financing American businesses expanding to Latin America and the Caribbean.

Banca Serfin has also established a "business immersion in

Mexico" consulting service for small and midsize foreign firms trying to get started in Mexico. These consulting services include:

- Mexican fact-finding tours with Serfin executives
- A feasibility study to select the appropriate location
- Assessments of labor availability and skills
- Referrals to legal, government, customs, and other agencies and professionals
- Consultation on alternative forms of financing the investment and operation

The bank charges from US$4,500 to US$7,000 for a typical two-month study that requires 150 man-hours from bank personnel.

A third approach was taken by Bancomer, which restructured itself along the lines of European universal banks to permit specialization in markets where it already had an established position: retail banking and Mexican capital markets.

Further information about Mexican bank financing can be obtained from the following U.S. offices directly:

Banca Serfin
88 Pine Street, Wall Street
  Plaza
New York, NY 10005
Phone: (212) 635-2320

Banco Mexicano Somex
63 Wall Street, 28th Floor
New York, NY 10005
Phone: (212) 425-2070

Banco Internacional
45 Broadway, 16th Floor
New York, NY 10006
Phone: (212) 480-0111

Banco Nacional de Mexico
375 Park Avenue, 12th
  Floor
New York, NY 10152
Phone: (212) 702-2588

Bancomer
444 South Flower Street,
  Suite 100
Los Angeles, CA 90071
Phone: (213) 489-7245

Multibanco Comermex
1 Exchange Plaza, 16th
  Floor
New York, NY 10006
Phone: (212) 701-0100

U.S. Financing Assistance

Many smaller U.S. companies prefer to use home-country banks, with or without assistance from government agencies. In the western United States and along the Mexican border, several U.S. regional banks actively encourage Mexican trade finance.

If a bank won't handle the transaction, Eximbank—the Export-Import Bank of the United States—generally will. Although Eximbank does not yet offer special programs for Mexican exports, it should be just a matter of time before it does. On the other hand, Mexican trade already receives a degree of preferential treatment. Even though such favoritism is vehemently disavowed by Eximbank officials, buyer and supplier credits and guarantees are generally easier to come by for sales to Mexican buyers than for other, less politically important trading partners.

Small businesses might try the Small Business Administration (SBA), although current funding restrictions are constraining the SBA's modest exporting assistance programs. Some offices are more active than others, however, so it can't hurt to try.

Venture Capital Funds

Nothing symbolizes the cutting edge of a country's developing financial system more than pioneer venture capitalists. Several U.S. funds have been established specifically to finance direct investment in Mexico by small and midsize firms. Many are located along the U.S.–Mexican border. Others find New York more to their liking. Here are three of the more adventurous pioneers:

1. *InterAmerican Holdings Co. (IAH), San Diego.* IAH specializes in small and midsize companies with labor-intensive processes that could increase profitability with a branch operation in Mexico. Raul Gomez, a partner in the firm, acknowledges that high-leverage deals don't fly in Mexico. As he states, "You can't get industrial revenue bonds like you might in West Virginia, and you can't get a 10-to-1 debt/equity ratio. It's 2-to-1 if you're lucky."

2. *Ventana Equity Expansion Partnership, San Diego.* This US$50-million venture fund has as its major partners Banco Nacional de Mexico (Banamex) and Nacional Financiera (Nafinsa), the Mexican development bank.

3. *Warwick Group, New York and Phoenix.* Executive Director

Tim Sprague says that the group's AmeriMex Fund, capitalized at US$20 million to US$50 million, helps "healthy U.S. small-to-medium-size companies with a large (greater than 25 percent) labor content in their cost of sales move some of their production off-shore." The fund specializes in companies in the garment and sporting goods manufacturing industries but will consider other applicants.

Chapter 4

Maquiladoras, Oil, and Headaches

In-bond, free trade zones along the nearly 2,000-mile stretch of the Mexican–U.S. border continue to be the most popular regions for U.S.–owned production facilities inside Mexico. This so-called maquiladora region is home to more than 3,000 foreign-owned assembly, processing, and manufacturing plants.

Maquila was the corn a farmer gave to a miller for grinding his crop: a toll for doing business in his mill. Today, companies pay a similar toll to industrial park management firms for assistance in conducting their businesses in Mexico's duty-free, maquiladora zones.

Nearly thirty years ago the Mexican government set up specific in-bond zones similar to the U.S. version of foreign trade zones. Within these zones, foreign companies can operate facilities called maquiladoras: shared-production or twin-plant manufacturing facilities similar to those operating in Puerto Rico and Caribbean Basin Initiative countries. Materials and products can be moved in and out of the zones nearly duty free.

Although labor-intensive assembly and light manufacturing remain the most popular types of production facility, many U.S. firms have expanded into agribusiness, telecommunications, chemical processing, capital goods manufacturing, and even service industries.

A maquiladora zone offers the same amenities as all industrial parks: plants built to client specifications as well as maintenance of roads, sewers, and power lines. For a fee, however, maquiladoras go one step further. They provide employee services, including recruiting workers, training them, and preparing payrolls. Management personnel employed by these Mexican versions of free trade zones will also handle relationships with the local community, government agencies, and tax collectors, and organize employee health care programs for foreign branches.

Subsidiaries of large and small U.S.–based companies make up the majority of maquiladora plants, but European and East Asian companies are also represented. Maquiladora facilities directly employ more than 500,000 Mexican workers. Another million or so work in peripheral and support businesses.

Although Mexican maquiladora workers earn wages and benefits that average US$1.85 per hour, cheap labor is only one reason for a Mexican facility. According to numerous surveys conducted by trade groups and the U.S. Department of Commerce, many U.S. companies set up shop in maquiladora zones because of lower *total* costs of production—including facilities, freight, and supervision as well as labor costs—than can be achieved in the United States. This enables them to be more competitive with suppliers in other low-cost parts of the world, notably East Asia. As one report stated, today's competition is "no longer just the rival down the street; it's the lower-cost company halfway around the world in Taiwan or South Korea."

Twin plant facilities mean big business to the Mexican economy, bringing in more than US$3 billion a year in foreign exchange. Since 1988, growth in the maquiladora industry has averaged nearly 30 percent per year.

The mechanics of operating maquiladoras are quite simple:

1. A foreign company acquires or builds a production facility in a maquiladora zone. Mexican law allows 100 percent foreign ownership.
2. The company then ships raw materials or components to the plant, either from the United States, Canada, or another country, duty free, or acquires materials within Mexico.
3. Materials and parts are then processed into finished or semi-finished products and shipped back to the United States.
4. U.S. duty is paid only on value added in Mexico. Similar provisions apply when shipping to other countries.

The maquiladora program is about as close to free trade as

possible without a formal government-to-government agreement. This fact may partially explain why the U.S. business community has lacked universal enthusiasm for a formal free trade accord.

In addition to permitting 100 percent foreign ownership of the facility, the Mexican government provides three incentives for companies to locate in maquiladora zones:

1. Duty-free entry of machinery and equipment to be used in the production of export goods
2. No restrictions on the type of goods produced for export
3. Authorization to lease land and facilities under a thirty-year beneficial trust arrangement

Maquiladora Sales and Purchases Within Mexico

In addition to producing finished or semifinished products for export, maquiladoras assemble and process goods for Mexican consumption.

A little-publicized Mexican program—the Program for Temporary Import for Export (PITEX)—permits foreign companies to combine domestic and export sales in one facility. Maquiladora firms have three choices:

1. Spin off a new company within the zone to produce exclusively for the Mexican market.
2. Expand production in an existing maquiladora facility and sell the additional products within Mexico.
3. Switch an entire plant over to the PITEX program.

In each case, the same maquiladora benefits accrue.

Maquiladoras also benefit from a reverse condition. Original supporters of the program argued that duty-free zones would not only provide jobs for Mexican laborers but would create an additional market for Mexican manufactured goods and materials. Thirty years later this prediction came true.

Toilet paper, soap, cardboard boxes, and other nonproduction materials have always been purchased locally. Now an American Chamber of Commerce survey shows a significant rise in the local supply of materials and components used in the production process, to nearly 10 percent of all maquiladora purchases. At substantially lower prices than similar U.S. goods imported from the United States, and delivery times significantly better, it's not surprising that more and more maquiladora plant managers are actively developing networks of local vendors.

Labor-Intensive Production

While access to domestic markets, duty-free imports of materials and equipment, and reduced duties on products imported back to the United States are certainly added premiums, they are not the main reasons why foreign firms have flocked to these zones for nearly thirty years. The main attraction has been and continues to be abundant, cheap labor. Foreign companies are willing to put up with all the hassles of operating a Mexican facility as long as real labor-cost savings can be achieved.

Most foreign companies in maquiladora zones have traditionally produced labor-intensive products, such as commercial electronics, auto parts and components (air conditioners, engines, transmissions), apparel, and furniture.

Within the consumer electronics category, maquiladora plants successfully manufacture a wide range of products: electric can openers, hair dryers, toasters, coffeemakers, toys, sporting goods, outboard motors, and pleasure boats, to mention only a few. Several companies have also discovered that the production of televisions, lamps, ceramics, and large appliances fit the Mexican mold. Somewhat surprisingly, so does the growing of cut flowers.

Many products made by foreign companies in East Asia can be more efficiently produced at a higher quality in Mexico. Labor is cheaper, workers more trainable, cultural differences less, shipping easier and less costly, and in some cases local markets are much larger.

Starting a Maquiladora

Several administrative steps must be taken to qualify a maquiladora facility under both U.S. and Mexican law. The first step requires obtaining an official "exemption from duty" certificate from the U.S. Customs Service. This exemption authorizes a U.S. company to assemble U.S.–origin products abroad and pay import duty only on the value added—usually labor and locally purchased raw materials—when finished products are exported back to the United States.

A company must also get approval from the Mexican Ministry of Commerce and Industrial Development (SECOFI) whether all products are manufactured for export or whether primary capacity will be used for domestic production and excess capacity for exports.

Companies must provide the following documentation:

- General information about the business and company
- Description of the manufacturing or assembly process
- Characteristics of the product or service
- List of commodities to be imported, temporarily, for use in the maquiladora facility
- Financial statements showing the company's investment plan, estimated operating costs, and estimated Mexican value to be added

A maquiladora agreement must be executed between the foreign parent company and the maquiladora zone management. It must be duly notarized, registered in the U.S. county of residence and with the Mexican Consul, and be translated into Spanish.

Once the maquiladora is in operation, it must adhere to the following rules:

- Generate at least twenty-five jobs in a one-year period.
- Not reduce the value-added amount previously generated in Mexico.
- Not relocate without prior approval of SECOFI.
- File information with SECOFI regularly, confirming that the company is complying with the applicable exchange-control regulations.

Smaller companies, perhaps inexperienced in international trade, generally find that the maquiladora startup process can be made easier and less costly by subcontracting personnel and administrative duties to a Mexican company—either a maquiladora management company or one not affiliated with the zone.

These subcontractors function as a combination labor broker and administrative partner, in an arrangement commonly used for managing smaller foreign facilities in the Middle East, Asia, and certain Caribbean and South American locations. They usually bill a flat rate based on the number of direct labor hours worked. Current Mexican rates range from US$2.50 to US$4.50 per hour.

Mexican Border/U.S. Foreign Trade Zones

Although nearly every trading country in the world utilizes foreign trade zones (FTZs), or "free zones" as some are called, the United States sports the greatest number. At last count more than 150 fully licensed FTZs were operational. Only West Virginia and Idaho are without them. Texas has sixteen.

FTZs provide a means to transship goods between countries without paying customs duties. In the United States, FTZs may be used for storage, distribution, assembly, light manufacturing, modification of products, or transshipment. Goods held in FTZs may be sold, exhibited, broken up, repacked, repackaged, graded, cleaned, and mixed with other foreign or domestic merchandise. Value may be added to goods after they have been brought in. They can then be shipped to a foreign destination without customs duties in either direction. Of course, customs duties do apply when goods are shipped to U.S. markets.

Domestic materials, subassemblies, or other components may enter FTZs free of duty, quotas, or taxes, providing customs officials are notified. These U.S.–made goods can then be combined with foreign goods for ultimate shipment. Protective barriers prevent a few domestic items from being processed while in the zone, such as domestic distilled spirits, wine, beer, and a limited number of other kinds of merchandise.

Setting Up Maquiladora Twin Plants

Although FTZs are located throughout the United States, a disproportionate number adjoin the U.S.–Mexican border in Texas, New Mexico, Arizona, and California and are used by nearly every

Fortune 500 company with twin plants in the maquiladora zones. This is how to set up cross-border twin plants:

1. Select an appropriate maquiladora site, meeting the requirements for labor, building facilities, and proximity to markets and materials used in the production process.
2. Choose another site in one of the border states—California, Arizona, New Mexico, or Texas—for a complementary facility to perform testing and/or final assembly, duty free.
3. Ship finished goods to international markets, Mexican markets, or repackage them for domestic markets.

It is not surprising that one of the highest-volume general purpose FTZs in the country is located in the lower Rio Grande Valley town of McAllen, Texas. Practically every American city along the Mexican border has at least one FTZ. Laredo, San Diego, and El Paso each have several.

It's pretty hard to beat the combination of twin plants, using maquiladora zones on the Mexican side and FTZs on the American side. Shipping costs are significantly lower than they are for similar production-sharing operations in the Caribbean, and maquiladora wages show no sign of escalating as rapidly as they have in Taiwan, Hong Kong, Malaysia, and Singapore.

So far, at least, the supply of trainable labor in maquiladora zones exceeds that available in nearly all other accessible developing nations. Internal controls, communication between local managers and the home office, and government support on both sides of the border provide a competitive edge for serving U.S. markets that overshadows anything that East Asian locations can match. It is not surprising that so many companies—mostly U.S.-owned—are already operating in the maquiladora zones.

Oil: Savior or Curse?

Trying to conduct business in modern-day Mexico without understanding the role of oil in the Mexican culture is like trying to bail out a boat with a strainer: it can't be done. Meaningful trade or investment strategies must include provisions for the pervasive and unusual role that oil plays in everyday Mexican life.

The Role of Pemex

Since 1938, when the Mexican government expropriated all foreign oil trusts, the gargantuan state-owned oil company Petroleos Mexicanos (Pemex) has been a symbol of Mexican identity on a par with the Virgin of Guadalupe and the national flag. Through the years the bureaucracy of Pemex has more than matched that of the federal government, if not in actual number of employees, at least in social and political power.

Pemex's enormous political and social influence became a natural breeding ground for corrupt power barons dressed as union leaders. Indeed, even after the dramatic steps taken by President Salinas to defuse the political power of the Oil Worker's Union (STPRM) (exemplified by the 1989 arrest and incarceration of union kingpin Joaquin "La Quinta" Hernandez Galicia and the 1991 shutdown of Mexico City's biggest polluter, the Azcapotzalco refinery) neither the union membership, the citizenry, nor Mr. Salinas himself was willing to take on the STPRM machine in a full-blown confrontation.

The stranglehold that La Quinta and his henchmen held over the state oil monopoly rivaled that of Eastern Europe's Communist Party bosses. For example, more than 2,000 Pemex-paid, gun-toting bodyguards protected STPRM bigshots. Not dissimilar to the control exercised over unions in New York and Chicago by members of the Mafia during its heyday, these thugs intimidated foes while their leaders pocketed trillions of pesos through payoffs, fraudulent companies, and sweetheart contracts for oil-field drilling, transportation of crude and refined oil, and equipment maintenance contracts. After the jailing of La Quinta, other big shots and their thugs were replaced by a less violent team and government reforms proceeded.

Will There Be Enough Oil?

Mexico produces approximately 2.5 million barrels of crude oil per day. Since 1986, crude oil and petroleum by-products have accounted for 37 percent of Mexico's foreign exchange earnings. In the future, however, the combination of a rapidly increasing population, a ballooning consumer demand for energy, and the government's emphasis on building the country's industrial base could have a devastating effect on Mexico's oil exports. Although the precise effects remain unclear, startling figures have been revealed by a former Pemex official, Francisco Inguano Suarez.

According to Suarez, the use of petroleum for domestic energy consumption is growing by 5 to 6 percent a year. At the same time, crude oil output decreases at the rate of 3 percent per year. At these rates, a lack of new wells will virtually put an end to Mexico's oil export business in 1994 or 1995.

If crude oil exports are stopped or severely diminished, it doesn't take a mathematician to calculate the devastating effect on Mexico's economy, much less the impact on the government's growth plans. The result would be a shattering of foreign investor confidence leading to a renewed flight of capital.

Mexico still bans foreign companies from competing with Pemex for oil exploration and production. Pemex also owns all refineries and retail outlets. Without major changes in the government's attitude toward foreign investment in the nation's oil reserves, the one commodity that has kept Mexico afloat for three decades could become its Achilles' heel.

NAFTA negotiations opened old wounds when U.S. negotiators took the position that free trade is impossible as long as Mexico protects its most important commodity. Mexican free trade advocates also recognize this and go one step further, acknowledging that without U.S. investment in oil exploration, production, refining, and distribution, Mexico's days as a major oil supplier are numbered.

The country already imports natural gas from U.S. companies, primarily those located in Texas. Imports rose from 2.2 billion cubic feet in 1988 to a whopping 35.6 billion cubic feet in 1990; the rate of acceleration continues unabated. Pemex uses Texas natural gas to fuel industrial growth in Monterrey and other northern cities where energy demand continues to escalate.

Imported coal is also needed to generate electricity in northern states. Until laws governing the Mexican oil industry change, U.S. companies will continue to find substantial markets in natural gas and coal, as well as all peripheral products and services that support the two industries.

No one really knows how big Mexico's oil reserves may be. Virtually no exploration was conducted during the 1980s. Known reserves are wearing thin, however, and unless significant new fields can be discovered, the nation's energy program will certainly undergo radical changes, creating even greater market openings for foreign companies.

The arrest of La Quinta opened the door a crack. A Houston consulting and engineering firm, Triton International, was invited to drill exploratory wells in Campeche Sound employing U.S. workers. This was the first turnkey deal signed with a foreign company.

When Triton completed the US$18 million contract in 127 days—half the time that Pemex takes to drill a well of similar depth—the gross inefficiency of the state monopoly was exposed.

Subsequently, the U.S. Eximbank put up US$1.3 billion in credit guarantees to enable U.S. firms to drill and service 113 new wells in Campeche Sound. Canadian Ex-Im Bank also came forward with a US$500 million credit guarantee to support Canadian drilling companies.

Granted, these steps do not fully open the Mexican oil industry to foreign competition, but at least they signify a start. Only time will tell the extent to which such competition will be permitted to develop.

The petroleum industry, maquiladoras, and many other sectors of the Mexican economy offer enormous opportunities. Nevertheless, a number of obstacles still confront foreign trade with and direct investment in Mexico. Some are more serious than others, but all must be addressed by foreign companies planning to test Mexican waters.

Headaches and Hurdles

Certainly burgeoning markets, abundant natural resources, and plentiful cheap labor are attracting an increasing number of foreign companies, not only to maquiladora zones, but to Mexico City, the resort areas, and other sections of the country as well. (General Motors, with twenty-five plants, is the largest foreign producer in Mexico.)

Although Mexico's population of 92 million is an attractive market, it can no longer be considered easy pickings, available to any foreign firm willing to come in. Consumers are becoming more sophisticated and demanding more choices, better prices, and more complete after-sale service. Price, delivery, and even quality competition from foreign multinationals and large Mexican firms is heating up. Price competition is becoming especially intense and has begun to drive margins down in most industries (except for envibusiness, health care, and specialized financial services).

Furthermore, Mexico is still a developing nation. The same obstacles to efficient business operations exist here as in other Third World nations. Although the relative aggravation varies with facility location and industry, most foreign companies find infrastructure deficiencies, labor unions, political corruption, taxes, and piracy of intellectual property the most troublesome issues, whether selling to domestic markets or producing goods for export.

Infrastructure

Two infrastructure deficiencies cause the biggest headaches: inferior telecommunications and unreliable electricity.

Except for Mexico City and a few coastal resort areas, erratic and often nonexistent telephone service remains an abysmal reminder of the underdevelopment of the country's infrastructure. Placing local calls from a rural area can be nearly impossible. International calls get through more frequently, but connections are often bad and line breaks common.

Since the American business community depends on frequent, reliable, and cost-effective telephone service to conduct even the most cursory activities, poor telecommunications usually presents an even bigger problem for U.S. firms than for their European or East Asian counterparts.

A good example occurred in maquiladora areas when the Mexican telephone company, Telefonos de Mexico (Telmex), was acquired by an international consortium that included Southwestern Bell, Cable and Radio from France, British Telecom, and Mexico's own Grupo Carson. Maquiladora managers cheered and U.S. home offices breathed a sigh of relief. But their euphoria was short-lived.

Service did not improve, and while service remained unchanged, rates escalated. Maquiladora facilities now pay much higher rates for inefficient services that range from a busy signal that backgrounds a conversation to the inability of either party to hear each other.

The reliability of electric power is not much better. Frequent outages bring production facilities to a halt. Brownouts and prolonged surges destroy computer files. Most foreign companies already in Mexico have learned to provide their own backup generator. It is not unusual for larger manufacturing facilities to generate 100 percent of their own power, especially in rural areas.

Mexico is not alone in suffering telecommunications and electric power deficiencies. Such conditions prevail throughout Latin America and the Caribbean.

Labor Unions

Mexican labor unions exert enormous power in major industries such as cement, oil, telecommunications, electricity, gas, water utilities, automobile manufacturing, and mining. They also control inland transport and port facilities. In this regard, union power isn't much different from that found in similar industries in the United States. The major difference is the amount of control the larger Mexican unions exert over members and nonmembers in many rural areas. It is not unusual for union bosses to be a more powerful force in the community than local governments.

One good example of union strength is the powerful Telmex union. When Telmex was privatized, union members were dissatisfied with wage and benefit arrangements. To voice their displeasure, they saw to it that telephone service throughout the country not only didn't improve, but in fact became worse than when Telmex was under state ownership.

Experienced foreign companies have learned that more progress can be made in dealing with union leaders through hired intermediaries than by handling union relations internally. Not infrequently such intermediaries are labor lawyers or the previously discussed administrative subcontractors.

Corruption

Although under the Salinas administration corruption in government agencies isn't even close to what it was before 1988, it still exists. This is especially true in rural areas or in maquiladora zones, where foreign managers continue to be frustrated by the corruption and delays at Mexican customs border stations.

In an experimental solution to the problem, entrepreneurs took over the management of import warehouses, thus denying customs officials access to the goods. The effort proved futile. The government's next solution was to replace all customs officials with new recruits. Although this helped somewhat, companies still report losses at border stations.

Taxes

Some progress has been reached in reducing Mexico's tax rates, historically among the highest in North America. The top rate, applied to personal income, dropped to 35 percent in 1991. The corporate rate was sliced to 35 percent from an exorbitant 56 percent.

Only the federal government levies income taxes, not the states. Although resident corporations are taxed on their worldwide income from all sources, nonresident corporations pay only on Mexican-source income. Special provisions ensure that income is not taxed twice, as dividend income is in the United States. Corporations also get relief from inflationary increases, again contrary to the IRS Code, which taxes inflationary gains.

Mexican tax laws have been structured to encourage corporations to invest in the shares of other Mexican companies, adding impetus to the growth of the Mexican stock exchange. Dividends received from another Mexican corporation are not taxed, provided that the distribution was made from taxable income.

Mexico imposes several other taxes on business activity. The most significant are as follows:

Value-added tax on any supply of goods or services except for exports and imports:	6 to 15 percent
Real estate acquisition tax on the market value of real estate transferred:	8 percent
Tax on salaries:	federal, 1 percent; state, various percentages

Residence tax on each em-ployee's salary up to ten times the minimum salary of the region:	5 percent
Employee profit sharing on taxable profits (excluding the effect of inflation):	10 percent
Social Security contributions on salaries:	employer, approximately 12.6 percent; employee, approximately 4.5 percent

Mexico does not have tax treaties with other jurisdictions, although it has agreed with the U.S. Internal Revenue Service to exchange tax information.

Intellectual Property

Many foreign companies have experienced piracy of their intellectual property throughout the Third World, including Latin America. Until countries began moving toward market economies and became dependent on U.S. aid to make the conversion, foreigners had little leverage to demand protection.

Now, with U.S. aid eagerly sought by virtually all Latin American and Caribbean governments and with the prospect of hemispheric free trade on the horizon, the pendulum has begun to swing. During the NAFTA negotiations, U.S. representatives made it clear that without reasonable protection against intellectual piracy, free trade agreements with any country will not be enacted and financial aid will be curtailed.

The Advisory Committee for Trade Policy and Negotiations recommended to the U.S. Congress that protection for intellectual property must be incorporated in any trade agreement and that it must include:

- Moral rights—the right to protect copyrighted work from unauthorized adulteration
- Works for hire—the rights involved when an employee or consultant originates an idea which the employer wants to patent or copyright

- Protection from the copying of computer programs
- Terms of protection and rental rights for copyrighted sound recordings
- Term and product protection for pharmaceutical and biotechnological products
- Limitations on compulsory licensing—a rule requiring foreign companies to license a product to a local business as a condition for getting a local patent
- Protection against third-party disclosure of data provided to governments with respect to trade secrets
- Protection for industrial designs, semiconductor layouts, and trademarks
- Effective internal and border enforcement procedures

Acquiescing to U.S. pressures, the Mexican government took the bull by the horns and passed legislation to protect intellectual property. This legislation—the Law of Promotion and Protection of Industrial Property—comes close to meeting U.S. demands. It protects inventions, technical product improvements, and innovations in products and processes, as well as trademarks, service marks, trade names, commercial slogans, and denominations of origin. Patent protection extends for twenty years from the date of filing; trademark protection, for ten years; and copyright protection, for fifty years.

Despite these improvements, many foreign companies, especially those from the United States, feel Mexico still has a long way to go. U.S. companies in the computer and computer software industries are particularly concerned about inadequate protection.

The managing director of the largest trade association in the U.S. computer software industry, Business Software Alliance, whose membership includes WordPerfect, Ashton-Tate, Aldus, Microsoft, Autodesk, and Lotus, claims that the industry loses more than US$100 million a year from Mexican software piracy. He also claims that only one out of eight programs used in Mexico is *not* pirated.

Management at Lotus and Microsoft decided to curtail business in Mexico until the rules are tightened. It's the enforcement side that concerns these companies, not the lack of laws.

PART III
The Caribbean and Central America

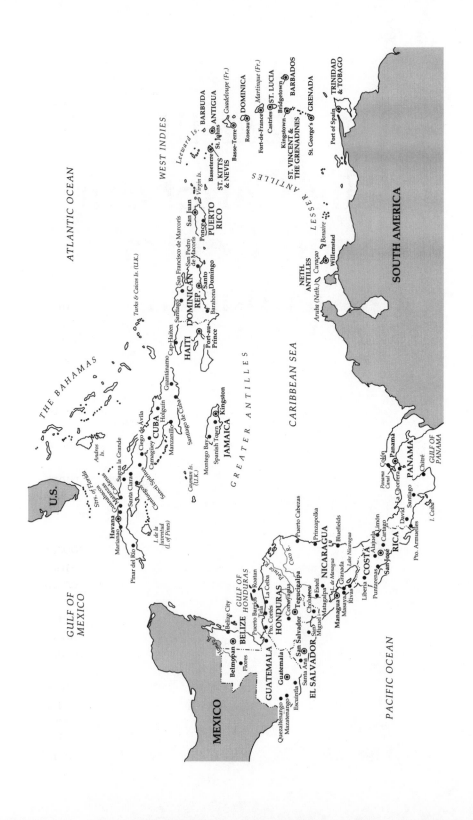

Chapter 5

A Profile of
the Caribbean Basin

For small businesses or companies inexperienced in international trade, it's hard to beat the Caribbean region, which includes all the island states and Central America. Here are just a few reasons why this area makes a good training ground in which to learn international trade:

- English used as the language of business everywhere but in the French islands
- The best tax benefits in the entire Western Hemisphere
- Small and easily accessible local markets
- Negligible competition from multinational corporations
- Abundant marketing, technical, and financial assistance from the U.S. Government

For brevity, the U.S. Government refers to the Caribbean islands and Central America jointly as the "Caribbean Basin." Although the region's population of 64 million, spread over thirty-eight political entities, does not rival that of Mexico or South America, it has become an important (albeit small) market for a variety of U.S. and Canadian exports. Additionally several countries have valuable natural resources, including oil, bauxite, timber, and seafood.

Once the outposts of European colonial powers, a number of Caribbean island states still have political ties to their parent countries. Martinique, Guadeloupe, and St. Martin are departments of France. The Cayman Islands, the Turks and Caicos Islands, Anguilla, Montserrat, and the British Virgin Islands are dependent territories of Great Britain. Curaçao, Bonaire, Sint Maarten, Saba, and St. Eustatius (and, until recently, Aruba) are Dutch parliamentary democracies, grouped as the Netherlands Antilles. The United States has granted the U.S. Virgin Islands territorial status and Puerto Rico commonwealth privileges.

A Few Negatives

Except for the Cayman Islands, Bermuda, and the American-affiliated island states, the region is desperately poor. Without a constant stream of foreign aid, few of these countries would survive, much less be capable of developing economies that can compete in the twenty-first century. Fortunately, the United States and European parent countries are permanently committed to supporting the financial needs of their wards. In a country without such ties (Haiti) and in those apparently abandoned by their former colonial rulers (Suriname and Guyana) conditions can be Dickensian and the suffering severe.

Smaller island states, such as Montserrat and St. Vincent and the Grenadines, have virtually no resources other than cheap labor and sandy beaches, and no means of sustaining economic self-sufficiency. Barbados, Trinidad and Tobago, Jamaica, and the Dominican Republic are doing much better, with fairly well-developed private sectors, but here too, infrastructures are failing.

In Central America, the only reasonably accessible consumer markets are comprised of a relatively minor part of the population—government bureaucrats, the business elite, and foreign retirees. The political stability of all Central American countries except Costa Rica, and perhaps Panama, remains in doubt.

Many Caribbean Basin countries suffer from slow growth and foreign exchange shortages. Although several factors contribute to this dilemma, low commodity prices for traditional exports (mostly agricultural products and natural resources) are the main culprit.

On the other hand, these same factors have forced most countries to develop free trade zones or other incentives to attract foreign investment in manufacturing and tourism as the only way to bring in hard currency and stimulate economic growth.

Throughout the Caribbean Basin, each of the thirty-eight separate countries, territories, colonies, departments, and dependencies has its own legal, tax, and financial system, which complicates matters for any type of regional corporate strategy. Cuba and Haiti have erected their own unique deterrents to foreign trade and investment.

On the Plus Side

For generations the Caribbean Basin has been alternately treated as a group of "banana republics" (connoting inconsequential status as satellites of the United States and European colonial powers), a dumping ground for American waste, and a U.S. buffer zone against invasion from foreign powers. Earlier generations of Americans and Europeans stripped the Caribbean Basin of its natural resources and agricultural products, and took cruel advantage of its very cheap, uneducated labor.

More recently, billions of U.S. dollars have been poured into Central America, theoretically to stop the spread of communism but inadvertently lining the pockets of ruthless military dictators, drug kingpins, and corporate patriarchs. Several Caribbean islands have become a combination playground and tax shelter for the rich and famous.

The Caribbean Basin began maturing as a viable region for trade and investment during the 1960s. Today, as various countries emerge from "puppet-state" status, unusual opportunities arise for tapping a rich base of natural resources, skilled low-cost labor, and small but growing local markets (although the latter is of less importance to U.S. companies than the former two).

As a side benefit, several countries maintain tax-haven status and actively encourage companies and individual investors from high-tax jurisdictions (including the United States and Canada) to take advantage of this unique arrangement.

Companies from the United States and Canada will find the Caribbean Basin a quick, easy, and inexpensive entrée to global trade, as well as a key site from which to utilize the strength of hemispheric trading blocs for tapping European and East Asian markets.

Concurrently, many European and Asian companies are learning to avoid costly and time-consuming direct investments in the United States, Mexico, or Canada. Instead, they are gaining entry to these markets through Caribbean Basin sites, while simultaneously eluding external barriers created by North American free trade agreements (e.g. NAFTA).

Every Caribbean Basin country, including Cuba, concentrates on export-oriented development policies and actively seeks foreign direct investment. Skilled and semiskilled labor is readily available in nearly all countries. Many have international airports and deep-water ports. Although electricity, telecommunications, and potable water are still unreliable, infrastructure development certainly surpasses anything Africa or South Asia has to offer. Health care and education standards are generally far superior to those in most other developing regions.

Target Markets and Investment Locations

The Caribbean Basin's population of 64 million includes nearly 11 million Cubans, so in reality a reachable consumer market of 53 million is a more accurate total. (This should be compared with Mexico's 92 million, Canada's 27 million, and the United States' nearly 260 million.) Complicating any overall business strategies, however, is the fact that the Caribbean Basin's 53 million people are spread over thirty-eight countries and hundreds of miles of open ocean.

To give some idea of potential market sizes, the Central American nations account for roughly 29 million people and the Caribbean island states (excluding Cuba) about 24 million. The largest island nations are the Dominican Republic (7 million), Haiti (6 million), Puerto Rico (3 million), Jamaica (2 million), and Trinidad and Tobago (1 million). The remaining 5 million live on twenty-five island states.

No other region in the world presents such a panorama of cultures, languages, and economic variance in such a small geographic area. Per capita GDP ranges from less than US$400 in Guyana and Haiti to more than US$17,000 in the Cayman Islands and US$23,000 in Bermuda.

The languages of the region include Spanish, which is spoken throughout Central America, the Dominican Republic, and Puerto Rico; Dutch, which is spoken in Curaçao, Aruba, and Bonaire; French, which is spoken in Martinique, Guadeloupe, and St. Martin; and English, which is spoken throughout the rest of the Caribbean states. English is the language of business everywhere in the Caribbean except in the French islands, and Spanish is the language of business throughout Central America.

Such a wide divergence in language, government structure, market size, and resources makes it difficult, if not impossible, to develop strategic objectives that fit the Caribbean Basin as a whole. Corporate strategies must target individual countries or focus on a group of countries, such as the group of English-speaking island states that make up the Caribbean Common Market (CARICOM).

In the Caribbean islands the greatest opportunities for either trade or direct investment reside in a rather limited number of larger states: Puerto Rico, the U.S. Virgin Islands, the Dominican Republic, and Jamaica. (The French and Dutch islands remain part of their respective parent countries, and trade and investment opportunities there must be viewed in conjunction with those offered by France and the Netherlands.)

Nearly all Central American countries are beginning to realize benefits from the revived Central American Common Market. However, Costa Rica warrants special attention as a good example of what can be accomplished with a market economy. The Panamanian economy is starting to revitalize and Honduras offers some interesting possibilities. The political and economic stability of the other Central American nations precludes significant market opportunities, although natural resources remain abundant and can be exploited with more adventurous direct investment strategies.

The Best Products and Industries for Foreign Companies

Since the inception of the Caribbean Basin Initiative (reviewed later in this chapter), the Caribbean island states have become very popular with smaller U.S. companies as a testing ground for international expansion. Smaller and midsize companies have also found an abundance of low-cost labor and valuable natural resources in Central American nations. According to the U.S. Department of Commerce, 789 new foreign-exchange generating investments by foreign companies (mostly American) in the Caribbean Basin have totaled an estimated $2.2 billion, creating more than 142,000 new jobs.

Although revenues from traditional industries like tourism, petroleum, and sugar production have declined, exports of nontraditional products have increased, indicating a reawakening for the region. Over time, this should sustain a more balanced production and export base. Exports of nontraditional products such as apparel, winter vegetables, fruits, seafood, and wood furnishings (primarily to the United States) have grown in excess of 14 percent per year since 1983. Apparel exports have nearly tripled.

As for exporting to the region from Canada, the United States, or Europe, the Caribbean island states offer very meager domestic markets. Costa Rica, Panama, and Guatemala, whose populations include larger groups of affluent bureaucrats and businesspeople, offer only slightly larger domestic markets.

Small exporters, however, benefit directly from small markets. Since major competitors cannot economically ship minimal quantities, the door is wide open for small companies to satisfy the consumer and commercial demand that does exist.

A thriving tourist industry in virtually every country is the one exception to the minimal domestic market in the region. Practically all goods must be imported: hotel and restaurant supplies and equipment; liquor, wine, and beer; processed food and fresh food; building materials; health care products and services; and infrastructure equipment. In addition, automobile, bus, and truck spare parts are in short supply everywhere.

Other than servicing the tourist industry and supplying small local populations with basic consumer products, the main benefit for foreign companies (especially those from the United States and Canada) lies in setting up local production facilities for the exploitation of low-cost labor, natural resources, and virtually duty-free exports to the United States and Canada.

Although each nation has its own peculiarities, the region's most successful industries are those that can make use of indigenous materials and skills to manufacture products for export to the

United States, Canada, and to a lesser extent Europe. Common exports are:

- Apparel and other made-up textile items
- Electronic and electromechanical assemblies
- Handicrafts, giftware, and decorative items
- Wood products, including furniture and building materials
- Recreational items, sporting goods, and toys
- Seafood
- Tropical fruit products
- Winter vegetables
- Ethnic and specialty foods—e.g., sauces, spices, liquor, jams, confectionery items
- Ornamental horticulture
- Leather goods
- Medical and surgical supplies
- Footwear

Some locations, notably the Dominican Republic and Jamaica, have gone out of their way to attract U.S. companies that need large numbers of low-cost employees to prepare data for computer entry or to handle high volumes of telecommunications transactions. Both island states have developed significant industries in data processing/keystroke businesses and in telephone switching services (such as handling 800 calls). Major U.S. companies in the airlines, telephone, insurance, and similar high-transaction-volume industries are profitably using twin-plant facilities in these island states.

Because of the U.S. Government's intense interest in developing the Caribbean Basin's economic base, virtually all federal agencies with responsibilities for the promotion of U.S. foreign trade or investment, as well as those commissioned to protect the environment and to further U.S. international policy, take an active role in promoting the region's development.

This active U.S. involvement takes the form of financial and technical assistance, environmental protection measures, special market studies, labor training, and assistance for developing transportation and infrastructures. The principal U.S. Government program under which various agencies function is called the Caribbean Basin Initiative.

The Caribbean Basin Initiative

In 1983, the U.S. Congress passed the Caribbean Basin Economic Recovery Act, which included the Caribbean Basin Initiative (CBI). In 1990, CBI provisions were made a permanent part of U.S. foreign trade policy.

Originally, the CBI was designed to promote economic growth, stability, and diversification in the Caribbean and Central America through private-sector investment and trade. Its primary tool was duty-free access to U.S. markets. In recent years, however, it has been expanded to include preferential treatment for U.S. exports to the region and a variety of special financing arrangements through Eximbank, Overseas Private Investment Corporation (OPIC), the special IRS Section 936 program (described in Chapter 7), the Inter-American Development Bank, and other, less-universal U.S. Government and multilateral aid programs.

The major elements of the CBI program are:

1. Duty-free entry into the United States, in perpetuity, for a wide range of products manufactured in CBI countries, except for those listed below (unless they are made from 100 percent U.S. components):

- Most textiles and apparel
- Canned tuna
- Petroleum and petroleum products
- Footwear (except disposable items and footwear parts such as uppers)
- Certain leather, rubber, and plastic gloves
- Luggage, handbags, and flat goods
- Certain leather wearing apparel
- Watches and watch parts, if any component originated in a Communist country

(Special conditions apply to ethanol, sugar, beef, and veal.)

2. U.S. economic assistance to the region to aid private-sector

development by financing essential imports and by establishing development banks, chambers of commerce, skills-training programs, industrial free zones, and other essential infrastructure

3. Caribbean Basin country self-help efforts to improve local business environment and support efforts by investors and exporters

4. A deduction against U.S. taxes for companies holding business conventions in qualifying CBI countries

5. A wide range of U.S. Government, state government, and private-sector promotion programs, including trade and investment financing, business development missions, technical assistance programs, and a U.S. Government special access program for textiles and apparel

6. Support from other trading partners and institutions, such as:

- The Caribbean-Canada Free Trade Agreement (CARIBCAN), a trade development and assistance program, which includes duty-free entry for products to Canadian markets
- The European Community's Lomé Convention, which allows duty-free entry to EC countries for a multitude of mostly nonmanufactured products

During 1991, the United States provided new or expanded duty-free treatment to ninety-four product categories, including bandages, wall coverings, plastic sheets, certain meats, plastic articles, mattresses, and athletic equipment. Information about continuing changes in CBI-qualified goods can be obtained from Mr. John Melle, Caribbean Office of U.S. Trade Representative, at (202) 395-6135.

Countries Qualifying for CBI Status

- Antigua and Barbuda
- Aruba
- Bahamas
- Barbados
- Belize
- British Virgin Islands
- Costa Rica
- Dominica
- Dominican Republic
- El Salvador

- Grenada
- Guatemala
- Guyana
- Haiti
- Honduras
- Jamaica
- Montserrat
- Netherlands Antilles

(Curaçao, Bonaire,
Sint Maarten)
- Nicaragua
- Panama
- St. Kitts-Nevis
- St. Lucia
- St. Vincent/Grenadines
- Trinidad and Tobago

Anguilla, the Cayman Islands, Suriname, and the Turks and Caicos Islands are potentially eligible but have not as yet applied for entrance to the program. To qualify for admission, countries must execute a Tax Information Exchange Agreement (TIEA), granting the IRS the right to examine records relating to the trade transactions of U.S. companies. Table 5-1 presents key economic statistics for members and nonmembers of the Caribbean Basin Initiative.

For further information, ask for the most recent *CBI Guidebook* when contacting:

Caribbean Basin Information Center
International Trade Administration
U.S. Department of Commerce
14th Street and Constitution Avenue, NW
Washington, DC 20230
Phone: (202) 377-2527

The Impact of Free Trade Agreements

Although it is still too early to measure the effect on CBI countries of new regional free trade agreements involving the United States, Mexico, Canada, and several South American common market groups, leaders of several smaller Caribbean states are increasingly uneasy over potential harm to their fragile economies.

The North American Free Trade Agreement (NAFTA) is viewed with special concern. It is feared that open access to U.S. and Canadian markets by Mexican companies will give competing

Table 5-1. Key Caribbean Basin Statistics ($US).

	Population (000)	Per Capita GDP ($000)	Growth Rate	Unemployment Rate
CARIBBEAN BASIN INITIATIVE MEMBERS				
CARICOM states				
Antigua and Barbuda	79	$ 5.1	6.2%	5%
Bahamas	246	9.1	2.0	12
Barbados	263	5.1	3.5	18
Belize	220	1.2	6.0	15
Dominica	84	1.2	−1.4	10
Grenada	84	1.7	5.6	N/A
Guyana	765	0.4	−3.5	30
Jamaica	2.441	1.4	2.6	18
Montserrat	12	3.7	12.0	3
St. Kitts-Nevis	45	3.8	6.0	15
St. Lucia	150	1.2	6.0	20
St. Vincent/ Grenadines	114	1.4	8.4	30
Trinidad and Tobago	1.3	3.3	−2.4	22
Non-CARICOM states				
Aruba	63	11.9	16.0%	3%
British Virgin Islands	12	7.7	2.5	N/A
Dominican Republic	7.241	1.0	0.6	30
Haiti	6.263	0.4	−1.5	50
Netherlands Antilles				
Curaçao	151	6.4	3.5	21
Bonaire, Saba, and Sint Eustatius	27	5.2	2.0	25
Sint Maarten	27	5.2	2.0	25
Central America				
Costa Rica	3.033	1.9	3.8	5
El Salvador	5.33	0.9	1.1	20

Table 5-1. (*continued*)

	Population (000)	Per Capita GDP ($000)	Growth Rate	Unemployment Rate
CARIBBEAN BASIN INITIATIVE MEMBERS (*continued*)				
Guatemala	9.098	1.2	3.0	43
Honduras	5.26	1.0	2.1	25
Nicaragua	3.723	0.5	− 5.0	25
Panama	2.314	1.9	3.0	25
NON-CARIBBEAN BASIN INITIATIVE MEMBERS				
United States affiliates				
Puerto Rico	3.3	6.1	7.3	15
U.S. Virgin Islands	110	8.7	N/A	3
British dependent territories				
Anguilla	7	4.1	6.0	N/A
Bermuda	58	23.0	2.0	2
Cayman Islands	26	17.2	13.0	-0-
Turks and Caicos Islands	10	4.5	3.0	N/A
French departments				
French Guiana	115	2.0	N/A	15
Guadeloupe (including St. Martin)	342	4.8	N/A	28
Martinique	340	4.4	7.0	31
Nonaffiliated				
Suriname	397	3.2	3.6	27
Cuba	10.7	2.0	− 2.0	N/A

Source: Caribbean/Latin American Action.

Mexican products an unfair advantage over Caribbean Basin products currently enjoying preferential tariff arrangements under both the CBI and CARIBCAN. In addition, it is feared that new direct investment from the United States, Canada, Japan, and the European Community will be diverted from the smaller island states to Mexico.

Although slow in starting, public- and private-sector groups have now been formed to reach a consensus on regional responses to these challenges. At a minimum, intraregional trade will be enhanced and dependence on U.S. favoritism reduced. This bodes well for companies from the United States and other foreign countries investing in the Caribbean Basin. Local markets will undoubtedly be strengthened without the loss of traditional CBI and Lomé Convention trade preferences.

Chapter 6

The French Islands, Cayman Islands, and Turks and Caicos Islands

Although Caribbean Basin Initiative member states offer a broad range of benefits to U.S. companies, a few nonmember Caribbean islands are equally attractive to companies from both the United States and Canada. Although every island state has advantages, those with the most unusual benefits are the French islands (Martinique and Guadeloupe), the Cayman Islands, and the rejuvenated Turks and Caicos Islands. This chapter examines each in light of the special circumstances that bring foreign exports and facilities to their shores.

Martinique and Guadeloupe

The two French islands, Martinique and Guadeloupe, are departments of France—the equivalent of U.S. states. As such, they operate under the same laws and systems that exist in France. Although these islands cannot boast the special trade preferences and aid packages available to CBI nations, they do offer one advantage not available elsewhere. As part of France, they enjoy the benefits (and in some cases, the disadvantages) of belonging to the European Community. A company investing in Martinique or Guadeloupe enjoys the same privileges of EC membership as if the investment were being made in an EC country.

The two islands' ability to provide an entrée to the European Community, combined with their well-educated populace and excellent port facilities and roads, make them favorite locations for offshore production facilities for companies from non-EC European countries, East Asia, and the United States. American companies interested in exploiting both Caribbean Basin and European Community advantages find these French departments an excellent alternative to CBI locations.

Consumer markets are very American-oriented. The islands boast significant U.S. tourism. With satellite access to U.S. television, residents are very aware of American products, and many consumers have adopted American tastes.

Martinique's population of 340,000 and Guadeloupe's 342,000 offer larger local markets than most CBI island nations. Annual U.S. exports to Martinique exceed US$20 million—primarily in food, paper products, and consumer hard and soft goods with a value of less than US$500. Many smaller U.S. firms (as well as French companies) are already serving these markets, so competition is keener than in other island states.

Martinique boasts industrial parks, a cruise ship port, and a modern (by island standards) convention center. Guadeloupe's excellent shipping facilities make it the third-largest French container port.

Tax and subsidy incentives are in place to help foreign companies create jobs, start up businesses, and import business equipment. To date, most U.S. investment has gone into petroleum refining, banking, and the production of rum, packaging materials, and batteries.

Good opportunities for direct investment and trade also exist in hotel franchises, clothing, fast food, sporting goods, refrigeration and air conditioning equipment, automobile accessories, satellite dishes, and a wide range of entertainment products, including audio and video tapes, compact discs, records, and magazine and book publication.

One notable feature of conducting business in the French islands (apart from the use of the French language and currency, of course) is the amount of competition from large and midsize French companies. While they do not present stiff competition in the rest of the Caribbean Basin, they certainly do in Martinique and Guadeloupe. Non-French companies seeking to expand there need to recognize that favorable pricing and delivery advantages will be difficult to achieve. U.S. companies bent on pursuing either trade or direct investment would be well advised to join up with a French partner that has the market intelligence to compete with much larger companies from the mother country.

Further information about investment and trade opportunities in Martinique and Guadeloupe, as well as help in reaching appropriate French partners or agents, can be obtained from:

Martinique/Guadeloupe
Invest-in-France Agency
610 Fifth Avenue, Suite 301
New York, NY 10020
Phone: (212) 757-9340
Fax: (212) 765-2632

The Cayman Islands

With zero unemployment, a population of only 26,000, and a per capita GDP of more than US$17,000, the Cayman Islands is the richest island state in the Caribbean, even though it has only two industries: finance and tourism. Tourists thrive here in a superb family vacation environment surrounded by some of the world's best diving waters.

The island state is also recognized throughout the world as a legitimate tax haven and offshore financial center with political stability guaranteed by the United Kingdom. For well over two decades, companies and individuals from the United States, Canada, Europe, and Latin America have flocked to the Caymans to open offshore subsidiaries, trusts, and bank accounts.

At last count, the island state boasted nearly 20,000 registered companies, more than 400 offshore insurance companies, and 550 banks and trust companies from more than thirty countries, including twenty-five of the world's top thirty banks. With a few minor exceptions, these establishments do not produce goods or provide services for local markets. From a business perspective, the three main objectives of a Cayman facility should be as follows:

1. Serve as a vehicle for reducing taxes on foreign transactions.
2. Provide a means for foreign currency convertibility.
3. Act as a depositary for protecting monetary assets.

Because the Cayman Islands depend on their international reputation as an offshore financial center and tax haven, the Cayman government has been extremely careful not to allow drug trafficking or money laundering schemes to filter in. Although bank security and confidentiality are vital to its reputation, any transaction suspected of being tainted is immediately opened and disqualified. Severe sentences are imposed on those caught in such nefarious activities.

Using Offshore Financial Center Facilities

Pragmatically, the Caymans are wide open to foreign investors. Profits and capital are freely repatriated. The island state has no exchange controls. Taxes of any kind are unheard-of. And island banking laws provide tight security for foreign deposits and trusts.

The law requires that any corporation set up to do business in the Cayman Islands (as opposed to engaging in offshore transactions) that is not at least 60 percent owned by Caymanians must obtain a license from the Caymanian Protection Board—a license that is both costly and discretionary on the part of the board. Several broad exclusions exist, however. In general, a Cayman corporation need not obtain a license if its purpose is to enter into investments on behalf of a foreign person or company.

Nearly all U.S. Fortune 500 companies have branches in the Caymans, as do hundreds of smaller firms. All major international banks, insurance companies, and public accounting firms maintain offices there. Most international fund management firms operate from Grand Cayman.

Advantages of the Cayman Islands

- A political stability unmatched in the region
- Security—in terms of physical plant, personnel, and bank deposits
- Confidentiality

- Zero taxes of any kind
- Excellent telecommunications
- No exchange controls
- A very pro-American population, with English the only language used throughout the islands
- Major insurance, trust, and banking facilities
- A very high standard of living
- Free import of components and equipment
- Outstanding electric power generation and distribution
- Efficient and honest customs officials
- Modern, well-developed infrastructure

Drawbacks of the Cayman Islands

- A small population and, consequently, a severe labor shortage
- A very high cost of living by any standards
- An erratic water supply during the dry season
- Ineligible for assistance from the U.S. Agency for International Development, the Overseas Private Investment Corporation, the Caribbean Basin Initiative, or the Section 936 programs
- A very small internal market

Virtually anyone from any country may open a bank account in the Caymans upon presentation of a reference letter from a home country bank. For obvious reasons, however, banks will not accept large cash deposits. Funds may be deposited in U.S. dollars or other currencies by check, bank draft, or wire transfer. With no exchange controls or reporting requirements, funds may be withdrawn at any time. They may also be converted into other currencies and freely moved in and out of the country.

Direct Investment

Some foreign companies (primarily British and Canadian) have found the Caymans an attractive location for direct investment. Although laws restrict foreign companies from producing for local consumption or export, they are manageable. It does, however, require a bit of patience to get licenses approved.

Without question, the best industries for direct investment focus on high-value products requiring low-labor content. Examples include:

- Cosmetics
- Security devices
- Small electronics products
- Research and development centers
- Computer software development
- Certain types of data processing
- Flowers (orchids)
- Hybrid seeds and fruit trees
- Seafood

Aquaculture offers the highest potential for export growth. The waters surrounding the islands are rich in every conceivable type of seafood, including an abundance of farm-raised turtles. Although the aquaculture industry has not caught on to any significant extent yet, it will very likely be a big winner in the future.

The United States takes about three fourths of the Caymans' exports. Another 9 percent go to Europe, 3 percent to Japan, and 8 percent to other Caribbean nations. The Cayman Islands do not have any unemployment. Everyone who wants to work can find a job.

Export Trade

With virtually no natural resources other than aquaculture products, a severe shortage of labor (at very high wages), and no indigenous agriculture, the Cayman Islands must import virtually everything, mostly from U.S. companies. The best exports to the Caymans, in addition to all the supplies and equipment needed in the tourist industry, include:

- Virtually all types of consumer manufactured goods
- Processed food and beverages
- Tobacco
- Petroleum products
- A variety of machinery and equipment

- Vehicles and parts
- Building materials
- Computers, peripherals, and spare parts
- Health care supplies and equipment

The tourist industry has been booming for the last eight years. Many luxurious hotels have been built, all requiring imported furnishings, equipment, supplies (cleaning, maintenance, bar, and restaurant), and office equipment and computers. But hotels are not the only tourist facility. Tourism on Grand Cayman is unique in two respects: first, most accommodations are condominiums and villas rather than hotels or resorts; and second, most of the owners are affluent U.S. citizens who come to the island a few times a year to check out their investment portfolio, assigning their condo or villa to local management companies for tourist rentals the rest of the year.

The big building boom is now completed, but the same residential conveniences demanded by American consumers are needed to supply and maintain these part-time residences: appliances, furnishings, floor and wall coverings, air conditioning, and so on. Market demand for these products will not abate as the structures age. Constant use, combined with salt air, makes everything deteriorate rapidly. Since none of these goods are manufactured on the island, there will be a steady market for imported products for many years to come. And with Miami just an hour's flight away, U.S. companies are the foremost exporters.

Competition is keen, however. Affluent U.S. owners are willing to pay top dollar for first-class merchandise. Many hotels are at least three-star and some are even higher class; they, too, are willing to pay for top-of-the-line goods. Such high margins are already attracting a surfeit of exporters. To compete, a new entrant will have to offer quality, delivery, or product uniqueness. This is not a price-sensitive market.

Grand Cayman is very small, easy to get around, and very British—with an American flavor. Agents and distributors are not needed. The island is a mere 460 miles south of Miami and easy to cover for U.S. sales personnel. It does help to get to know local Cayman business families, however. They know exactly how to manage the bureaucracy, which, by island or Latin American standards, is extremely honest (though slow).

Grand Cayman is also a favorite cruise ship stop, and duty-free shops abound. This offers another lucrative opportunity to export jewelry, perfume, watches, and all the rest of typical cruise ship boutique products. And again, prices are at the top of the range.

Import duties range from 5 to 38 percent. Duty-free status, however, is accorded agricultural machinery and supplies, certain basic foodstuffs, and various luxury items resold to cruise ship tourists: perfumes, cameras, china and crystal, and stereo and audio equipment and components.

Further information about opportunities in the Cayman Islands can be obtained from:

Cayman Islands Government Information Service
Tower Building
Grand Cayman, BWI
Phone: (809) 949-8092
Fax: (809) 949-8487

The Turks and Caicos Islands

During the 1980s the Turks and Caicos Islands developed a reputation as a major drop-off point for drugs from South America. Situated at the bottom of the Bahamian chain of islands, just an hour and a half away from Miami by plane and not far from the north coast of the Dominican Republic (yet isolated by lack of commercial air service and few outside visitors), the Turks and Caicos proved too convenient for drug smugglers to ignore. By 1990, however, the government had cleaned house and begun turning the island state into another tax haven and tourist mecca.

The Turks and Caicos Islands are not as developed as the Caymans, but they are being promoted as the newest Caribbean tax haven and eventually as an offshore financial center. The island state has no direct taxes of any kind, either on income or capital, for individuals or companies. In addition, upon request, the government will issue permanent guarantees against the future imposition of taxes.

A variety of incentives are offered to attract foreign tourism projects, including the availability of Crown land, exemption from customs duties on building materials and supplies, and an "open and even-handed immigration policy" (the official government line).

The Turks and Caicos government also actively pushes foreign direct investment in fish farms and aquaculture. The world's first conch farm is already operating. Projects for farming Caribbean king crab, sponge, and shrimp are also strongly encouraged.

A small agricultural industry is currently developing in cassava (the manioc or tapioca root), citrus fruits, maize, and beans. High technology methods currently produce tomatoes and salad vegetables. Potential exports of aragonite, a mineral used in the production of gypsum products, and fine concrete are also beginning.

Since the Turks and Caicos have no manufacturing industry and very limited agriculture, everything must be imported. Products deemed by the government to be essential to the island state's well-being are admitted duty free. Infrastructure, health care, construction, and tourism products are especially welcome.

For further information contact:

Private Sector Development Office
Hibiscus Square, Grand Turk
Turks and Caicos Islands
Phone: (809) 946-2732
Fax: (809) 946-2556

Chapter 7

Puerto Rico: The Shining Star

In many respects, Puerto Rico is the best-kept secret in the Western Hemisphere. Located slightly more than two hours' flying time from Miami, it forms the head of the Antilles chain that contains most of the island states in the Caribbean Basin. A U.S. commonwealth, this "shining star of the Caribbean" (the official motto) offers more special advantages to companies from the United States and elsewhere in the world than can be described in the space available.

Commonwealth status was conferred by the U.S. Congress in 1952, granting Puerto Rico essentially the same level of control over its internal affairs as the fifty U.S. states have over theirs. In a 1962 plebiscite vote, 60.5 percent of the population opted for continuance of commonwealth status in preference to either independence or statehood.

Citizens of Puerto Rico hold full U.S. citizenship and send elected representatives to the U.S. Congress (although they may cast votes only in committee, not on the House floor). Puerto Ricans serve in the U.S. armed forces. Even though Puerto Rico has its own constitution, it falls under the jurisdiction of the U.S. federal court system, the Internal Revenue Service, and the U.S. Postal System. Travelers between the United States and Puerto Rico do not pass through U.S. customs. As a U.S. commonwealth, Puerto Rico's political stability is as secure as if it were one of the fifty states.

Nothing about Puerto Rico is second-rate, and no one should make the mistake of judging the commonwealth by Third World standards. The usual reaction of first-time visitors is that Puerto Rico resembles southern Europe far more than it does the Caribbean or Latin America. Four-lane superhighways carry thousands of late-model cars. Glass and steel office buildings anchor clusters of modern shopping centers, new residential communities, and high-tech industries. And most businesspeople are articulate, aggressive, and courteous.

The Domestic Market Potential

Not only is Puerto Rico's political stability comparable to any of the fifty states, so is its economy. Consumer markets are virtually identical to those in a mainland region of equal size and population. So are classes of consumers. The affluent live in large homes, drive expensive cars, belong to the best clubs, dress in designer clothes, and frequent upscale restaurants and cultural events. Middle-class businesspeople, educators, government employees, and professionals also have the same consumer tastes as their northern brethren. And—again as in the United States—there are pockets of dire poverty.

Industrial demand in Puerto Rico is not quite as varied as it is in the States, but it's close. When matched against regions of comparable size, Puerto Rican manufacturing is already considered one of the most proficient, high-tech industrial bases in the hemisphere.

The Commonwealth has now embarked on the road to developing a major R&D capability and world-class manufacturing companies. This means a blossoming need for state-of-the-art manufacturing equipment, business computers, testing and diagnostic instrumentation, robotic controlled material and production handling equipment, and the like. Very few such products are currently produced in Puerto Rico. That means an export market for U.S. companies—at least for an interim period, until the commonwealth catches up.

To go beyond these few industrial markets and attempt a stratification of products to meet this varied consumer and industrial demand is impossible. The best advice to foreign export companies might be to develop market penetration strategies that mirror those applied in the fifty states.

The same can be said for selling techniques. The same type of advertising, sales representation, pricing tactics, after-sale customer service, sales literature, catalogs, and product standards that work on the mainland will work here. Only two caveats need to be borne in mind:

1. If U.S. sales personnel are employed in Puerto Rico, they had better be bilingual. Without fluency in Spanish, they won't stand a chance.
2. All sales literature, advertising, catalogs, product specifications, price sheets, warranties, and so on must also be printed in both Spanish and English. If they aren't, they'll be thrown in the garbage.

Practically all Puerto Ricans are bilingual, but Spanish is preferred in most circles. When in Rome, do as the Romans do.

Although many U.S. companies find that exporting to Puerto Rico can be as lucrative as selling in Europe, they also find intense competition from local manufacturers and American multinationals. The list of American corporations with active facilities in Puerto Rico reads like a Who's Who of global industry.

The Puerto Rico Economic Development Administration lists the leading U.S. manufacturing companies in Puerto Rico with 1,000 or more employees as follows:

Pharmaceuticals

- Baxter International
- Johnson and Johnson
- Abbott Laboratories
- Bristol Myers Squibb
- Warner Lambert
- American Cyanamid
- American Home Products
- Schering Plough
- Eli Lilly

Food

- H. J. Heinz
- Uni Group

Chemicals

- DuPont

Apparel

- Sara Lee (Hanes Menswear)
- Propper International
- P. O. Industries
- Wickes Companies

Electrical/Electronic Products

- General Electric
- Westinghouse
- Digital Equipment
- Motorola

Jewelry

- Avon Products

Scientific Instruments

- U.S. Surgical

More than 240 Fortune 500 companies have set up shop in Puerto Rico, creating 115,000 new jobs. Although the exact number of small and midsize firms following suit is unavailable, estimates place the number at more than 2,000.

Puerto Rico's principal industries are pharmaceuticals, food processing, electrical/electronic manufacturing, computers and software, scientific instrumentation, and apparel. Most labor-intensive assembly industries have now moved offshore to CBI nations, where the cost of labor is lower. So have basic industries such as heavy equipment manufacturing, steel, aluminum, and mining.

With such an array of competitors, not to mention local Puerto Rican firms, it's fairly clear why Puerto Rican domestic markets are not the main attraction for new entrants.

Foreign companies (and especially those from the United States) are attracted to Puerto Rico for four primary reasons:

1. An absurdly low tax rate
2. A dynamic, skilled, and low-cost labor force
3. A deep well of management talent
4. A unique opportunity to borrow from a more than US$10 billion kitty with interest rates at a mere 85 percent of the London Interbank Offered Rate (LIBOR)

For smaller companies, the Section 936 program outweighs all other advantages for locating in Puerto Rico.

These features permit Puerto Rican facilities to compete in global trade on more than an equal footing with any country other than the twenty-four nations in the Organisation of Economic Cooperation and Development. And foreign trade statistics prove the point.

Puerto Rico's total foreign trade—more than US$35 billion—is greater than that of all other Caribbean Basin nations combined. To place it in perspective, Puerto Rico's foreign trade exceeds that of every Western Hemisphere country south of the U.S. mainland except Mexico and Brazil.

The approximate values of major exports break down as follows:

	(US$ billion)
Drugs and pharmaceuticals	US$6.4
Food products (excluding fish)	2.1
Chemical products	1.9
Electrical machinery	1.9
Electronics/computers	1.8
Professional and scientific instruments	1.2

	(US$ million)
Apparel and textiles	US$797.9
Petroleum refining products	645.0
Fish processing	573.7
Leather and leather products	268.1

Unique Direct Investment Opportunities

Puerto Rico has finally outstripped Taiwan, Hong Kong, Singapore, Thailand, Malaysia, and Indonesia as the lowest-cost, highest-quality, and most politically stable manufacturing location for American firms. It has not accomplished this feat on its own, however. Without the Caribbean Basin Initiative duty-free incentives and financing programs, the Commonwealth would be facing many of the same limitations as the newly industrialized countries in East Asia.

By exploiting attractive CBI incentives, U.S. companies can have the best of both worlds: a virtually tax-free location, a high-tech labor and management base, and a state-of-the-art infrastructure for offshore manufacturing, plus a second location in a very low-cost, labor-rich, and duty-free CBI-member state.

Companies typically utilize the twin-plant arrangement by locating high-tech, capital-intensive production in Puerto Rico—where labor costs run about 50 to 60 percent of those in the United States. A modern transportation and communications infrastructure ensures the coordinating convenience of a plant on the mainland. They then set up labor-intensive plants in a neighboring CBI country—perhaps Jamaica, the Dominican Republic, or Barbados—where labor and facility costs are even lower. The resulting blended cost is competitive with almost any site location in the world.

As an added advantage, Puerto Rico's free trade zones provide convenient light-manufacturing and distribution transshipment points for exports to other Latin American countries, Europe, East Asia, or back to the United States.

The island state's gross domestic product of US$22 billion is roughly comprised of manufacturing (40 percent), wholesale/retail (16 percent), transportation and communications (5 percent), construction (2 percent), and agriculture (1 percent). The balance of 36 percent is spread over a variety of industries.

The key statistics in Table 7-1 provide insight into the vibrant nature of Puerto Rico's economy.

Puerto Rico's Economic Development in Perspective

Puerto Rico's modern era began in 1947 when the legislature passed laws exempting profits made from goods manufactured in Puerto Rico from all island taxation. Since the 1950s, business and financial incentives have attracted billions in foreign capital under one of the most successful development programs in the world—fondly dubbed "Operation Bootstrap" by residents.

**Table 7-1. Key Puerto Rican
Statistics ($US).**

Population	3.3 million
Labor force	1.1 million
Unemployment rate, including rural areas	16%
Literacy	89%
Land mass	3,400 sq.mi.
GDP	$21.5 billion
Inflation rate	3%
Total annual exports	$19.1 billion
Total annual imports	$14.6 billion

Like many other developing countries, Puerto Rico initially attracted labor-intensive industries: textiles, apparel, food processing, machinery and components, and paper production. Then, like the newly industrialized countries of East Asia, the commonwealth began to focus on heavy industry, primarily oil refining and petrochemical operations.

The late 1970s and 1980s saw a shift to high-tech industries: pharmaceuticals, scientific instruments, electrical appliances, consumer electronics, computers, and medial products. Of the Commonwealth's US$20 billion annual exports, 73 percent are high-tech products. Manufacturing now accounts for 40 percent of Puerto Rico's GDP (compared with 20 percent in the United States). The sheer breadth of American, European, and Japanese manufacturing operations in Puerto Rico has given the island a distinctly international flavor.

Labor, Management, and Infrastructure

In addition to a nearly zero tax structure, two important features attract foreign investment:

1. A highly educated, skilled work force
2. A trained cadre of managerial talent

The 1991 average hourly wage rate of US$6.45 (including fringes) compares favorably with an average US$10.96 (without fringes) paid on the mainland.

Although trade unions represent many hourly job classifications, they are not a serious threat to stability. In addition, only 6 percent of salaried workers belong to unions. Most unions are unaffiliated or independent labor organizations, permitting collective bargaining at the company level rather than industrywide.

Public education is compulsory through age 16. Even though instruction is conducted in Spanish, the official language, English has always been a required subject. The highly regarded state university system consists of three principal campuses, two university colleges, three technological university colleges, and three regional colleges.

Telecommunications are excellent, with direct dialing to and from the United States, Canada, and Europe. Other infrastructure development—electricity, potable water, medical care, waste disposal, and so on—is the best in the Caribbean and rivals that of many U.S. states. A modern highway system links all cities and towns along the coast and cross-country. Major ports at San Juan, Mayagüez, and Ponce are supplemented with smaller ports on the northwest and east coasts. More than thirty shipping lines and twenty-three airlines service the Commonwealth.

Industrial Incentives for Foreign Companies

The Puerto Rican government supports a variety of foreign investment incentives including: cash grants for employee training, government-paid leasehold improvements, defrayal of equipment transportation charges, tax holidays, free trade zones, and superior financing.

Three free trade zones, located in Mayagüez, Ponce, and San Juan, offer local and foreign companies the opportunity to import equipment and supplies duty free, if they are used for export production. In addition, ninety-nine industrial parks are administered by the Puerto Rican Industrial Development Corporation (PRIDO)—far and away the greatest number in any Caribbean or Latin American nation.

The Puerto Rican government grants tax exemptions of up to 90 percent for specific periods of time (generally ten to twenty-five years). When combined with the special provisions of the Internal Revenue Code's Section 936 (described later in this chapter), the exemptions mean that U.S. companies operate in the Commonwealth essentially tax free.

Puerto Rico now stands ready to enter the fourth phase of its economic development: the stimulation of R&D projects and the continued pursuit of world-class excellence in manufacturing. In addition to hundreds of U.S. companies that find Puerto Rico an excellent Caribbean location, European and Japanese businesses have begun to recognize the competitive advantages of Commonwealth sites.

Over the last four years European companies have invested more than US$500 million in Puerto Rican facilities, while Japanese companies have invested some US$80 million. To date, major Japanese interest has centered in the tourist industry, and, to a lesser extent, on manufacturing facilities, but that will change as Japan's economy strengthens.

Promoting Puerto Rico's entrance into its fourth phase of development, the renowned development magazine *Plants, Sites and Parks* acknowledges new advantages to would-be investors:

- State-of-the-art machinery and technology
- Capable managers and technicians
- An ample supply of high-tech workers
- A productive manufacturing work force of 160,000
- A US$4 billion state-of-the-art telecommunications system
- World-class transportation facilities and services

Within the last decade, Puerto Rico has established itself as the hub of the Caribbean. According to Stephen H. Long, Citibank's senior officer for the Caribbean and Central American Region, the Commonwealth has developed into the prime site for U.S. and foreign companies doing business in the Caribbean Basin and is rapidly becoming the gateway to the Americas.

The Section 936 Program

Although a solid, state-of-the-art industrial base and highly qualified economic and trade officials exert a major influence on Puerto

Rico's growth potential, special financing from the Section 936 program continues to be a prime attraction for U.S. investors.

Section 936 of the Internal Revenue Code designates as 936 companies certain U.S. corporations that derive a significant portion of their income from Puerto Rican business activities. These companies are effectively exempt from U.S. income tax on the portion of their income derived from sources within Puerto Rico.

Funds repatriated to the mainland parent are subject to a Puerto Rican tollgate tax at a maximum rate of 10 percent. The average tollgate tax actually paid, however, has been substantially less—approximately 4 percent—which in effect saves at least 90 percent of normal federal taxes.

Quipsy Funds

As long as these funds remain on deposit in Puerto Rico they are tax free and many companies have complied (mostly large U.S. corporations). This has resulted in a substantial amount of Section 936 funds, referred to as "qualified possession source investment income" or QPSII (quipsy) funds. This money is available for company use in Puerto Rico or by the financial institutions holding the deposits.

Financial institutions holding quipsy funds may grant loans to companies investing in qualified projects in any CBI country that has executed a Tax Information Exchange Agreement (TIEA) with the United States. The loans carry below-market interest rates approximating 85 percent of LIBOR. Furthermore, the government of Puerto Rico has committed to provide a minimum of $100 million per year of 936 funds for private-sector investments.

Many American companies are using 936 funds to set up twin plants in qualified CBI countries such as Jamaica, Grenada, or the U.S. Virgin Islands. These facilities operate in ways similar to those of the Mexican–U.S. maquiladora free-trade zone program. Under the Section 936 program, however, the capital cost of twin plants is substantially less than it is in Mexico.

The Puerto Rican government's stated objective is to maximize both the number and the dollar value of 936 loans "as part of Puerto Rico's ongoing mission to promote economic welfare in the Commonwealth and the Caribbean Basin."

Either new business or expansion projects are eligible for 936 funding. They may be in manufacturing, information processing, agroprocessing, hotels, or tourism. Funding is also available for the development of roads, airports, telecommunications, and low-cost housing. Current estimates place the quipsy pool at more than US$10 billion. Private placements, however, continue to augment the original pool.

The following countries qualify for investment of Section 936 funds: Jamaica, Barbados, Grenada, Dominica, Trinidad and Tobago, the Dominican Republic, Costa Rica, Honduras, and the U.S. Virgin Islands. Nicaragua, El Salvador, and other CBI countries are in various stages of consideration.

Qualifying for 936 Funding

The same criteria used by mainland banks applies to 936 loan approval: namely, a sound credit history and a demonstratable ability to repay. Furthermore, 936 applicants must provide guarantees from home-country banks. The primary advantage of using quipsy funds is not that loans are easier to obtain, but that the interest rate is substantially lower than that charged on conventional bank loans.

Although no minimum loan value is prescribed, the larger the loan, the greater the benefits. With interest rates of approximately 85 percent of LIBOR, a five-year-term loan for $500,000 saves the borrower at least $8,000 per year: a $50 million loan results in savings of more than $800,000 each year.

Special Funding Arrangements

Smaller companies, or those needing lesser amounts, might do better to work through a private Puerto Rican venture capital fund, the Caribbean Basin Partners for Progress, Ltd. (CBPP). This venture fund is a partnership of 936 companies formed specifically to invest up to US$100 million of quipsy funds in small and midsize private-sector projects with job-creating potential.

CBPP grants loans of US$1 million to US$10 million for up to 75 percent of the financing requirement. Terms extend to ten years. According to Andrew Markey, international treasurer of Johnson and Johnson, a large majority of the loans have been under US$1 million. During 1991, its first year of operations, CBPP financed four projects: a US$300,000 manufacturing plant in Barbados, a US$600,000 banana farm and a US$900,000 tourism project in Costa Rica, and a US$520,000 apparel project in the Dominican Republic.

To further expedite the flow of 936 funds, the Puerto Rican government established a bond-issuing agency, the Caribbean Basin Projects Financing Authority (CARIFA). By tailoring a bond issue to the needs of a qualified borrower and selling the bonds to 936 companies (mostly Fortune 500), CARIFA provides a mechanism for companies to invest directly in specific projects. Banks holding 936 funds can also invest in CARIFA bonds.

The One Major Deterrent

The greatest deterrent smaller companies face in qualifying for 936 funds is the requirement for home-country bank guarantees, which in many cases are just not available. To circumvent the problem, several public agencies stand ready to offer guarantees, albeit each with its own restrictions:

- The Overseas Private Investment Corporation (OPIC) offers guarantees of up to US$50 million, provided that the investment project is at least 25 percent U.S.–owned and the loan/equity ratio does not exceed 60 percent.
- The World Bank's Multilateral Investment Guarantee Agency (MIGA) issues loan guarantees, provided that it also issues equity guarantees in the same project. Also, the borrower must either be from a country that has joined MIGA or be a national of a developing country bringing equity from a foreign source. Unfortunately, most countries have not yet ratified MIGA, and of course MIGA cannot grant loans without participating in equity guarantees.
- The USAID Small Business Loan Portfolio Guarantee program covers up to 50 percent of the commercial risk for projects in the US$1 million to US$3 million range.

In 1991, the U.S. Government threw a monkey wrench into the use of public agency guarantees. It ruled that U.S. agencies, namely OPIC and USAID, cannot guarantee loans of Section 936 funds because doing so would confer a double tax benefit—using tax dollars to back a tax-exempt investment.

A year later, under pressure from the Commonwealth of Puerto Rico and agencies in the U.S. executive branch, the rule was changed to allow OPIC guarantees to continue through 1995. Such guarantees are limited to a total of US$100 million for each year.

In addition, CARIFA is setting up its own guarantee program.

For further information about the Section 936 program, contact either of the following:

Caribbean Development
  Program
Economic Development
  Administration
Department of State, P.O.
  Box 3271
Old San Juan, PR 00902
Phone: (809) 758-4747
Fax: (809) 723-3305

Caribbean Development
  Program
Economic Development
  Administration
1290 Avenue of the
  Americas
New York, NY 10104-0092
Phone: (212) 245-1200
Fax: (212) 581-2667

Chapter 8

The U.S. Virgin Islands: American Paradise

If Puerto Rico is the best-kept secret in the Western Hemisphere, the U.S. Virgin Islands, commonly referred to as the USVI, rank a close second. For small and midsize businesses, the Virgin Islands offer even more benefits and fewer headaches than the more congested, cosmopolitan Commonwealth.

Although an unincorporated territory of the United States, the USVI has retained its most-favored-nation status with Denmark, which owned the islands prior to 1917. This provides companies located in the USVI with a unique entrance to European Community markets duty free, or, in some cases, under preferential tariffs. The USVI also qualifies under the multilateral General System of Preference (GSP) from several countries, including Japan and Canada, and may ship selected products duty free to those countries.

But that's only the tip of the iceberg. U.S. direct investments in the USVI qualify for the following benefits:

- Section 936 financing
- Duty-free exports to the United States, Puerto Rico, and many Caribbean Basin countries
- Virtually tax-free income
- IRS foreign sales corporation status

Historical and Political Perspectives

In 1993, the U.S. Virgin Islands celebrates its quincentennial. Discovered by Christopher Columbus in 1493 and named "St. Ursula and Her Eleven Thousand Virgins," the USVI was alternately claimed by Spain, England, the Netherlands, France, and the Knights of Malta. In 1670, Denmark finally gained control of St. Thomas and then St. John. In 1733, it purchased St. Croix from the French.

Eager to protect its Panama Canal shipping lanes from the German threat during World War I, the United States purchased the Virgin Islands from Denmark in 1917 and established naval bases on St. Thomas and St. Croix. From that date until the 1960s, the islands slumbered under the Caribbean sun. Except for fragmented agricultural products and modest tourism, few considered this American paradise anything more than a playground for industrious Puerto Ricans.

The closing of Cuba to U.S. travel, coupled with sustained economic growth in the United States during the 1960s, 1970s, and 1980s, brought about a substantial development of the USVI tourist industry and a general revitalization of the islands' business life.

The U.S. Virgin Islands are located forty miles east of Puerto Rico, 1,100 miles south/southeast of Miami (2.5 hours' flying time), and 1,500 miles from New York (3.5 hours' flying time). They are 600 miles from Caracas, 3,400 miles from Los Angeles, 2,300 miles from Mexico City, and 4,200 miles from London.

The Virgin Islands have always been attuned to international trade. They first developed as slave-holding sugar cane estates. To this day, the geography of the islands is divided into "estates." St. Thomas also became a key Caribbean port for transshipment between the Americas and Europe. Raw materials were assembled from the Caribbean region and exchanged for processed goods in the United States and Europe. Sugar production eventually gave birth to a rum-distilling industry that is still thriving.

The USVI is comprised of the three main islands and sixty-five small cays. Three miles separate St. Thomas from St. John, of which 75 percent is national parkland administered by the U.S. Park Service. St. Thomas, with one of the best natural deep-water harbors in the Caribbean, services a thriving cruise ship trade. It is also a major shipping port for trade with the United States and Europe.

St. Croix, the largest and the most industrialized of the three

Table 8-1. Key U.S. Virgin Islands Statistics.

Capital city	Charlotte Amalie, St. Thomas
Total land mass	137.5 sq.mi.
Population	110,000
Labor force	45,000
Minimum wage	$4.65/hr
Unemployment rate	4.7%
Literacy rate	90%
Per capita income	$9,030
Annual imports (principally from the United States, Africa, and the Middle East)	$3.3 billion
Annual exports (principally to the United States)	$2.8 billion

Source: U.S. Virgin Islands Industrial Development Corporation, U.S. Virgin Islands Chamber of Commerce.

islands, lies 40 miles south of St. Thomas. It is the home of Hess Oil (Caribbean), the largest oil refinery in the Caribbean Basin.

As a territory of the United States, the USVI falls under the U.S. federal court system, the Internal Revenue Service, the U.S. Postal Service, the U.S. Customs Service, the U.S. banking system, and the accreditation system of the U.S. public school and university systems. The USVI uses the U.S. dollar as its currency, and its citizens carry a U.S. passport.

A politically stable government under the jurisdiction of the U.S. Congress, executive branch, and judicial system eliminates investment risk. Security provided by the U.S. armed forces further reduces the possibility of local or foreign power expropriation. The U.S. Army's protection of St. Croix businesses from looting after Hurricane Hugo in 1990 is a good example of the importance of such security measures.

Table 8-1 shows the territory's key statistics.

Local Markets for Imported Products

Most USVI manufacturing and processing facilities produce goods exclusively for export. Natural resources are scarce, although until its shutdown in the mid-1980s, the Martin-Marietta facility on St. Croix used indigenous minerals to produce alumina. A very modest agricultural base produces small amounts of produce and livestock for local consumption. Until recently, local waters were rich in crustaceans and a variety of fish, but overproduction has driven fishing boats farther and farther into the open ocean.

Such scarcities mean that domestic demand must be satisfied almost entirely from imports. A growing number of Americans, some of them retirees, are setting up residence in the USVI, either part-time or full-time. These residents comprise a relatively small consumer base, but one that demands the products that are available on the mainland. Émigrés from "down-island"—Antigua, St. Kitts-Nevis, Trinidad and Tobago, and so on—have adopted American tastes, as, of course, have USVI natives. All construction materials, hard goods, spare parts, capital equipment, food, clothing, and general supplies, including a portion of the potable water requirements, must be imported.

Here is a sampling of products in the highest demand. All of them must be imported, primarily from U.S. and Puerto Rican companies:

Consumer Products

- Electronics
  - VCRs
  - TVs
  - Radios
  - Computers (and computer software)
  - Typewriters
  - Copying machines
- Appliances
  - Ranges
  - Refrigerators
  - Freezers
  - Microwave ovens
  - Telephones
- Vehicles
  - Automobiles
  - Buses
  - Trucks
  - Vans
  - Mopeds
  - Bicycles
- Athletic and physical fitness equipment
- Repair parts for electronics, appliances, and vehicles
- Office supplies
- Clothing
  - Work clothes
  - Dress clothes
  - Shoes
  - Boots
- Medical and pharmaceutical supplies

Capital Equipment

- Medical diagnostic and treatment
- Waste disposal
- Water purification and treatment
- Construction: Graters, dozers, haulers, cranes, dump trucks
- Welding
- Electricity generators
- Plumbing, electrical, and carpentry supplies
- Plumbing and electrical fixtures

Food

- Meats and poultry
- Fresh produce
- Frozen foods
- Soft drinks
- Liquor, beer, and wine
- Paper products
- Cereals
- Candies
- Dairy products

When virtually every type of product (except rum) sold on the islands must be imported, prioritization of product demand means nothing. When the USVI economy is up (and it follows the U.S. economy very closely) freighters from Miami and Puerto Rico make daily runs carrying everything from automobiles to ice cream, from plumbing fixtures to California wine, from New York designer clothes to rattan furniture, from color television sets to sailboat masts, and from laundry detergent to milk and fresh produce. You name it, it's imported.

A few categories stand out, however, as being in such high demand that price levels are practically irrelevant. The used car market is a good example. Local car dealers fly to Miami specifically to buy used cars at auctions and ship them down. The condition of the cars is immaterial. So is price. U.S. firms in the used car business can make a fortune here.

The same holds true for building materials. For more than a decade, a residential and commercial building boom has been going on in St. Croix, and, to a lesser extent, in St. John. Because of the exploding demand for hotels, condominiums, and second (or retiree) homes for affluent Americans, there has been a constant demand for all types of construction materials, furnishings, and building trades services—even during the 1989–1992 recession. Add the rebuilding necessary after periodic storms and hurricanes (such as that occasioned by Hugo in 1990) and the construction industry has reason to anticipate an ongoing boom for years to come. None of it would be possible without imported supplies.

Consumer electronics, household appliances, and auto and bus repair parts are always in demand. All foods, liquors (the USVI is a duty-free port for liquor), beer, and wine to service the local markets and the tourist industry do very well too.

Competition in most of these products and services is very weak. No multinationals have set up shop to service local markets, as happened in Puerto Rico. Local firms are all small. Margins are broader than in the states, although pricing cannot be as exorbitant as on some of the less-developed islands.

No sales agents are necessary, or even desirable. Stateside sales personnel can handle the USVI more than adequately and local businesses expect to deal with Americans.

Service Markets

The insurance industry has not yet discovered the USVI, and all insurance underwriting is done off-island. A handful of insurance brokers service all three islands. Other financial services are represented, although they are somewhat few in number. Barclays, Banco Popular, Citibank, Chase Manhattan, First Pennsylvania, First Virgin Islands Federal Savings, and Bank of Nova Scotia all maintain active branches. Fund management is nonexistent, although Merrill Lynch and Prudential Bache handle securities investment transactions. The USVI does not have a stock exchange.

The islands are rife with attorneys; there were over one hundred firms at last count. Major international accounting firms have not yet discovered the USVI, although several small firms of certified and noncertified accountants practice in the islands. Additional experienced CPAs with extensive U.S. and foreign tax credentials are desperately needed.

Other well-represented businesses include advertising and public relations, commercial printing (but no quick-print shops), data processing, architectural and engineering, secretarial, and telephone answering services. A small number of firms offer very rudimentary business consulting services. To date, the USVI has not caught on to the value of specialized consulting fields, although the market will expand in time.

Two markets in the service area stand out as generating the greatest demand and the least competition:

1. Electrical, electronic, and mechanical repair services
2. Environmental engineering services

It is virtually impossible to get anything repaired, or repaired properly, in the USVI. Repair services are in very high demand for autos, computers, home appliances, office equipment, production equipment, construction and off-road vehicles, swimming pool equipment, hotel equipment, aircraft, power boats, and sailboats. For some businesses the closest repair facilities are in Puerto Rico; for many they're in Miami.

Environmental Markets

The boom in environmental services seen in the United States has not yet hit the islands. However, the current trickle of market demand will inevitably turn into a torrent as the U.S. Environmental Protection Agency increases pressure on local government and businesses to clean up their acts. Getting in at the beginning ensures a very lucrative market in the years ahead in such fields as solid waste management, resource recovery/recycling, water treatment, hazardous waste management, environmental engineering and consulting, and air pollution control.

Direct Investment Opportunities and Incentives

The main industries currently active in the USVI are:

- Tourism
- Government service
- Petroleum refining
- Watch assembly
- Rum distilling
- Construction
- Pharmaceuticals
- Textiles
- Electronics assembly

Virtually all goods are produced for export—mainly to the United States—not for local consumption.

The USVI does not have any free trade zones. However, several trade and tax incentives more than make up for this omission. With the blessing of the U.S. Internal Revenue Service, the U.S. Department of Commerce, and the U.S. Treasury Department, the local government actively solicits direct investment from American firms. To this end, a variety of tax and other incentives make the USVI a unique business location in the Caribbean Basin.

Products Exported to the United States

The General Headnote 3(a)(iv) of the Harmonized Tariff Schedule of the United States grants USVI companies special privileges not available to Puerto Rican companies or those from CBI countries. This provision permits any product eligible for CBI preferential tariff treatment to be imported into the United States from the USVI free of any duty.

In addition, as long as a company in the USVI substantially transforms the product into a different product than that imported to the territory, up to 70 percent of the product's value may consist of foreign dutiable components.

Second, products that do not fall under the CBI duty-free provisions, such as textiles and leather goods, may be imported to the United States from the USVI duty free, provided that no more than 50 percent of the value is comprised of foreign dutiable components.

The USVI offers yet a third unique stimulus for the manufacture of exports to the United States. A USVI company can import CBI-qualified products with up to 65 percent dutiable foreign materials, and then combine them in an assembly or other manufacturing process with non-CBI imports, transforming these materials and components into a new finished product that qualifies for duty-free export to the United States. Such finished products remain duty free even though they consist of more than 70 percent of foreign materials that would normally be subject to U.S. duty.

As a further incentive, companies in the USVI are exempted from the protectionist provisions of the Jones Act, which specifies that goods moving between U.S. ports must be carried on U.S.

vessels. Since companies shipping goods from the USVI or Puerto Rico need not comply, more competitive rates are frequently available from foreign carriers.

Tax Incentives

The Industrial Development Act of the U.S. Virgin Islands, together with Section 934 of the U.S. Internal Revenue Code, offers a variety of business tax incentives for U.S. direct investment.

Section 934 relates to companies domiciled in the USVI. Such companies that invest 100 percent of their earnings in capital projects on any of the three islands for five years can, from the sixth year forward, exclude 98 percent of profits from U.S. or Virgin Islands income tax.

The five major investment incentives from the Industrial Development Commission include:

1. A 100 percent exemption for USVI gross receipts, property, and excise taxes
2. A 90 percent exclusion from the USVI corporate income tax*
3. A reduction of USVI customs duties to 1 percent
4. Tax benefits available for terms of ten to fifteen years, depending on the location of the facility, with five-year extension normally granted upon request
5. Repatriation of earnings to a U.S. parent company tax-free under IRS Code Section 936

In 1991, according to the Industrial Development Commission (IDC), over seventy companies with more than 5,000 employees enjoyed these tax benefits. The companies represented a complete cross section of industries: hotels, guest houses, tourist attractions, communications, transportation, specialized services, and manufacturers.

The twenty-five manufacturing companies that qualified for the benefits included companies producing watch assemblies, phar-

---

* It should be noted that even though the USVI falls under the U.S. Internal Revenue Code, taxes are paid to the USVI government and retained in the territory. The rates and regulations are identical to those applied to U.S. mainland corporations.

maceuticals, alumina, oil refining, electronics, and rum and liquor products. Some of the better-known manufacturing firms included Hess Oil, Allied Signal, Zenith Laboratories, Timex, Clarendon, Pharmacia, Brown Forman, and Benrus.

The following three classes of business qualify for IDC benefits:

Tourism

- Hotels
- Guest houses
- Transportation services
- Selected recreation facilities

Goods Production

- Manufacturing of all types
- Raw material processing
- Assembly operations
- Utilities
- Agribusiness
- Aquaculture

Service Businesses
(all of whose services must be provided to customers located outside the Virgin Islands)

- International commercial distribution and trading companies
- International public relations firms
- Publicity firms
- Economic, scientific, or management consulting companies
- Public auditing firms
- Companies that process, edit, and dub motion pictures
- Commercial and graphic artists
- News syndicates
- Mail-order businesses
- Assembly, bottling and/or export packing operations
- Computer service centers
- Maritime vessels servicing operations
- Aircraft repair and maintenance companies
- Machinery and heavy equipment repair companies
- Electrical, electronic, and watch repair businesses
- Architectural design and engineering firms
- Photographic labs
- Dental labs
- Optical and ophthalmological labs

- Companies that install prefabricated houses
- Captive insurance companies

A company in one of these industries qualifies for benefits, provided that it meets the following four standards:

1. Provides full-time employment to at least ten island residents who have resided in the USVI for at least one year prior to being hired.
2. Invests at least $50,000, exclusive of inventory, in an industry or business that advances the well-being of the USVI. ("Well-being" is undefined.) For a company leasing equipment, its fair market value is included in determining compliance with the $50,000 minimum investment.
3. Meets the requirements of IRS Code Section 934 for a USVI corporation, individual or partnership, or Section 936 for a USVI subsidiary of a U.S. corporation.
4. Is an actual investor in the enterprise, not a contractor, subcontractor, or other person or corporation acting as an agent.

A simple example best demonstrates how these incentives benefit a foreign direct investment. Assume the existence of a manufacturing subsidiary of a U.S. corporation with sales of $2 million, making products using imports from CBI and non-CBI countries in its products.

Gross receipts tax

Sales	$2,000,000
Tax rate	4%
Tax liability	$ 80,000
Exemption	$ 80,000

Property tax

Real property assessed value at 60 percent	$250,000
Tax rate	1.25%
Tax liability	$ 3,125
Exemption	$ 3,125

Excise tax

Value of imported materials and components	$750,000
Ad valorum assessment	105%
Assessed value	787,500
Excise tax rate	4%
Tax liability	$ 31,500
Exemption	$ 31,500

Customs duty reduction

Value of non-U.S. imported materials and components	$600,000
Customs duty rate	6%
Normal customs duty	36,000
Duty at 1 percent of value	6,000
Duty savings	$ 30,000

Corporate income tax

Assume net profit of 15% of sales	$300,000
Virgin Islands tax calculation:	
15% × $50,000	$ 7,500
25% × $25,000	6,250
34% × $25,000	8,500
39% × $200,000	78,000
10% × 61,250 (USVI surcharge)	6,125
Tax liability	106,375
Exemption at 90%	95,737
Actual tax	$ 10,639

The total benefits from investment incentives in this example are:

Gross receipts tax exemption	$ 80,000
Property tax exemption	3,125
Excise tax exemption	31,500
1 percent customs duty savings	30,000
USVI income tax exemption	95,737
Total benefits	$240,362

In addition to these savings, the mainland parent company would benefit by importing USVI finished products duty free and by a 100 percent exemption from U.S. corporate income taxes on the subsidiary's net income under Section 936 of the Internal Revenue Code.

To qualify under Section 936, the USVI business must be a wholly owned subsidiary of a U.S. corporation. In addition, the parent must make an election to be a 936 company for ten years and select a cost-sharing or profit-splitting accounting method to claim intangible income credit. At least 80 percent of the subsidiary's income must be from USVI sources and 75 percent from the active conduct of a USVI trade or business. Companies operating subsidiaries in both Puerto Rico and the USVI can combine the income of the two subsidiaries to meet this requirement.

Financial and Technical Assistance

The USVI encourages the formation of small businesses or small branches of foreign businesses (predominantly U.S. companies) through four local programs. They are:

1. *Small Business Development Agency (SBDA)*. The SBDA provides up to $150,000 in bank loan guarantees and up to $25,000 in direct loans. Guarantees cover 90 percent of the bank loan, with interest set by the lending institution. Interest on direct loans runs about two to three points above prime. Eligibility requirements include a maximum of $1 million annual sales and fifty or fewer employees. Individual borrowers must be owners working full-time in the business and meet one of the following criteria: born in the USVI; a ten-year USVI resident; or a five-year resident if one parent was born in the USVI.

The SBDA also administers several other programs:

- The Frederiksted Revolving Loan Fund (a $30,000 bank loan guarantee and a $20,000 maximum direct loan)
- The Economic Development Administration Loan Fund, with a maximum direct loan limit of $75,000
- The Farmer and Fisherman Loan Fund, with direct loans

up to $5,000 at 4 percent interest for farmers and fishermen with three years' USVI experience
- The Savan Revolving Loan Fund for direct loans up to $10,000, to be used for leasehold improvements by businesses located in Savan of St. Thomas

2. *Small Business Development Center (SBDC).* As part of the University of the Virgin Islands, the SBDC offers counseling, training, business information research, business planning, market feasibility evaluation, and technical assistance under eligibility requirements of the U.S. Small Business Administration, mostly free of charge. In conjunction with Barclays Bank, the SBDC operates a Small Business Assistance Loan Program with loans up to $10,000, with no interest the first year and 5 percent interest thereafter.

3. *Tri-Island Economic Development Council (TIEDC).* The TIEDC is a community based, nonprofit organization that operates the Rural Development Loan Fund under the auspices of the U.S. Department of Agriculture. It makes direct loans of up to $99,500 at 10.78 percent interest to companies meeting SBDA eligibility requirements. The TIEDC, through its subsidiary, VITIED, Inc., operates the Minority Business Development Center under a grant from the U.S. Department of Commerce. The center provides a wide range of services to qualified applicants, including management and technical assistance, business counseling, brokering, marketing services, and procurement and contracting assistance.

4. *Film Promotion Office.* The Film Promotion Office is a division of the Department of Economic Development and Agriculture and provides a range of services to producers of films, TV shows and features, TV commercials, print, and other media from the U.S. mainland and other countries.

In addition to these local programs, the U.S. Small Business Administration and the Farmers Home Administration (FmHA) offer the same types of assistance in the USVI as in the United States.

Local banks are equipped to handle a full range of trade finance, short-term working capital loans, and long-term loans for capital purchases. They also make real estate mortgage loans for industrial and residential property.

The Virgin Islands' Infrastructure

The United States has heavily subsidized the construction and maintenance of the USVI infrastructure. Streets and rural roads on both St. Thomas and St. Croix are as good or better than those in many sections of the U.S. mainland. Each island has a hospital, although there is a lack of state-of-the-art equipment and medical specialists.

As island states go, telephone service to and from the USVI ranks near the top of the list. Companies accustomed to the failsafe systems in the United States, however, will be disappointed. Foul weather causes frequent outages and interruptions. Installation and repair services from telephone company personnel are abysmally slow—not unlike other service-oriented businesses in tropical locations.

Nevertheless, the USVI does have many modern communications conveniences, including an international fax system, satellite service, the U.S. long-distance network, digital switching, and fiberoptic transmission.

Electricity generation is probably the greatest infrastructure deficiency. Growing island populations have pushed relatively primitive generating facilities to their very limits. All three islands need additional power capacity to sustain continuously expanding residential requirements, tourist facilities, and industrial/commercial demands. Very frequent electric spikes, brownouts, and complete shutdowns make it necessary for industrial facilities, and many commercial ones, to keep their own standby generator systems.

Fresh water supply and waste disposal facilities, although meager, are no worse in the Virgin Islands than on other Caribbean islands, and a big improvement over most.

Labor, Management, and Facilities

Out of a population of 110,000, approximately 45,000 men and women are counted in the labor force. Although predominantly a service economy, the government is actively pursuing private investment in manufacturing, construction, and transportation sectors. Government statistics break the labor force into the following industries.

Government service (territory and federal)	16,700
Retail	8,850
Service industries (including hotels)	8,100
Construction	2,950
Transportation and utilities	2,900
Manufacturing	2,600
Finance, insurance, real estate, and banking	2,300
Wholesale	700
	45,000

Representative average wage rates are as follows:

Manufacturing (instruments and related products)	$ 6.95
Hotels	7.00
Banking	8.10
Construction	11.80
Transportation and utilities	10.20

St. Croix is the largest and most populous of the Virgins (approximately 60 percent of the population). It boasts a large pool of skilled manufacturing labor, much of it extensively trained by the large Hess Oil refinery and the now-defunct Martin-Marietta alumina facility.

A Vocational and Technical Education Division of the public school system provides a full range of programs to train youths and adults. The Private Industry Council and the Federal Job Training Partnership Act provide funding and technical assistance for company training programs.

Local management talent is not as abundant as hourly labor. The University of the Virgin Islands, with campuses on both St. Thomas and St. Croix, offers degree programs but not much in the way of business courses. Expats from the United States and Europe who have settled in the islands provide a very small management base. Most managers must be brought in from the U.S. mainland or Puerto Rico. Average salaries run approximately 30 to 60 percent less than for comparable positions on the mainland.

Industrial sites and facilities are in very short supply on St. Thomas (and virtually nonexistent on St. John). When office space can be found, it runs $15 to $30 per square foot (according to 1990 figures). Office rents in St. Croix for comparable space run approximately one third less.

St. Croix offers the best opportunity for industrial or commercial facilities. The island has a variety of industrial sites, including the modern twenty-five-acre V.I. Light Industrial Park, operated by the Industrial Development Commission. Rentals start at $2.50 per square foot. St. Croix also offers a wide selection of commercial, office, wholesale, and retail space, ranging from 400 square feet to 25,000 square feet. Plentiful truck fleets and good roads make transport around the island's eighty-five square miles easy and inexpensive.

Small and midsize U.S. companies hoping to exploit Caribbean Basin resources, duty-free incentives, and enormous tax breaks, but not wanting to compete with multinationals for labor and government incentives, should seriously consider St. Croix as a good place to learn the ropes. While it is true that labor rates are higher than those in the Dominican Republic, Jamaica, Honduras, and any of the small English-speaking island states, the other incentives more than offset this drawback.

One very important but frequently overlooked strategic consideration is the effect a foreign location can have on expatriate managers. While some are certainly adventurous and long to experience unusual, out-of-the way places, more prefer to relocate where family members feel safe, living accommodations are comfortable, and educational and cultural facilities are similar to those enjoyed at home. St. Croix meets each of these criteria.

A second very crucial consideration must be the attitude of government bureaucrats toward foreigners and foreign companies. More than one Latin American and Caribbean country has experienced social upheaval, resulting in antiforeigner vendettas, or, more often, simply anti-Americanism. This does not and cannot happen in the USVI, whose citizens are also U.S. citizens.

A third strategic decision (and the one that points to St. Croix rather than St. Thomas or St. John) is the diversity of the business community. The other two islands are basically vacation spots. St. Croix is business-oriented. Local government and chamber of commerce officials do everything possible to make a new foreign company feel at home, including providing special security protection if desired. Martin-Marietta and Hess Oil have called St. Croix home for decades. They would not do so if it weren't making them money.

Quality-of-Life Considerations

The USVI advertises its biggest selling point to U.S. businesses as "the opportunity to run a profitable business in an island location where it's like being on vacation every day."

The USVI is more Americanized than any other Caribbean or Latin American location. It boasts physical fitness clubs, a glittering nightlife on St. Thomas, camping on St. John, the most prolific charter sailboat facilities in the world, scuba diving, snorkeling, a plethora of beaches, championship golf and tennis facilities, legitimate theater, big-game sportfishing, and probably the best shopping in the Caribbean. The islands also offer frequent and competitive air service direct to Puerto Rico, Miami, New York, Atlanta, and Philadelphia.

Accommodation rentals run upward from $400 per month for a one-bedroom apartment and $1,000 per month for a beachfront two-bedroom condominium. Purchase prices for condominiums run from $65,000 to $1 million; houses run from about $100,000 to well over $1 million. Indeed, the USVI offers something for everyone, regardless of taste.

Families will appreciate the territory's public school system (which boasts a total of 34 elementary and secondary schools) and its many private schools (both religious-affiliated and nonsectarian). Music, theater, and dance groups exist on both St. Thomas and St. Croix. Many American and European artists and writers make the USVI their year-round home.

In 1988, the Industrial Development Commission conducted a survey of 200 U.S. manufacturing companies to determine the major elements they considered when choosing an offshore location. Respondents overwhelmingly ranked attractive tax incentives as the most important. They also preferred not to be subjected to currency inconvertibility, communications failures, time differences, travel expense, and executive downtime. The IDC claims that the USVI meets all these requirements item by item.

Foreign Sales Corporations

One of the special features of the USVI is that, other than the U.S. Pacific possessions of American Samoa, Guam, and the Northern Marianas, it is the only American location that qualifies as a "foreign country" under the foreign sales corporation provisions of the Internal Revenue Code.

A foreign sales corporation (FSC) is a separate company formed by a U.S. exporter (or others under contract), incorporated in a qualified foreign country (of which there are 30), with an operating office in that country. Theoretically, this is an administrative and bookkeeping office. It prepares export invoices to foreign customers and deposits collections in a local bank. When the parent corporation files its annual tax return, it can exclude a portion of export income from taxable income. The result is a maximum tax reduction of 15 percent on export income.

Large FSCs are used by nearly all of the Fortune 500; small FSCs, by companies exporting less than $5 million annually. The administrative procedures and reporting requirements are substantially less complex for small FSCs.

Companies with less than $50,000 in export sales generally use "shared FSCs" set up by several states and trade associations.

Companies frequently find that it is not practical to set up a foreign office, staff it, and maintain local accounting records. As an alternative, a local FSC management company can be engaged to handle the administrative details at a very low cost: $1,500 to $5,000 per year, depending on the volume of transactions. The USVI has approximately twenty to twenty-five FSC management companies—local branches of U.S. banks, law firms, and accounting firms—as well as several independent FSC management companies.

Chapter 9

CARICOM and the Smaller English-Speaking States

The wave of trading blocks sweeping the hemisphere encouraged the rebirth of the Caribbean Common Market (CARICOM). Also referred to as the Caribbean Community, CARICOM was originally formed in 1973 under the Treaty of Chaguaramas to create a common commercial market for duty-free trade between member nations and aid in the drive for economic unification. Now, twenty years later, regional leaders have set January 1, 1994, as the deadline to complete the integration, in order to present a stronger voice in negotiations with representatives of other trading blocs and decrease the region's dependence on U.S. and European financial and other economic assistance.

Current CARICOM membership consists of Antigua and Barbuda, the Bahamas, Barbados, Belize, Dominica, Grenada, Guyana, Jamaica, Montserrat, St. Kitts-Nevis, St. Lucia, St. Vincent and the Grenadines, and Trinidad and Tobago. In addition to duty-free trade and economic integration, the CARICOM nations are working toward establishing:

- Common incentives to attract foreign investment
- Tax treaties between member nations
- A common set of external tariffs

In addition to its role as a coordinating body, CARICOM sponsors the Eastern Caribbean Association of Commerce and Industry to actively promote foreign trade and investment in the region and the Caribbean Development Bank (CDB) to facilitate financing of investment projects. In 1992 it created a third organization, the Caribbean Council for Europe (CCE), to bring together Caribbean and European private-sector leaders to lobby and monitor developments flowing from the implementation of the European Community (EC) economic policies on January 1, 1993, as they affect the Caribbean.

The CCE is of special interest to potential U.S. investors in that it establishes a formal, private-sector link to Europe that will undoubtedly open trade possibilities previously ignored. Its major thrust is to "provide an umbrella to enable Caribbean companies to seek investment, arrange joint ventures, and identify markets for export to Europe." The Lomé Convention already permits the duty-free export of many categories of goods. However, with the CCE as a coordinating body, companies with facilities in a CARICOM country should be in an excellent competitive position to tap EC markets.

CARICOM members that qualify under CBI and the Canadian-Caribbean free trade agreement (CARIBCAN) get a triple-barreled opportunity: duty-free exports to the United States, to Canada, and to Europe. In recognition of the single CARICOM voice, representatives from the United States and CARICOM executed a free trade framework agreement in 1991 as part of the Enterprise for the Americas Initiative.

The World's Smallest Common Market

The Organization of Eastern Caribbean States (OECS), referred to as the "world's smallest common market," was established in 1981 as a subcommon market within CARICOM to promote trade and investment for its smaller member nations. It is comprised of Antigua and Barbuda, Dominica, Grenada, Montserrat, St. Kitts-Nevis, St. Lucia, St. Vincent and the Grenadines, and the British Virgin Islands (a recent addition).

These tiny nations share:

- A common currency, the Eastern Caribbean dollar, pegged at EC$2.70 = US$1

- A common form of government, the British parliamentary system
- A common language, English
- Similar foreign investment incentives

Together, they have a population of less than 600,000, a labor force of 240,000, and a GDP of US$1.3 billion.

All OECS members solicit foreign investment, primarily in their target industries: hotel and resort development, data entry, information processing, electronics assembly, apparel, agribusiness, and (recently) aquaculture. However, with very small markets and an even smaller labor base, microbusinesses are about the only foreign investment that makes sense, other than tourism facilities, of course.

Toward the end of 1991, the OECS, in conjunction with USAID, established the Environment and Coastal Resources Project (EN-CORE) to devote special attention to community-oriented environment management in Dominica and St. Lucia. USAID has funded the project with US$11 million over a six-year period. Although not a large sum, it is a start, and signifies the region's increasing interest in developing new measures to protect the fragile environment of these microstates. This bodes well for foreign businesses capable of supplying appropriate goods and services, none of which are available locally.

The Best Market Prospects for Foreign Companies

Thirteen very small domestic markets (excluding Jamaica), separated by vast stretches of ocean and possessed of varying degrees of income capabilities, do not offer much opportunity for large export orders. Although every island imports nearly all its basic goods and services, market size restricts any meaningful export opportunities. However, certain markets are worth considering for small shipments to meet specific demands.

In the Bahamas, an excellent market exists for virtually all consumer durables (appliances, automobiles, electronics); a wide range of consumer soft goods, including work clothes and dress clothes for men, women, and children, leather goods, and processed foods; and petroleum products, including fuel oil, detergents, and gas.

The best products for export to Barbados are personal computers, peripherals, and software, especially business software; grains of all types; and paper products—newsprint, consumer paper goods, shipping boxes, and industrial packaging.

Although tiny and well removed from the rest of the Caribbean states, Belize needs all the consumer goods mentioned for the Bahamas plus on- and off-road construction vehicles and equipment (earthmoving, drilling, gas and electricity generating, and lifting) and automobile parts and accessories (most cars and trucks in Belize are falling apart).

Impoverished Guyana's most dire import need, in addition to foodstuffs, is all types of mining and construction equipment.

Although well-developed by island standards, Jamaica continues to import substantial quantities of industrial chemicals, petroleum for fuel, machine tools (such as grinders, lathes, milling machines, drills), and a wide range of agricultural equipment and spare parts. Chapter 10 reviews additional opportunities in this, one of the largest of the Caribbean nations.

Oil-rich Trinidad and Tobago is developing its own industrial base. A good import market also exists there for electrical machinery, food processing equipment (freezers, mixers, packaging equipment, and storage facilities), and personal computers, including peripherals and business-oriented software.

A sizable demand exists in all CARICOM nations for the following products:

- Processed food
- Apparel
- Medical supplies and equipment
- Construction equipment and services
- Power generating and distribution equipment
- Water purification and storage equipment
- Educational supplies
- Telecommunications equipment and services
- Building materials
- Frozen meats
- Basic computer hardware and software

- Security equipment
- Vehicles and parts
- Hotel and restaurant supplies and equipment
- Water sports products
- Building materials
- Chemicals
- Fuels and lubricants

Foreign companies interested in exporting to the Caribbean must adjust pricing strategies to account for small quantities and sometimes noncompetitive shipping costs. Also, delivery times must be matched to available carrier schedules, which to some islands is erratic.

In-house sales personnel must manage marketing programs on most islands. Reliable agents or representatives just don't exist. The exceptions are Trinidad and Tobago, where local representation is practically mandatory, and Jamaica, where it is highly desirable.

Competition from a cadre of smaller U.S. suppliers is keen in most product lines, although the large companies generally don't bother with these small markets. Effective local competition is non-existent.

The implementation of CARICOM's common external tariff has significant implications for foreign exporters and investors. Managing a single set of tariffs for the entire CARICOM market minimizes the exporter's paperwork and traffic cost and provides easier access to a broad market base. Foreign companies with facilities in the region benefit from reduced costs of raw materials and capital goods imports.

Unfortunately, not all member nations met the original October 1, 1991, deadline for implementing the common tariffs. Although the Bahamas is a member of the Caribbean Community, it has elected not to join the common market. Antigua and Barbuda and Montserrat have not set implementation dates. St. Lucia and St. Kitts-Nevis plan to take the step in early 1993.

The Export Development Program (CEDP) was set up in 1989 to encourage foreign exporters to focus on the CARICOM nations. CEDP offers a variety of services, including commercial training programs, coordination of trade fairs, and assistance to companies interested in obtaining information on regional markets. More information on CEDP's services can be obtained from:

Export Development Program
Caribbean Community Secretariat
Bay Street, P.O. Box 34B
Brittons Hill Post Office
St. Michael, Barbados
Phone: (809) 436-0578
Fax: (809) 436-9999

The Best Direct Investment Prospects for Foreign Companies

Most local manufacturing and processing is directed toward export products. Some products, but very few, are produced for local consumption. Adequate labor supply and appropriate skills are lacking on many of the smaller islands, deterring any serious consideration by foreign companies for manufacturing investments.

Most CARICOM nations have always welcomed foreign investment. However, recent moves toward integration and fears of being left out of NAFTA and other important hemispheric trade blocs have created an almost frenetic drive to bring U.S. companies to their shores.

The best prospects for foreign investment are as follows:

In all CARICOM nations:	Tourism
St. Kitts-Nevis and St. Vincent and the Grenadines:	Electronics and apparel manufacturing
Dominica and St. Lucia:	Agricultural products, food processing
Grenada and St. Lucia:	Light manufacturing in labor-intensive industries
Trinidad and Tobago:	Petroleum-related products and services, including dredges

Belize:	Forestry, aquaculture, and ecotourism
Antigua, Barbados, and Mont-serrat:	Financial services to support each nation's policy of developing offshore financial center capabilities

In virtually all CARICOM nations, other excellent opportunities exist for foreign investment in sugar production, apparel assembly, handicrafts, infrastructure development and maintenance, aquaculture, rum distilling, furniture assembly, and food processing.

Tourism continues to be the predominant industry in most CARICOM countries. Hotel development projects have been substantial over the last four years. Even in more developed countries, such as Barbados, tourism accounts for more than 50 percent of GNP; in the Bahamas, it reaches 70 percent. Although recessionary pressures from the United States, Canada, and Europe directly affect tourism, island states seem to weather economic downturns as well or better as do developed countries.

Financing investment should not be a problem. Plenty of funds are available from the Puerto Rican Section 936 program (see Chapter 7); from the United States' Eximbank; from the Overseas Private Investment Corporation (OPIC); from the British Commonwealth Development Corporation (CDC); and from local branches of American, British, and Canadian banks. Financing for major infrastructure and local-government-sponsored development projects can be obtained from local development banks, which in turn receive funding from the Inter-American Development Bank (IDB).

Assistance in locating the best markets and resources (appropriate labor, management, facilities, and raw materials) can be obtained quickly by contacting the Eastern Caribbean Investment Promotion Service (ECIPS). This regional organization promotes general investments throughout the region. In addition to helping foreign investors source markets and resources, it can be of enormous help in identifying the need and location for specific projects, and in sourcing appropriate joint-venture partners. ECIPS can be reached at:

Eastern Caribbean Investment Promotion Service
1730 M Street, NW, Suite 901
Washington, DC 20036
Phone: (202) 659-8689
Fax: (202) 659-9127

Investment Incentives for Foreign Companies

Nearly all CARICOM members have enacted foreign investment incentives—some very good, some mediocre. Here is a rundown of important incentives in the five larger states (see Chapter 10 for investing in Jamaica):

Bahamas:	No taxes of any kind except on real property (exempted for ten years on new hotels); exemption from import duties; full encouragement for offshore investment companies and other financial services firms.
Barbados:	A tax holiday for ten years; exemption from import duties; full repatriation of profits and capital; subsidized factory space; a labor training program; full tax exemption for captive insurance companies; a tax of only 1–2.5 percent for offshore investment companies, 2.5 percent for offshore corporations, and 2.5 percent for data processing companies; and full exemption for foreign sales corporations.

Belize:	Equal treatment for foreign and local companies; full tax holiday up to twenty-five years; exemption from income tax during holiday period up to contributed capital; exemption from import duties; guaranteed repatriation of original investment, profits, and capital gains; rental of facilities on concessionary terms; free trade zone on Mexican border.
St. Lucia:	Two free trade zones; exemption from import duties; tax holiday for ten to fifteen years in manufacturing and tourism sectors; unrestricted repatriation of profits and capital.
Trinidad and Tobago:	The assistance of the Industrial Development Corporation, a one-stop office set up to help foreign investors complete official paperwork and identify opportunities; 100 percent foreign ownership if investor provides all the capital and technology, exports 75 percent of production to earn hard currency, uses local raw materials, and creates jobs (but joint ventures are preferred and a long list of industries is reserved exclusively for nationals); various tax holiday arrangements; import duty exemptions; two free trade zones (at Point Lisas and Piarco).

No special visas are required for Americans or Canadians in any CARICOM nation.

Infrastructure, Labor, and Management

Infrastructure development in other than the larger states of Barbados, Jamaica, the Bahamas, and to a lesser extent Trinidad and Tobago has not progressed as rapidly as private-sector industries. Electricity generation and distribution, while adequate, remain unreliable. Water systems and telecommunications have improved considerably over the past decade but, like electricity, haven't kept up with population growth and economic development. Also, hurricanes and other storms batter the islands now and then and tend to knock out everything.

While education is far better in these states than it is in rural Central and South America, new schools and teachers are desperately needed throughout the region. Medical facilities are not good, but major cities like Caracas, Miami, and San Juan are relatively short flights away in emergencies.

Basic labor is available even in the smaller states, although modern industrial skills are lacking. Trade unions in Trinidad and Tobago have traditionally been obstreperous, and the use of intermediary labor negotiators is a prerequisite. Conversely, unions in Barbados tend to be cooperative.

Management pools may not be large, but supervisory talent is increasing rapidly throughout the region. Many high school graduates attend American universities and return to their island homes for business careers. If anything, management talent probably outstrips job opportunities in most of these island states.

Chapter 10

Jamaica: Land of Higglers* and Miracles

Compared with other CARICOM members, Jamaica is a highly developed nation. It has an active stock market in Kingston and many British, Canadian, and American commercial and merchant banks. The work force in the Kingston and Montego Bay areas is plentiful and skilled.

In Jamaica, as in other island states, tourism remains a major industry, but bauxite mining runs a close second. Over fifty major companies from the United States and Europe have established businesses in Jamaica, including such well-known names as IBM, American Airlines, Nestle, W. R. Grace, and Sterling Drug. The reason for their locating in Jamaica is not to provide goods and services for domestic markets but to reap the benefits of abundant low-cost labor and natural resources to make goods for export back to the United States and Europe.

Jamaica has accomplished one of the most dramatic economic turnarounds the region has seen, and it boasts the most successful economic liberalization record. In the late 1980s, a highly successful privatization program sharply reduced the government's role in the business sector. State-owned businesses of all types and sizes were sold off, including those in the telecommunications, cement, hotel, urban transportation, radio, sugar, and agricultural sectors.

In addition, tariffs were sharply cut to a range of 5 to 45 percent. Very few imports now require licenses, although a 1991 law assesses

* Jamaica's pavement vendors.

imports a general consumption tax of 10 percent. Foreign exchange has been completely liberalized. The Jamaican dollar now floats at market rates.

Foreign Trade and Investment Incentives

These incentives attracted foreign imports all right, but foreign exchange was hurt. External debt still ate up about 50 cents of every export dollar earned. A different approach was needed to increase exports. The administration determined that the best way to raise hard currency for use in reducing the overwhelming debt load was to bring in more foreign investment. Accordingly, the government abandoned exchange laws that required exporters to sell their foreign currency, often at a loss, to the Central Bank. The government also enacted a series of laws to facilitate foreign investment. These laws can be summarized as follows:

- Profits can be freely repatriated and exporters are allowed to retain 7.5 percent of earnings to import new raw materials and capital goods, often without import duties.
- New ten-year corporate income tax exemptions are in effect for foreign investors in horticulture, fruit farming, tree farming, livestock, fishing, and fish farming.
- An initial 20 percent tax allowance applies to new industrial buildings and machinery.
- A 12.5 percent tax deduction is permitted for vehicles used in business.

The new incentives have worked. Foreign investors have taken the bait, bringing in welcome hard currency and creating a burgeoning export-oriented industrial and service base. External debt has come down and Jamaica has been able to meet the IMF's austere structural adjustment requirements, returning the nation to good standing—and new funding.

Foreign Investment Support

As a result of investment incentives, U.S. companies have poured more than US$1 billion of new investment into Jamaica, mostly in bauxite mining, apparel operations, a variety of manufacturing companies, and data entry businesses. Most companies have been impressed by the results of their branch operations. As major benefits, they cite the absence of labor or customs problems and a high degree of employee loyalty and integrity. Best of all, they are no longer required to make payments under the table to keep their businesses rolling.

The average minimum wage stands at approximately US$18 per forty-hour week for a total labor force of more than 1 million people. Unemployment runs at approximately 16 percent.

Jamaican businesses have also benefited from a growing economy. Although their product range remains narrow, they are steadily increasing exports of bauxite and alumina, sugar, bananas, citrus fruits, rum, cocoa, and coffee.

Infrastructure

Foreign companies also speak favorably about a relatively well-developed infrastructure (telephones and electricity work most of the time). Exports from Jamaica also get preferential market access to the United States through CBI, to Canada through CARIBCAN, and to Europe through the Lomé Convention. Annual exports to the EC now account for US$17 million of Jamaica's foreign exchange.

Free Trade Zones

Jamaica has four government-owned and -operated free trade zones: two in Kingston, one in Montego Bay, and one in Clarendon. The biggest, at 724,000 square feet, is located in Kingston, next to Port Bustamante. Fifteen American, European, and East Asian companies use the facilities to warehouse, assemble electronics and apparel, and process food. The Montego Bay free trade zone houses thirteen companies engaged in data processing, telemarketing, and apparel assembly. In addition, twenty-eight information service companies use the Jamaica Digiport International campus and its earth satellite. No charge is made for factory space. In addition, one privately owned free trade zone operates at Spanish Fort. Rents there run about US$4.25 per square foot.

Foreign companies located in free trade zones are entitled to special incentives, including:

- A 100 percent tax exemption forever
- Complete exemption from import licensing
- Exemption from import duties
- Full freedom to repatriate profits up to original capital without approval of the Central Bank

By far the greatest boom markets are telemarketing and information data services. Jamaica Digiport International (JDI), owned jointly by AT&T, Cable & Wireless, and Telecommunications of Jamaica, operates its earth-satellite station from the Montego Bay Free Zone. It provides a wide range of services, including credit authorization, reservation services, toll-free calls, high-speed switched and dedicated services, and facsimile, voice, and data transmissions.

The facility owns a 35-foot satellite dish that handles 20,000 telephone lines—sufficient for a city of 60,000 people. A great many 800 calls and telemarketing transmissions made in the United States get routed through this facility.

According to Winston Gooden, director of service industries for Jamaican Promotions (Jampro), other offshoot services are also adaptable: image processing; custom-built software programming; electronic publishing; mailing lists; and coupon coding for airlines, credit card companies, banks, and other financial institutions. Jampro is the government's one-stop-shop development agency and can be reached at:

Jamaican Promotions
35 Trafalgar Road
Kingston 5
Phone: (809) 929-7190
Fax: (809) 924-9650

Since the government opened tourism to private-sector development, many new opportunities have sprung up. Already ten of the twelve state-owned hotels have been sold to private investors. Permit applications for constructing new hotels and resort complexes are being accepted.

The Best Potential for Foreign Exports

Jamaica's population of nearly 2.5 million makes the nation's consumer base similar to that of Costa Rica and Panama and about three fourths that of Puerto Rico. A very low per capita GDP, however, reflects the nation's continuing battle with poverty. Compared to a per capita GDP of US$3,300 for Trinidad and Tobago and a per capita GDP of US$5,100 for Barbados, Jamaica's meager US$1,700 makes it one of the poorest states in the Caribbean.

The very limited means of most Jamaicans has an impact on market opportunities for exporting companies. Without question, consumers and the local business community desperately need a complete range of imported products and services, but their poverty, coupled with the shortage of hard currency, deprives exporters of an otherwise viable customer base.

Chapter 9 enumerated Jamaica's primary markets as industrial chemicals, petroleum, machine tools, and agricultural equipment and spare parts. Additional strong import markets include:

- Processed food
- Apparel
- A variety of consumer goods
- Hotel and restaurant supplies
- Equipment for construction
- Vehicles and spare parts
- Building supplies
- Computers, peripherals, and business software

Local sales representation is essential to tap capital goods markets. Selling to retail establishments can normally be accomplished satisfactorily with company sales personnel traveling from the States. It's always a good idea to engage a local attorney, however, to pave the way with obstinate bureaucrats and customs officials.

Higglers Who Haggle

Jamaica wouldn't be Jamaica without its *higglers*—or pavement vendors. Mostly women, and mainly found in Kingston, Jamaica's higglers account for much of the competition in the domestic consumer markets because the majority of the population cannot afford retail store prices. Higglers sell everything imaginable: shoes, clothes, radios, cosmetics, buttons, watches, umbrellas, and U.S. dollars (bought and sold at a premium). You name it, they have it. Sometimes the bargaining get a bit brisk and bad-tempered, but a lot of money changes hands. While the formal economy suffered through a lengthy recession, this informal economy boomed.

Reportedly, Dunstan Whittingham, general secretary of the Higgler's Association, reckons that higglers import some US$100 million in goods each year. He also estimates that 300,000 people work in the trade—out of a total population of about 2.5 million. Although established traders complain, airlines and travel agents are jubilant about the volume of higgler flights.

To get their cheap imports, higglers fly to places like Curaçao, Panama, and Miami. Armed with exports of fruits and vegetables, they fly to infertile places like the Cayman Islands to sell them. Whittingham claims that "intrepid middle-aged women think nothing of setting off with US$200 to track down smuggled bargains in Haiti."

The government recognizes what a formidable economic force higglers have become and would like to formalize the trade with taxes, insurance contributions, and import duties. (Could pension plans be far behind?) It will never happen, according to Whittingham: "I think they're trying to drag us into the formal sector. Not everyone wants that." (To put it mildly.) (Those who may not be familiar with the fine art of higgling may enjoy the article in *The Economist*, November 30, 1991, from which Whittingham's remarks were excerpted.)

On my last trip to the island in 1992, the higglers were still plying their wares, beating merchant prices, and haggling continually. Truly, they are one of the livelier aspects of life in the Caribbean.

Chapter 11

The Dominican Republic: One of a Kind

By the end of the 1950s, after thirty-one years of dictatorship, Rafael L. Trujillo counted most of the country's assets—including businesses, agricultural land, mineral deposits, and cash—as part of his own treasury. When Trujillo was executed and his family exiled to Europe and the United States, the government of the Dominican Republic confiscated these assets. Instead of a dictator owning everything, the state did.

Successive administrations followed the same state-ownership and economic-intervention policies as those of other Latin American nations. Not only were nearly all businesses of any significance run by inefficient, corrupt state managers, but stringent regulations on investment, taxes, and foreign trade kept most foreigners out.

But politics breeds strange bedfellows . . .

The Strange Role of the United States

Gaining its independence from Spain in 1865, the Dominican Republic was bankrupt by the turn of the century—a situation that ended in the creation of a receivership by the U.S. Government in 1905. Fears of a German invasion led to occupation by the U.S. Navy in 1916. Citing internal disorders, the U.S. Government installed a military government that ruled in the name of the United States from 1916 to 1924.

The ruthless General Rafael Trujillo Molina took over in 1930 and ruled with an iron fist until his assassination in 1961. Civil wars erupted until 1965, when order was restored by 23,000 U.S.

troops (which were subsequently incorporated into an Inter-American Peace Force by the Organization of American States).

Given the more or less constant intervention by the United States for the last sixty years, it's not surprising that during the later 1960s and 1970s special favors were granted to the giant Gulf + Western Corporation. The corporation soon spread its conglomerate tentacles throughout the republic's business community, despite government laws to keep foreigners out.

The infrastructure deteriorated, external debt skyrocketed, and Dominicans grew poorer. The dawning of Latin American economic liberalization forced the Dominican government to acknowledge that it had better join the parade or face economic disaster—or perhaps another U.S. intervention. With the United States by its side, the administration of President Joaquin Balaguer (elected in 1990) enacted an austerity program that met the IMF's structural adjustment requirements. This, in turn, resulted in new funding that saved the day.

The Dominican Republic's population of 7.2 million ranks second in the entire Caribbean Basin behind Guatemala's 9.1 million. The nation boasts a wealth of minerals, primarily gold, silver, and ferrous nickel.

Representing the eastern two thirds of the island of Hispaniola, the Dominican Republic has matured into a viable Caribbean trading partner, while neighboring Haiti (the other third of Hispaniola) marches straight to oblivion.

By 1992, inflation dropped from triple digits to zero, real growth went from 0 to 3 percent, and imports surged. However, the nation still suffers from an abysmally low per capita GDP of under US$1,000 and unemployment approaching 30 percent.

Nevertheless, the list of foreign companies now operating in the Dominican Republic reads like a Who's Who of American business: Johnson & Johnson, Bristol Myers, Abbott Laboratories, Sara Lee/Haynes Knitwear, Westinghouse, Sylvania, Ayerst Wyeth Pharmaceutical, 3M, American Airlines, Xerox, Exxon, Holiday Inn, and Young & Rubicam, to mention a few. Well over 300 foreign firms are represented, mainly in twenty-three free trade zones (FTZs), producing a wide range of products and services for export to the United States and global markets.

Three characteristics typify the economy of the Dominican Republic:

1. Free trade zones, in which foreign firms produce goods and services for export
2. A booming tourist/second-home industry
3. A majority of the population with incomes below the poverty level

Domestic Markets

U.S. exports to the Dominican Republic ran around US$1.6 billion in both 1991 and 1992, much of the total going to the tourist industry and supporting businesses, and to foreign free trade zone companies. The best market prospects continue to be:

- Processed food
- Basic foods such as wheat and corn
- Animal feeds
- Fuels
- Industrial raw materials
- Machinery and equipment of virtually all types (especially power generating and telecommunications)
- Fabrics
- Medical equipment and supplies
- Automotive parts and service equipment
- Pharmaceuticals
- Agricultural chemicals (primarily fertilizers and herbicides)

The burgeoning tourist industry has created a high demand for a wide range of imported goods, including:

- Fabrics
- Furniture
- Kitchen and bar equipment
- Processed food
- Hotel operating equipment and supplies

- Air conditioning and refrigeration equipment (and spare parts)
- Computers and peripherals

Other than imports for the tourist industry and FTZ foreign companies, the consumer base is too poor to afford very many foreign-made products. Much of the clothing and housing consumed by the bulk of the population comes from local producers and street peddlers. Food for this segment comes primarily from local farms. It is very difficult to reach this market with foreign products other than the bare essentials, such as used cars, TV sets, and radios.

A minority of the population, living around Santo Domingo or on the north shore, makes up the business, military, and government elite. The imported products demanded by this group are practically identical to those purchased by the average American middle-class household.

Government bureaucracy permeates every aspect of the business community. To do business in this environment, American exporters would be wise to sell through local distributors rather than to retail outlets or end users.

Foreign exporters looking for local marketing representation should definitely attend the annual REP-FIND Fair. It is generally held in the September-October period in the Dominican Republic. The whole purpose of the fair is to match foreign suppliers with local distributors and agents. Further information can be obtained from:

The Commercial Officer
U.S. Embassy, Dominican Republic
APO Miami, FL 34041–3470
Phone: (809) 541-2171
Fax: (809) 688-4838

Commercial contracts generally can't be enforced, but they are essential to maintain the proper "profile." English-speaking lawyers are plentiful in Santo Domingo. Many are expatriates from the United States. American banks and accounting firms can also be a big help in making the right contacts.

Free Trade Zones

Free trade zones were started as early as 1980, primarily to reap the hard currency benefits of foreign investment while avoiding foreign interference in the domestic economy. Today, the Dominican Republic boasts one of the world's most successful FTZ programs. Free trade zone sales volume reached US$838 million by 1990. Employment exceeded 120,000.

Nearly all new foreign investment over the last few years has been concentrated in FTZs. To date, 325 separate production facilities are in full operation, two thirds of them belonging to U.S. companies. Industry representation is very broad, including textiles and apparel assembly, sporting goods, pharmaceuticals, furniture manufacturing, electronics, and footwear. Information services has shown the greatest recent growth in such activities as data entry, computer-aided digitation, and telemarketing.

The twenty-three free trade zones are a mixture of public- and private-sector management, although the government looks to the private sector for additional FTZ development. Five new zones were under construction in 1992. Seven additional ones are being developed for operation in 1993–1994.

Local merchants also benefit. Domestic sales of goods and services to FTZ companies tops US$200 million annually, about half in basic-production raw materials and the balance spread among textiles, packing materials, office equipment, leather, adhesives and plastics, labels and tickets, threads, and elastic for clothing. Most raw materials and operating equipment must be imported, however.

The Dominican Republic business community is very close. Without personal contacts in high levels of the government, foreign companies generally are not welcome and have a hard time breaking in. The exceptions are the tourist, agribusiness, and mining sectors. Even in agribusiness and mining, however, which are being pushed by the government as viable sectors for foreign investment, small and midsize foreign firms will have a hard time without friends in high places.

Although FTZ firms have the option of selling up to 20 percent of production output in the Dominican market, most goods are exported—mainly to the United States and Canada, but also to Europe under the duty-free Lomé Convention.

The Dominican Republic Investment Promotion Council (IPC) is available to assist companies set up FTZ operations. It offers assistance in the selection of local suppliers and in the preparation of official paperwork. It also provides marketing assistance in the form of statistical information and customer sourcing.

In addition, the council provides in-plant consulting to local companies for improving manufacturing processes, business planning, and cost controls. It can be contacted at:

Dominican Republic Investment
  Promotion Council
P.O. Box 25438
Washington, DC 20007
Phone: (703) 247-8445
Fax: (703) 247-8569

Free Trade Zone Incentives

In an effort to stimulate foreign interest in Dominican free trade zones as opposed to investments in the domestic economy, the government enacted a series of incentives that included:

- Duty-free imports of machinery and equipment, spare parts, construction material, and other items needed to construct and operate a facility
- Duty-free import of raw materials, supplies, and other goods destined for reexport
- A 100 percent exemption from all taxes for fifteen to twenty years
- A 100 percent tax exemption for expatriate workers
- Exclusion from foreign currency holding and exchange restrictions
- Exemption from any financial reporting requirements, except those detailing local expenses

Wage rates run a meager US$0.56 per hour, including fringes. Labor supply is plentiful, although skills are at the lower end of the spectrum. Management talent is very scarce and expatriate managers are a necessity. Foreign companies may freely repatriate profits and capital and own 100 percent of free trade zone businesses.

Direct Investment Outside the Dominican Free Trade Zones

Business conditions are not as attractive outside the FTZs, although good opportunities do exist in tourism and, to a much lesser extent, agribusiness.

The 1989–1992 recessions in the United States and Europe hurt the Dominican export trade and tourism business. In addition, continued political strife between the Reformist Party, the Dominican Revolutionary Party, and the Dominican Labor Party, all of which hold commanding positions in the government, has delayed the implementation of much-needed economic reforms.

Although fiscal discipline has begun to take hold, the country still suffers from an external debt approximating US$4 billion—a very high figure for a country this size. Exchange controls were relaxed in 1991 and the currency was allowed to float at market rates. Restrictions on the use of foreign exchange have generally been eliminated, although Central Bank permission is still required for import payments. The loudest complaint from foreign investors continues to be that poorly managed customs operations and corrupt customs officials hamper the movement of goods in and out of the country.

In 1991, the government enacted a new set of tariffs. The schedule was simplified to six categories, with seven tariffs ranging from 5 to 35 percent. In addition, a temporary import surcharge of 30 percent was imposed. This is expected to drop to 10 percent during 1993.

In addition, tariff exonerations were suspended for tourism, mining companies, and import-substitution industries. A 15 percent foreign exchange surcharge and a 2.5 percent foreign exchange commission were imposed instead.

Despite these unrealistic impediments to foreign investment, the government still insists that direct investment is welcome in three sectors outside the free zones: agriculture, mining, and tourism.

Agribusiness is potentially a dynamite investment, assuming the government ever straightens out its regulations and ownership laws. So far, the law requires 51 percent local ownership of any land or agribusiness. Even meeting this requirement doesn't guarantee trouble-free contractual problems. Numerous conflicts have been reported over contractual rights and land tenure.

The government has done little to correct either impediment. However, a joint U.S.–DR group has been set up to help agricultural investors: the Santo Domingo-based Joint Advisory Committee, working in tandem with the U.S. Embassy's Agricultural Counselor. Further information can be obtained by contacting either of the following:

Oscar Benitez, Executive Director
Joint Agricultural Consultative Committee
Apartado Postal 38809
Santo Domingo, Dominican Republic
Phone: (809) 567-7207
Fax: (809) 541-4564

Lawrence Eisenberg, Commercial Officer
U.S. Embassy, Santo Domingo
APO Miami, FL 34041-3470
Phone: (809) 541-2171
Fax: (809) 688-4838

It should be noted that government price controls keep agricultural exports from being competitive in international markets, severely restricting the development of this sector.

The Dominican Republic exports more to the United States than any other independent country in the Caribbean basin, exceeding US$2 billion annually. Slightly less than half this comes from companies in the free trade zones. The balance mostly comes from local firms outside the zones, shipping sugar and sugar by-products, ferronickel, gold, silver, coffee, cocoa and by-products, and bauxite.

The eventual restoration of gold and silver production at the Rosario Dominicana Company and increasing demand for ferrous nickel are expected to boost exports substantially in the future. In addition, as Europe 1992 becomes fully functional, demand in the

European Community for all traditional products should increase exports even further.

The Importance of Tourism

Tourism generates approximately 30 percent of the nation's foreign exchange, represents 12.5 percent of gross national product, and employs more than 5 percent of the population. Official estimates place 1991 revenues from tourism at a whopping US$880 million. Growth projections for 1992 were optimistic, with 1.3 million visitors expected for the 500th anniversary of the discovery of Hispaniola by Christopher Columbus.

Tourism isn't restricted to hotels and resorts. The Dominican Republic actively solicits foreign investment in a spread of villa and condominium developments on the nation's north shore. The town of Puerto Plata now has airport facilities capable of handling any size commercial aircraft. Direct flights arrive from New York, Miami, and several European capitals.

As discussed previously, hotel development and foreign-owned villas and condominiums have what is probably the most vibrant market for American exports. All varieties of supplies, consumer hard goods, furnishings, and maintenance supplies and parts must be brought in from outside the country.

Foreign contractors can also participate in this building boom, either through subcontracting with a multinational prime contractor or by successfully bidding against local suppliers for smaller jobs. For all except the major North American, European, or Japanese international contractors, however, it's difficult to penetrate the prime market for large projects.

During 1991, the Dominican Republic and the United States signed a free trade framework agreement under the Enterprise for the Americas Initiative. Meetings between representatives of the two nations during 1992 resulted in a mutual determination to push for free trade throughout the hemisphere.

The government also executed a Tax Information Exchange Agreement (TIEA) with the United States permitting the use of Puerto Rican Section 936 funds for investment projects. Within the first year, more than US$131 million of Section 936 funds were used. Negotiations are currently under way to reach a bilateral investment treaty with the United States. It appears that the "big brother" relationship has not changed.

The Impact of Taxes

Tax laws continue to be a major deterrent, both to foreign investment outside the free trade zones and to local development. The Dominican Republic's top corporate tax rate of 46 percent is one of the highest in the Caribbean Basin. Foreign branches pay the same.

Withholding rates on dividends are equally outrageous, hitting 12 percent when paid to Dominican companies, 20 percent for foreign companies, 35 percent for foreign companies without a DR presence, and 20 percent for nonresident individuals. The branch remittance tax is also 20 percent. Furthermore, the government charges a value-added tax (VAT) of 6 percent. Employers pay a social security tax of 7 percent; employees pay 2.5 percent.

The Dominican Central Bank has a monopoly on all foreign exchange transactions (excluding the free zones), both incoming and outgoing. All individuals or businesses generating foreign exchange are required to exchange it with the Central Bank through commercial banks. Imports can be purchased only with dollars furnished by the Central Bank.

It seems obvious that these policies will be modified eventually. Some are already being reviewed for change. In the meantime, as in any country that mandates tight foreign currency controls, the Dominican Republic has a thriving dollar black market. Although it is strictly illegal, anyone can exchange U.S. dollars for local currency and vice versa at any time of the day or night, simply by stepping outside a hotel or office building. Street merchants are everywhere. Just be careful not to get taken on the exchange rate. It can easily be verified at any major hotel or commercial bank.

Chapter 12

A New Central America

The period was 1990-1991, and for the first time in decades, most of the Central American nations were optimistic about rejoining the international community. Peaceful Costa Rica led the way toward economic reforms, political stability, and fiscal responsibility. With Panama's Manuel Noriega safely behind bars in Miami, American troops had pulled out of the war zone. Even sleepy Honduras—referred to by some as the "USS *Honduras*"—was beginning to stir.

All was not serene, however; some nations still had a long way to go. Nicaragua's new administration faced an uphill battle trying to sort out a role for the Sandinistas in the nation's political spectrum. Although winding down, El Salvador's now-ended civil war still disrupted the economy. And Guatemala's gangs of soldiers and guerrilla dissidents were more dedicated than ever to wiping each other out.

The Central American Common Market

Despite the unsettled political environment in three of the six Central American nations, the region was ready to move forward toward economic integration. As a first step, member countries Costa Rica, El Salvador, Guatemala, Honduras, and Nicaragua agreed to rejuvenate the long-dead Central American Common Market (CACM). The general feeling was that without a united front, these small nations could not compete individually with the newly forming free trade blocs to the north and south.

The CACM was originally conceived in 1961. It disintegrated, however, after minor conflicts arose between El Salvador and Honduras in the mid-1970s. The only segment of the agreement that remained functional was the Central American Bank for Economic Integration (CABEI), a variation on the common market/development bank theme.

Many protectionist features of the original CACM had been eliminated prior to 1990-1991, including the removal of 95 percent of all tariffs between the member countries. Today, the development of mutually satisfactory external tariffs and the harmonization of economic policies still must be negotiated. Many details need to be worked out, but progress is being made.

Although it appears reasonable to expect the CACM to play a role in the development of free trade in the region eventually, widely divergent political, social, and economic conditions among member countries stand in the way of a united front. For the foreseeable future, each country must look to its own efforts to improve its trade and investment climate.

The Pluses and Minuses of Doing Business in Central America

The Central American nations of Costa Rica, Panama, Honduras, Guatemala, Nicaragua, and El Salvador present a different and more complex business environment than do the Caribbean island states or Belize. Doing business in this isthmus of six contiguous countries totaling 29 million people poses a set of problems and opportunities wholly unlike those encountered in the island states.

On the plus side, the consumers of imported products—the bureaucrats, the military, the elite business community, and the expatriates of foreign companies—are much more numerous and wealthy than their island counterparts. And compared with shipping from the United States to the Caribbean, shipping to Central America takes less time, is generally less costly, and is even, in some cases, more frequent. Moreover, raw materials are substantially more plentiful and labor is generally more available in Central America than it is in the islands.

As offsets to these advantages, all Central American governments, having followed the Latin American economic model of protectionist self-sufficiency during the lost decade of the 1980s, are only now waking up to the realities of free trade and the benefits of foreign direct investment. Most administrations still harbor restrictive disincentives for foreign companies, ranging from burdensome tax structures and outdated tariff schedules to outrageous government approval processes.

Although each of these countries has a significantly larger population than any country in the Caribbean except the Dominican Republic, the majority of citizens are abysmally poor and unable to afford imported products. Also, the local business community attends to most of the product and service needs of these large underclasses, leaving only the middle- and upper-class elite as potentially viable consumers for foreign products.

Lastly, although competition from other foreign companies or from local producers isn't substantially greater here than in the islands, it is enough to dampen prices and demand a more rigorous marketing program for companies wishing to sell in local markets. The highest import volume is generated by U.S. multinationals who price with the market and make their margins on volume— the same strategy followed by many firms in the United States.

While there are pockets of consumers susceptible to U.S. standards of advertising (notably American and European expatriates) media advertising budgets are wasted in Central America. Nearly all selling is done through personal relationships. Trade shows in the Colón Free Zone of Panama and in a few of the zones in Costa Rica remain one of the best methods for introducing new products.

One final comment on business practices in Central America: Corruption and government red tape permeate the business structure of every country. Until a foreign firm recognizes which buttons to push to get things accomplished, it is a practical necessity to work with local partners who have the connections. Formal joint ventures aren't always necessary, but an arrangement with competent local traders, or *runners,* is the minimum requirement for success.

Foreign companies exploring the potential of Central America should recognize up front that the real benefits to be gained are not to be found in exporting to these countries or in tapping domestic markets with local facilities. The two primary attractions of the region are its wealth of natural resources and its large, low-cost labor base. Direct investments in free trade zone facilities to produce components or even finished goods for export back to the United States or Europe can give a small or midsize company significant cost advantages in its home-country markets.

Chapter 13

Costa Rica and Honduras: A Study in Contrasts

Costa Rica: Books, Not Arms

Costa Rica is a prime example of how the combined efforts of an enlightened government, a cooperative business community, and collaborative educators can raise a small, undeveloped country beyond the self-imposed constraints of its richer and larger neighbors. With a political structure and constitution adopted more than forty years ago, Costa Rica has enjoyed the longest period of stability and economic growth of any country in Latin America. The absence of a standing army since 1949 attests to Costa Rica's obsession with political tranquillity; the nation is often referred to as the "Switzerland of the Americas." The country's 95 percent literacy rate testifies to its preoccupation with education. Costa Ricans relate with pride that the only army they need or want is one comprised of teachers and books. Such a beneficent national philosophy has encouraged more than 20,000 American retirees to call Costa Rica their home. Table 13-1 shows the nation's key economic and trade statistics.

Costa Rica operates under the same three-tiered executive, legislative, and judicial system as the United States. In 1990, Rafael Angel Calderon replaced Nobel Peace Prize–winner Oscar Arias as the elected President.

Like other Latin American governments, the Costa Rican government has been busy trying to transform the country from a state-controlled economy to a free-market economy. As in other Latin American countries, this has been a long, difficult journey. Economic reforms are not yet completed, but of all the nations in Central America, Costa Rica has made the most progress.

Table 13-1. Key Costa Rican Statistics as of 1990–1991 ($US).

Population	3.0 million
Labor force	1.2 million
Unemployment rate	5.0%
Inflation rate	27.3%
Economic activity	
Industry	22.0%
Agriculture	19.0%
Commerce	17.0%
Total annual exports	$1.450 billion
Total annual imports	$2.000 billion

Source: Costa Rica Ministry of Trade.

The first action taken by President Calderon was to increase government revenues in an effort to reverse the growing deficit. This was achieved by raising utility, petroleum, and sales tax rates, eliminating 7,000 public sector jobs, and trimming agricultural subsidies.

Although economic liberalization has been going on for several years, there was a breakthrough in 1991 when, for the first time, the government reached a consensus with the opposition party that had a far-reaching impact on economic reform. According to the Ministry of National Planning and Economic Policy, the consensus involved a commitment by both parties to:

- Fiscal discipline
- Rationalization of public spending
- Liberalization of the financial system (although banks are still government-owned)
- A neutral foreign exchange policy
- An orientation toward international trade
- Deregulation in a variety of areas
- Tax and customs reform
- Privatization

Several important steps have already been taken to quantify

the bipartisan accord. Costa Rica joined the General Agreement on Tariffs and Trade (GATT). Under the Enterprise for the Americas Initiative, it signed a bilateral framework agreement on trade and investment with the United States. It agreed to cap its tariff rates at 20 percent by the end of 1992 (many have been reduced to 5 percent). It reduced import surcharges from 12 to 2 percent and eliminated import deposits.

In addition, the government scrapped many nontariff barriers, reformed its customs services, and agreed to privatize ports and the insurance industry (although dates have not been set). It also switched to the Harmonized Tariff System on January 1, 1992.

Privatization in Costa Rica began in 1984 and is still under way, albeit to a very minor extent. Only two companies were scheduled for privatization in 1992—a fertilizer company and a cement maker.

Direct Investment in Costa Rica

Costa Rica is the second-largest exporter in the Caribbean Basin, largely because of its thriving free trade zones, with the United States taking more than half of the US$1.5 billion total. Local producers export fruit, vegetables, bananas, coffee, plants, flowers, meat, and seafood.

Foreign investors claim the lion's share of exported manufactured products, primarily plastics, apparel, pharmaceuticals, and complex electronics, and mostly from free trade zone facilities. Most of these products are shipped back to parent company plants or distribution centers in the United States or other home countries, rather than being exported directly to global markets.

Given the nation's political stability and highly educated work force, it's not surprising that so many U.S., Canadian, European, and Asian companies are operating profitable facilities there. Within the past three years, several U.S. companies have moved their high-tech assembly facilities from East Asia to Costa Rica. They are willing to pay higher wages than they would have to pay in other Latin American countries in order to get the higher skills and far superior quality of workmanship available to them in Costa Rica.

Tourism is one of the fastest-growing segments of the economy.

The government hopes to make the tourism industry its largest foreign exchange earner, not merely via new hotels and beaches, but by tapping increasingly important ecotourism. Costa Rica has a larger percentage of its land in its twenty-three national parks than does any country in the Western Hemisphere. Continued emphasis on ecotourism is beginning to pay off, with an increasing number of foreign businesses participating.

Costa Rica's minimum wage rate, including fringe benefits, stands at US$1.07 per hour, as against US$0.56 per hour in the Dominican Republic and US$0.47 per hour in neighboring Honduras.

Free Trade Zones

In addition to labor advantages and political stability, Costa Rica attracts substantial foreign investment to its very active free trade zones, or FTZs.

Many years ago the Costa Rican government recognized the contribution free trade zones could make toward building the economy. Using FTZs, products could be imported for manufacturing, assembly, and packaging, and then exported, free of all duty and taxes.

Today, approximately 130 foreign companies (many of them American) operate facilities in Costa Rica's FTZs, producing mainly electronics products and pharmaceuticals, and employing about 11,000 workers. Six privately owned free trade zones offer a full range of services. Two of these are on the coasts: Moin, on the Atlantic, and Santa Rosa, on the Pacific. Four others are located near the San José international airport: Airport Intran S.A. Free Zone; Alajuela-Zeta Group Industrial Park; Alajuela Free Zone Industrial Park; and Metropolitan S.A. Free Zone. All the FTZs offer investors:

- A 100 percent exemption from import duties and export taxes
- Foreign exchange facilities independent of the Central Bank
- A 100 percent exemption from municipal and capital taxes for ten years
- A 100 percent exemption from income taxes for twelve years, plus a 50 percent exemption for an additional six years

Companies choosing FTZ locations outside the capital of San José enjoy even more benefits, including a 15 percent new-job bonus for the first five years (it drops by two points each year thereafter). Rents vary by industrial park but average about US$3.25 per square foot.

More information on free trade zones can be obtained from:

Corporación de la Zona Franca
  de Exportación S.A.
P.O. Box 96 Montes de Oca
San José, Costa Rica
Phone: (506) 22-58-55
Fax: (506) 33-50-90

Investment Incentives and Assistance

In addition to efficiently managed free trade zones, Costa Rica has enacted four other incentives to attract foreign investment:

- Tax exemption on the import of capital goods and raw materials
- Negotiable tax credits based on the volume of exports
- Free access to locally generated foreign currency
- A guarantee of profit and capital repatriation

The government's one-stop office, the Center for Export and Investment Promotion (CENPRO), assists prospective investors with information and with the completion of forms required to set up a facility. The organization's efforts to streamline investment regulatory procedures have been very helpful and effective. CENPRO also helps exporters secure the necessary export approvals and obtain marketing information. It can be contacted at:

Center for Export and Investment
  Promotion
Ministry of Foreign Trade
P.O. Box 5418-1000
San José, Costa Rica
Phone: (506) 21-71-66
Fax: (506) 23-57-22

The Costa Rica Investment Promotion Offices (CINDE), located in the United States, can also be of immense assistance. Funded by USAID, CINDE is a private, nonprofit organization dedicated to promoting Costa Rican exports and attracting foreign investment. It favors companies willing to invest in the production of ornamental plants, spices, fruits, nuts, apparel, and electronics for the export market. CINDE also helps identify and set up joint ventures. For information, contact one of the three U.S. locations of the Costa Rica Investment Promotion Offices:

992 High Ridge Road
Stamford, CT 06905
Phone: (203) 968-1448
Fax: (203) 968-2591

254 East Old Elm Road
Lake Forest, IL 60045
Phone: (708) 615-2202

7200 Northwest 19th Street,
   Suite 203
Miami, FL 33126
Phone: (305) 594-7446

Costa Rica has numerous attractions for foreign investors—as the country's trade commission is quick to point out. (It is noteworthy that in contrast to the claims made by other Latin American countries, most of those made by the Costa Rican trade commission are accurate.) As Costa Rica's primary advantages, the commission lists the following:

- A peaceful democracy (without a standing army)
- A high literacy rate (95 percent)
- A well-educated work force
- A very pleasant, moderate climate
- A pleasant living environment
- An absence of racial or religious problems
- An excellent telecommunications network
- Abundant water supplies and hydroelectric power
- Duty-free access to the United States under the Caribbean Basin Initiative

Since more than half of Costa Rica's trade is already transacted within North America, and all of Central America already qualifies under the CBI program, it appears that the region's eventual inclusion in NAFTA is a foregone conclusion.

Exporting to Costa Rica

Despite its long record of tranquility, a low per capita GDP of US$1,900 indicates that Costa Rica's 3 million people are not well-off. In terms of disposable income, Costa Rica and Panama are well ahead of their Central American neighbors. But when their per capita GDPs are compared to those of other Caribbean Basin states, such as Aruba (US$11,900), the Bahamas (US$9,100), and Barbados (US$5,100), they look like laggards.

Consumer income becomes an important consideration when developing strategic export plans, and Costa Rica's shortfall bears heavily on marketing strategies to tap the national markets of its 3 million people.

On the plus side, the country boasts a sizable cadre of expatriate managers and workers in its very active free trade zones. It also attracts thousands of North American and European retirees to its tranquil setting and temperate climate. Finally, the local business and financial community, as well as government workers, enjoy a comfortable middle-class life-style.

About half of the country's total imports of US$2 billion come from the United States. Venezuela ships about 8 percent (mainly oil); Japan, 7 percent; Mexico, 6 percent; and Guatemala, about 4 percent.

The imported products in greatest demand by the consumer segment are auto parts; paper products; drugs and pharmaceuticals; disposable health care products; and air conditioning and refrigeration equipment. Multinationals in each of these industries are the prime suppliers, making it difficult—but not impossible—for smaller companies to gain entry.

As in practically any consumer market controlled by large suppliers, niche markets offer the best opportunities for smaller competitors. The trick is to complete sufficient market research to determine which niche products are called for in given markets. The only way to accomplish this in Costa Rica—or in any Central American nation—is to go there. Hiring an outsider to do market research won't work effectively. Nine out of ten times, the answers received are flawed. These same principles hold true when entering industrial and commercial markets.

On the commercial and industrial front, imports of medical diagnostic and treatment equipment, food processing and packaging machinery, textile machinery, and plastic materials and resins are all in high demand.

Advertising in Costa Rica

Advertising does not receive much emphasis in Costa Rica—nor in any Central American country for that matter. Most business is conducted via personal relationships and direct sales. However, some companies report that a limited amount of advertising does pay off.

One of the most popular forms of promotion is the ads that appear just before the showing of a movie at local theaters. Other popular media used for special purposes (depending on the particular product and market location) are outdoor billboards along major thoroughfares, loudspeakers on roving trucks and cars, and direct mail (although mail service is spotty at best).

Trade publications are not big in Costa Rica. Some companies do advertise in newspapers and television in urban areas. Costa Rica's major newspapers are: *La Nacion*, with a circulation of 160,000; *La Republica*, with a circulation of 70,000; *La Prensa*, with a circulation of 35,000; and the *Tico Times*, the only English-language paper.

Six television channels hit 81 percent of urban households. Radio commercials reach 275,000 households and more than 1 million listeners, chiefly in the countryside.

Honduras: U.S. Stepchild

Honduras is an especially attractive vacation spot, with the most congenial people in Latin America. The Bay Islands of Roatán and Utila are one of the few unspoiled vacation spots remaining in the Caribbean. They are also a popular yachting haven for American and Canadian private boats. No cruise ships, no fancy hotels, no crowds—just sandy beaches, easy-going inhabitants, and safety. For vacationers interested in Mayan history, the Cabon ruins on the Guatemalan border are worth the flight down all by themselves.

But Honduras is extremely poor. One sees many people living in one-room shanties without electricity, plumbing, or water, wearing ragged clothing, and in some cases, going without shoes. Certainly this pains the conscience of affluent tourists—or it should. On the other hand, most Hondurans appear to be well-fed and healthy. No widespread discontent or military repression disrupts the tranquillity, as it does in Guatemala to the north.

Checkpoints and military personnel are still seen in Honduran cities; but they seem to be there for the protection of the average citizen, not to harass passersby. Best of all, most Hondurans are very pro-American, and recently, very pro-Canadian as well. They are a proud people and genuinely want outsiders to share the pleasure of their beautiful country.

Lastly, as in neighboring Guatemala, everything is very, very inexpensive: the lempira is worth about US$0.20 and has been pegged to the U.S. dollar for seventy-five years. A busy, illegal gray market, largely ignored by the government, flourishes in the cities and airports. Money changers hawk their wares and usually pay a few more lempira for a Yankee or Canadian dollar.

But vacationing only applies to tourists. Businesspeople don't have time. And on the business side, Honduras doesn't offer very much yet, although conditions are improving.

Exporting to Honduras

Honduras suffers from a chronic shortage of foreign exchange, and this limits hard currency payment for imports. In addition, the government still has a very convoluted approach to foreign trade, attaching prohibitive import duties and surcharges to a wide range of goods—in some cases up to 100 percent of invoice value. Imports from Central American Common Market countries fare much better, with tariffs ranging from zero to 35 percent.

Foreign traders soon find that the outdated bureaucratic labyrinth can delay almost any transaction; it actually kills many deals. Import permits and licenses are required for everything, including letters of credit. Documentation is extremely weighty. For all these reasons, illicit contraband floods the borders.

Companies willing to cope with the extraordinarily complex import procedures will find relatively little competition for most product sales. Local production facilities are scarce and primeval. Most multinationals have chosen to pass up Honduras for more lucrative local markets and better trade incentives.

It's almost impossible for small exporters to do business here without local affiliation. The distribution of products isn't so difficult, but dealing with the bureaucratic paperwork is. It's best to work either through the Honduran Consulate General or through the several specialized aid agencies to arrange meetings with potential local partners or representatives. Pricing must be kept low, however, because of the lack of hard currency and the near-poverty level of consumer income.

The best product opportunities are in:

- Plastic materials and resins
- Paper and paperboard
- Organic and agricultural chemicals
- Health care equipment and supplies (the country is also desperately in need of doctors, nurses, and dentists)
- Pharmaceuticals
- Machinery of all types and spare parts
- Vehicles and spare parts
- Virtually any consumer durables

Direct Investment Opportunities

The government encourages foreign investment as the only feasible way to generate foreign exchange. To this end it has enacted a few important investment incentives. The most crucial are:

- A permanent tax holiday
- No import quota restrictions
- A free trade zone

Empresa Nacional Portuaria (ENP), the National Port Authority, operates a free trade zone in Puerto Cortés, a well-supplied port on the Caribbean. Normal duty-free procedures apply to importing materials and equipment and exporting products. Sales within Honduras are treated as imports from abroad.

Excellent opportunities abound to exploit Honduran natural resources and low-cost labor. The best prospects are:

- Shrimp farming (especially on the Pacific coast)
- Fishing (especially scalefish and shrimp, since the high demand for lobster by various U.S. restaurant chains has practically stripped Honduran coastal waters bare)
- Fish processing
- Winter fruits and vegetables
- Food processing
- Tourism (in the Bay Islands and elsewhere)
- Wood products (especially furniture)
- Small electronic assemblies
- Apparel
- Mining

One of the surprising aspects of the Honduran business environment is the extensive number of options available for financing investment (mostly funded by USAID and the Overseas Private Investment Corporation and, to a lesser extent, for trade. Local banks can handle short-term trade finance, and the Central Bank of Honduras and USAID stand ready to assist with long-term investment financing. A variety of government aid programs will also help finance small projects.

Although the Honduran lempira has been pegged to the dollar, consistent overvaluation has created a thriving black market in foreign exchange. In recognition of the inevitability of such an unofficial market and in an attempt to stimulate exports, the Honduran government initiated the Transferable Export Certificate (CETRA) program.

Exporters are issued CETRA certificates equivalent to a percentage of their deposited export revenues. These certificates represent a claim on foreign exchange that may be used by the exporter to finance import requirements. Certificates can also be sold through commercial banks at market rates. These certificates have enabled more than 90 percent of the country's imports to be financed outside the official foreign exchange system.

For those interested in trading with or investing in Honduras, check with:

Honduran Consulate General
80 Wall Street, Suite 915
New York, NY 10005
Phone: (212) 269-3611

Chapter 14

Panama: "Crossroads of the World"

Historically, Panama has been one of the most open countries in Latin America toward foreign investment. Though it does enforce certain restrictions in the retailing sector and on foreign ownership of land near its borders, Panama generally welcomes foreign investors from virtually all countries and promises them the same treatment that local investors enjoy.

Panama's chief business attractions to foreigners are:

1. Its status as a reliable and secure offshore financial center and tax haven
2. The development of the Colón Free Zone, which provides the opportunity for foreign companies to display and sell their wares to the rest of Latin America
3. The Panama Canal, which is home to thousands of American expatriates and military personnel

Table 14-1 shows the country's main economic characteristics.

To develop effective corporate strategies for the utilization of these assets in expansion plans, it is necessary to understand the role the United States currently plays in this country that links north and south, east and west.

U.S. Assistance and Economic Reforms

As part of its commitment to rebuild Panama after the December 1989 invasion, the United States has poured more than US$1 billion

Table 14-1. Key Panamanian Statistics as of 1991–1992.

GDP	
Population	2.5 million
Labor force	0.8 million
Unemployment rate	16%
Inflation rate	1%
Economic activity	
Industry	30%
Agriculture	28%
Services (including banking)	30%
Public sector	12%
Minimum wage	
Panama City-Colón corridor	$0.78 per hour
Other areas	$0.65 per hour

Source: Panamanian Trade Development Institute.

into the economy, providing an enormous boost to economic growth. The U.S. government has also encouraged its handpicked successor to General Noriega, President Guillermo Endara, to implement a wide range of economic reforms designed to strengthen the Panamanian economy and thus secure the future safety of the Panama Canal.

The Endara administration has made several moves to stimulate foreign trade, but to date, most are meager compared with improvements put in place in other converting economies. For example, import duties and tariffs on manufactured goods have dropped to 60 percent; for the agroindustry, to 90 percent. Further reductions, to 40 and 50 percent respectively, went into effect January 1, 1993. It seems inconceivable that government officials believe such outrageous penalties will foster foreign trade, but they do.

Tax reform was also introduced as an investment incentive. Top corporate brackets were dropped from 50 percent to 34 percent, and individual rates, from 56 percent to 30 percent—again, hardly sufficient to attract swarms of foreign companies eager to produce products for local consumption.

For tax purposes, corporate profits fall into one of three categories.

1. *Panamanian source income:* Taxes at rates ranging from 20 to 50 percent.
2. *Export income from free trade zone:* Taxed at rates from 2.5 to 8.5 percent.
3. *Non-Panamanian source income:* No income tax. Non-Panamanian, or foreign-source income, includes the invoicing of exported products from abroad, directing transactions abroad, distributing dividends abroad, and receiving interest, commissions, or fees from financial operations conducted abroad.

Corporations in the Colón Free Zone are subject to the following tax rates:

Portion of Taxable Income	Tax Rate Percentages
Up to US$15,000	2.5%
US$15,000 to US$30,000	US$375 plus 4% over US$15,000
US$30,000 to US$100,000	US$975 plus 6% over US$30,000
Over US$100,000	US$5,175 plus 8.5% over US$100,000

The granting of discounts from taxable income is based on the number of Panamanian nationals a business employs. In addition, employers in or outside the free zones pay a social security tax of 12.25 percent on wages; employees pay 8.5 percent. The value-added tax (VAT) stands at 5 percent.

One surprising feature for a country intent on enticing international business is that its tax laws make no exception for expatriates. Non-Panamanian executives of foreign subsidiaries or branches pay the same personal income tax and other levies as any resident of Panama, whether the facility is in or out of the free zone.

Compared to the United States, personal tax rates are outrageous, reaching 56 percent for taxable income over US$200,000. At US$50,000, the rate is 34 percent. Another way of looking at this anomaly is to conclude that Panama wants foreign investment dollars but not foreign management to run the operations. Obviously, expatriate corporate executives should use tax-haven bank accounts as much as possible, or insist on being paid directly to a home-country account.

Panama's Role as an Offshore Financial Center and Tax Haven

For several decades, Panama has been a financial services–oriented economy. More than 145 banks from thirty countries form a thriving onshore and offshore financial center. Fifty-four banks are authorized to conduct onshore banking; the balance offer strictly offshore or representative facilities. As any executive responsible for maximizing gains on currency transactions or for raising offshore capital knows, a well-organized offshore financial center is the only way to go.

The most active Panamanian-owned onshore banks are: the Latin American Export Bank (BLADEX), Central America's version of Eximbank; Banco Cafetero (Panama); and Banco de Iberoamerica. Chase Manhattan is one of the most active U.S. banks and offers local onshore services covering virtually any need.

Panama's special tax exemptions for offshore transactions also give the nation a firm position as a tax haven. Foreign companies in need of banking confidentiality, tax-free status, and a strategically located site for trade with South America, the Caribbean Basin, and East Asia find Panama hard to beat.

Despite the decimation of Panama's economy by General Noriega's drug dealings and the U.S. invasion, the banking community continues to function. The nation's international reputation as a reliable offshore financial center remains intact. Panama is still a U.S. dollar economy protected by bank secrecy laws and is still free of any exchange controls.

To enhance its position as a longtime financial center, the U.S. dollar has been legal tender since 1904, and the balboa is permanently pegged to the dollar. This permits Panama to escape the currency exchange and devaluation problems so common in other Latin American nations. Passive and direct foreign investors can transfer capital in and out of the country freely, without any local approvals.

Free Trade Zones in Panama

Panama prides itself on well-developed free trade zones that attract foreign investment from the four corners of the world, mostly in search of Mexican-type maquiladora or twin-plant advantages. Although the United States and Canada account for the greatest number of companies, Taiwan, South Korea, and Hong Kong are also well represented, as are various European and Latin American nations.

Most foreign companies with strategies to utilize Panama's unique location and low-cost labor should begin with the free trade zones, preferably the Colón Free Zone. The incentives are better, the business amenities more available, and the shipping easier and less costly than can be found outside the zones.

Panama's free trade zones offer a wide range of investment, industrial, and tourism incentives, including:

- Exemptions from all import and export duties (although surcharges apply to all imports in or out of the free trade zones)
- Minimal income taxes on export operations
- A real estate tax holiday for twenty years
- Free repatriation of profits
- Open foreign exchange
- The beginnings of a stock market in Balboa

Most foreign companies elect to set up facilities in the largest FTZ zone in Latin America: the Colón Free Zone located at the Atlantic mouth of the Panama Canal. More than 1,400 foreign businesses use the zone for importing, warehousing, assembling, repacking, and reexporting a vast array of products, including electronic apparatus, pharmaceutical products, liquors, tobacco, furniture, clothing, shoes, and jewelry.

Panamanians like to think of their country as the "puente del mundo," the crossroads of the world. The Colón Free Zone advertises itself as the shop window for South and Central America and offers modern facilities in which companies may display their wares. In 1990 U.S. companies brought US$2.7 billion worth of goods into Colón and shipped another US$3.1 billion worth out. Some of this went to other free ports, such as San Andros, Colombia and Margarita Island, Venezuela, or direct to Aruba and other Caribbean Basin commercial centers.

PanExport is a privately owned free trade zone located on the Panama City side of the isthmus at Ojo de Agua. It is a ten-minute drive from the Tocumen International Airport. Detailed information about it can be obtained by calling (507) 69-2138, or faxing (507) 64-2459.

During 1992, a new innovation in FTZ structure was announced: a combination of zones to be called the Panama Teleport. When completed, it will include an international business park, an export processing zone, and a scientific and technological research zone. Its promoters envision tenant companies of all sizes, with operations in banking, financing, telemarketing, insurance, data entry, reservations centers, and credit-card databases. For more information, call (507) 20-4585, or fax (507) 64-7181.

Two ports—Balboa, serving Pacific Rim markets, and the Port of Cristobal on the Colón side—offer a full complement of services and give Panama a justifiable reputation as one of the world's greatest shipping crossroads.

The Labor Force and Labor Laws

Although Panama boasts a highly skilled labor force (including many bilingual workers), the country's onerous labor laws can be difficult to manage. The government restricts the number of non-Panamanian blue-collar workers to 10 percent of the work force in any one company, although no restrictions apply to senior management. Organized unions represent about 14 percent of Panama's work force and are concentrated in the transportation, services, construction, and energy sectors.

Perhaps the most important incentive for locating in a Panamanian free trade zone is being exempted from having to enter into collective bargaining agreements for the first four years of operation.

Direct Investment Outside Panama's Free Trade Zones

Outside the free trade zones, local companies and a few foreign investors produce goods for export, including sugar products, bananas, shrimp and sea products, coffee, melons, brooms and mops, tobacco, apparel, and a small amount of petroleum products. About 45 percent of these exports goes to the United States, another 21 percent goes to other Caribbean Basin countries, and 28 percent goes to Europe, with the balance spread among Mexico, South America, and Asia.

Foreign companies interested in forming joint ventures outside the FTZs will find the best opportunities in specialty fruits and vegetables, aquaculture (mainly shrimp farming), cut flowers, electronic assemblies, building materials, apparel, forestry, and mining. However, with all the advantages offered by free trade zones, it makes more sense for new entrants to locate there than in more restricted and competitive external sites.

Privatization

Privatization of state-owned industries is an essential part of President Endara's economic reforms. The program is just getting off the ground, although a few businesses have already been privatized, including Air Panama International, the Hotel Washington, the Hotel Toboga, and exclusive concessions to operate the dry dock of the National Port Authority. Although the government plans to put many businesses on the market over the next five years, it has identified only eleven outright sales or concessions during 1992–1993.

Local Conditions and Assistance

Of all Latin American countries, Panama probably has the most efficient and reliable telecommunications network—an absolutely essential ingredient for an offshore financial center. Panama also has the best health and sanitary conditions, at least where foreigners live. Once the shambles left by the U.S. invasion are fully cleared away and rebuilding is completed, Panama City will rank with many U.S. cities in sanitation, cultural amenities, and shopping.

In 1984, the government created a one-stop center, the Panamanian Trade Development Institute (IPCE), to assist foreign investors cut through government red tape. A branch office was recently opened in Miami, but the most complete information can be obtained by calling the institute's headquarters in Panama City at (507) 25-7244, or by faxing (507) 25-2193. Additional information can be obtained by contacting:

> The Embassy of Panama
> 2862 McGill Terrace NW
> Washington, DC 20008
> Phone: (202) 483-1407

Exporting to Panama

Panama's consumer base is very similar to Costa Rica's in that a large segment of the population of 2.3 million has an income below the poverty line; its per capital GDP is only US$1,900. The United States supplies about 40 percent of Panama's imports: the Caribbean Basin, 23 percent; Mexico, 10 percent; Europe, 11 percent; and South American countries, 14 percent.

A very large contingent of U.S. military and commercial families live in or near the Canal Zone. Like these expatriates, many Panamanian bureaucrats and business managers enjoy a standard of living considerably higher than that of the average citizen. This means that consumer-goods exporters would do well to target the expatriate and government/business elite markets rather than seek out Panama's mass markets. The competition—from local Japanese, Taiwanese, and Hong Kong business interests—is stiffer in Panama than it is in other Central American countries. Prices are still reasonably high and will probably remain so as long as the large contingent of Americans remains. Virtually all types of consumer goods, as well as food products, and health care supplies and equipment, must be imported.

On the commercial and industrial side, the country needs machine tools and materials handling equipment to jump-start its industrial expansion, as well as construction equipment and services to rebuild and upgrade its infrastructure.

Local agents should be engaged to handle the still-difficult maneuvers necessary to get customs clearance and import approvals and to keep abreast of East Asian competition.

The Panama Canal

Under an agreement reached with former U.S. President Jimmy Carter, the responsibility for managing the Panama Canal will be turned over to the Panamanian government in 1999. It seems that Mr. Carter is one of the few who still believe in the wisdom of his action. With the turnover nearing, an increasing number of U.S. and Panamanian government officials and business leaders are expressing concern over the fate of this vital link to the world's shipping lanes.

Former Panama Canal administrator Fernando Manfredo has proposed privatizing the operation as a way of avoiding the corruption and inefficiency prevalent in government-run businesses. As he told an international shipping conference, "Many people think that if it becomes a government entity, one will see the same problems of inefficiency, high costs, and even corruption that frequently takes place in Panamanian state companies."

A poll taken in 1991 showed that a majority of Panamanians believe that Panama is not qualified to run the canal efficiently. The United States and other major users are taking these poll results and Mr. Manfredo's suggestions very seriously. Some observers believe that before 1999 arrives, alternative arrangements will have to be negotiated, perhaps with the idea of turning the Panama Canal over to a joint commission consisting of the United States, Panama, and other major interested parties, such as the United Nations.

Clearly, with the world's shipping lanes at stake, it pays to keep an eye on these developments. The loss of crossocean access would most likely redirect the hemispheric trade strategies of many companies. Attempts to influence developments over the next three years could possibly be one of the most important contributions the

U.S. business community could make to hemispheric, and perhaps world, trade.

Whether via its efficient offshore financial center and free trade zones or as a select export market, Panama offers a range of competitive benefits to foreigners of all nationalities, including:

- A prime location at the entrance to both North and South America
- Access to crossocean shipping through the Panama Canal
- Very liberal laws relating to banking, taxation, insurance, corporations, and shipping (in fact, to commerce and trade of all types)
- A market economy based on free trade
- A complete absence of currency exchange controls
- An outstanding international communications network
- Easy access by air, sea, and land
- A highly trained and mostly bilingual population
- The strong commitment of a large middle class to a democratic, pluralistic society which, with the exception of the Noriega era, has strongly contributed to a politically stable government

Chapter 15

Nicaragua, El Salvador, and Guatemala: States Approaching Anarchy

While opportunities for foreign investors and traders are increasing rapidly in Costa Rica, Panama, and even Honduras, the same cannot be said for the rest of Central America. Although all administrations outwardly encourage foreign investment as the only feasible way to bring in hard currency, few are serious enough to make the effort worthwhile.

The era of Latin America's isolationism, violence, and economic degradation did not end with the advent of the 1990s—at least not in Nicaragua, El Salvador, and Guatemala. So far, the 1990s have seen a continuation of political, social, and economic upheaval—albeit with a different public face.

Political labels have changed. The shooting has stopped. American aid is pouring in. But in many respects, it is business as usual for the armies and the repressed peasant majorities. The rich continue to get richer, the poor, poorer. The gap continues to widen between the privileged few, who drive Mercedes and sports cars purchased with funds deposited in Miami accounts, and the decidedly unprivileged masses, who desperately need a broad range of consumer goods but cannot afford them.

A Painful Emergence From Civil Strife

While most of Latin America and the Caribbean countries were casting off the last vestiges of the lost decade of the 1980s and marching toward free-market economies, Nicaragua, El Salvador, and Guatemala remained impoverished, embattled nations struggling to regain their status as healthy political entities.

Not that major changes have not occurred since the 1980s; they have. For example:

- In Nicaragua, General Daniel Ortega and his ruling Sandinistas were overthrown in a peaceful election that installed Violeta Barrios de Chamorro as the nation's president.
- The government of El Salvador and the Farabundo Marti National Liberation Front (FMLN) signed an agreement to end the country's twelve-year civil war.
- Promising negotiations between the Guatemalan government and rebel guerrilla groups have been ongoing.
- All three nations have joined the rest of Central America in having duly elected democratic governments and functioning liberal democratic institutions.

The era of revolutionary insurgency seems to have ended. But this does not mean that future revolutions couldn't overthrow one or more of these teetering democracies, or that democracy has permanently triumphed. Major changes have definitely occurred in the social and economic fabric of these strife-torn nations, but long-term results are still indeterminable.

A few of the questions that remain unanswered are:

- What does it mean to El Salvador that 20 percent—one in five—of the population lives outside the country?
- What significance can be attached to the fact that one third of Guatemalans, traditionally devout Catholics, now belong to stridently evangelical churches?
- What impact will militant Sandinista labor organizations have on Nicaragua's economic growth potential?
- With Nicaragua's cotton crop (its prime foreign exchange and employment generator) reduced to one tenth of its 1977 level, can the nation regain any semblance of economic order with substitute exports?

Recovering but Not Recovered

The past fifteen years have certainly transformed these three countries, bringing radical changes to their political frameworks, social structures, and economies. Modern technology has been a willing servant of these changes. Strangely, pockets of affluence—complete with new luxury automobiles, television sets, cellular phones, computers, luxurious residences—are to be found amid the vast stretches of abject poverty.

Citizens are politically informed, active, and comparatively well-organized. A constant international flow of people, goods, and capital conflicts with preindustrial revolution working conditions. All three traditional agricultural/industrial economies are becoming increasingly dependent on services to generate income.

The setting is surreal. Traversing the streets of Guatemala City, San Salvador, or Managua, one has the feeling of being in two worlds—the very old and the very new—simultaneously, depending on which side of the street one uses. Political structures in the three countries have also changed, but not in the direction of democratically elected governments. When the ten-year Mexican civil war ended in 1920, opponents sought reconciliation and political accommodation. The same occurred after the Colombian civil war of 1946–1958. The exact opposite has occurred in the aftermath of the civil war in Nicaragua and the ongoing unrest in El Salvador and Guatemala. Instead of political accommodation and unification, the countries are splitting further into local, regional, and social, politically attuned factions. This lack of acceptance of any central authority makes it extremely difficult for their newly elected governments to govern.

The violence of the 1980s was accompanied by economic disintegration in all three nations. Production, and exports, of course, fell to dangerously low levels. Budget and trade deficits soared. Inflation skyrocketed and per capita income plummeted.

The Impact of Strife on Basic Economic Structures

Now, in the recovery period, it is clear that economic structures were also drastically altered. The prevailing attitude in the private

Table 15-1. Key Statistics for Nicaragua, El Salvador, and Guatemala ($US).

	Nicaragua	El Salvador	Guatemala
Population	3.9 million	5.3 million	9.3 million
Economically active	1.3 million	NA	2.8 million
Urban literacy	87%	65%	50%
Unemployment	20%	20%	6%
GDP	$1.6 billion	$4.8 billion	$11.1 billion
Per capita GDP (US$)	$394	$913	$1,215
GDP growth	3.7%	1.1%	3.5%
Exports	$322 million	$615 million	$1,161 million
Imports	$697 million	$1,050 million	$1,626 million

Sources: Caribbean and Latin American Data Book; Banco Central de Nicaragua; The Investors Services Center—Enterprise Chamber of Guatemala.

sector is a perfect example. Traditionally, the business communities concentrated on production output improvements and financial conservatism. Now, underscoring the previously unknown ability of money to flow to foreign bank accounts, one senses a pervasive skepticism about future prospects.

With the destruction of annual cotton crops and little incentive to replant and care for new crops, the area has become dependent on self-perpetuating coffee crops as the primary export. Little export diversification is evident.

Nicaragua and El Salvador pay for about one half of their imports with export foreign exchange. Export earnings cover about three fourths of Guatemala's imports. The balance of foreign exchange for all three countries comes from a combination of U.S. and multilateral financial aid, tourism, repatriation of hard currency from family members living in the United States, foreign embassy expenditures, and drug trafficking (especially in Guatemala).

Table 15-1 shows key comparative statistics for the three countries:

It doesn't take a genius to recognize the fragility of these economies. Without U.S. financial and trade support, all three countries would long ago have erupted into anarchial fiefdoms. Although this remains a possibility, as long as the United States pays hard currency for regional tranquillity, the three countries should gradually come out of their economic doldrums.

This may not be the time to actively pursue opportunities in these three countries, but looking to their future revival, corporate strategists might well begin planning for the day when conditions are more favorable. As far as the governments of Nicaragua, El Salvador, and Guatemala are concerned, each has consciously inaugurated promotion programs to attract foreign investment and trade. Nicaragua's is the most aggressive.

Nicaragua: Searching for Compromise

After the successful democratic election in February 1990, the U.S. lifted trade embargoes in effect since 1985. Furthermore, Nicaragua now qualifies under the Caribbean Basin Initiative, and meets the requirements for Eximbank credits and the Overseas Private Investment Corporation insurance and financing assistance.

Once installed, the Chamorro administration was quick to implement a series of economic reforms aimed at bringing Nicaragua back to the world community through a free-market system. Inflation was curtailed, the currency stabilized, and foreign exchange liberalized. A partially successful attempt was made to restore government-expropriated land and businesses to the private sector, although backroom concessions to Sandinista members negated much of this effort. Government export monopolies were disbanded and tight import restrictions were lifted. Although still in its infancy, a private banking system is beginning to emerge.

Prior to 1979, when the Sandinista regime took power, Nicaragua was a thriving center of trade and investment. In fact, it was a model for all of Central America, with the strongest, fastest-growing economy in the region. Major exports included coffee, tobacco, bananas, and various nontraditional agricultural products.

Its recent period of economic prominence has left Nicaragua with an infrastructure of roads, power utilities, telecommunications, and services that the emerging nations of Eastern Europe might envy. As Central Bank President Raul A. Lacayo states, Nicaragua "has a modern airport; seaports on both the Atlantic and Pacific; the longest coastline in Central America, with some of the best weather conditions on the continent; an abundance of rich volcanic agricultural land; a large, young work force; and a commitment from its government to foster economic growth and increased productivity."

Domestic Market Opportunities

The real question is not "What products should be exported to meet Nicaragua's market demands?" It is "Where do purchasers get hard currency to use for payment?" With a per capita GDP of less than $400, most consumers in this nation are as broke as those in many African countries. Commercial and industrial buyers can, with appropriate connections, tap into a modest share of the foreign aid pouring in from the United States and United Nations organizations.

However, in truth, only the business, military, and government elite can afford to buy imported goods. To be sure, these consumers are eager for practically all durables and soft goods, but they represent only a small percentage of an already meager population base of 3.9 million. This significantly reduces the benefits of even trying to export consumer goods. In most cases the small volume is not worth the aggravation of dealing with customs and transport officials. For companies willing to ship small quantities, the Caribbean island states offer much better opportunities.

In the future—hopefully the near future—as the economy stabilizes, the rest of the population will earn sufficient income to satisfy at least minimum needs. When that occurs, basic, low-end hard and soft goods should create presentable markets.

On the commercial and industrial side, though imported quantities are small, the best products for local markets are:

- Chemicals and resins
- Cereals
- Agricultural and industrial machinery
- Vehicles and parts
- Fertilizers
- Paper products

Maximum import duties have been dropped from rates   as

high as 350 percent in the 1980s to an average of 10 percent today. Duties have been completely eliminated on products from other Central American countries, under the terms of the Central American Free Trade Agreement.

The greatest local demand is for construction and agricultural equipment and materials to rebuild war-torn sections of the country and to expand the nation's free trade zones. Foreign contractors and skilled building trade expatriates should have little difficulty finding projects for the next ten years.

Direct Investment Opportunities

The Nicaraguan government's economic reform program specifically encourages foreign direct investment in virtually every industry. New commercial legislation includes the following key provisions:

Foreign Investment Law

- Guaranteed capital repatriation after three years
- Up to 100 percent repatriation of net profit
- Guarantees against expropriation for ten years, with just compensation if expropriated later
- Guarantees that the corporate tax rate in effect at the time of investment will not increase for earnings from that investment

Free Zone Law

- 100 percent duty exoneration on inputs, vehicles, facilities for employees, and packaging materials (if not available in Nicaragua)
- 100 percent corporate tax exemption for the first five years of investment, with 60 percent reduction thereafter
- No geographic restrictions for establishing free zones

Export Promotion Law

- Up to 100 percent import duty exemption, depending on percentage of output exported (the higher the percentage, the greater the exemption)

- Up to 80 percent reduction on property tax
- Export contract available for ten years
- Tax credit of 10 to 23 percent, depending on projected employment generation, export destination, and foreign exchange earnings, for up to six years

Nicaragua's large low-cost labor base offers North American investors a good opportunity to manufacture products such as light assemblies, apparel, and wooden furniture (all requiring extensive labor input but minimal skills) for export back to the United States or Canada.

Agribusiness is also a good industry to exploit Nicaragua's resources. Coffee is far and away the largest export commodity right now and, with a little attention, cotton crops could be brought back. In addition, the following commodities offer excellent potential for export back to the United States: honeydew melons, mango, pineapple, peanuts, cucumbers, cardamon, ginger, palm, sugar, bananas, and beef.

Nicaragua has one of the largest untapped fishery resources in the Caribbean basin. Government officials estimate that the current US$60 million annual exports of shrimp, lobster, and squid could be increased fivefold with minimal investment in boats and processing plants. Some shrimp farming has already begun in the northern sector.

Free Trade Zones

Nicaragua's first free trade zone, Las Mercedes, is alive and well, following a US$7 million loan from the Central American Economic Integration Bank. All eleven buildings on the 118-acre site near the Managua Airport are occupied by domestic and foreign firms, manufacturing primarily jeans and other apparel. An additional 300,000 square meters of land is available for development.

As is the case with Mexican maquiladora tenants, Nicaraguan FTZ occupants can delegate all government, labor, infrastructure, and community functions to the industrial park's management, allowing plant management to concentrate entirely on production activities. Space at Las Mercedes rents for US$1.75 per square meter.

Privatization

The goal of Nicaragua's privatization program is to get the government completely out of manufacturing, commodity production, and commercial banking activities. The program consists of selling over 300 government-controlled businesses and industries, and returning agricultural and aquacultural operations and commercial banks (all nationalized by the Sandinistas) to the private sector.

While backroom deals with the Sandinista party have slowed privatization efforts, one can see some progress in the recent sale of coffee plantations, a cattle holding company, a cotton grower and producer, and the fleets and processing facilities of a large fishing concern. Four banks have already been privatized, with more to come.

Any foreign company interested in expanding to Nicaragua through the privatization program can get specific guidance in Managua by contacting either of the following:

Dayton Caldera
Corporation for
   Privatization
KM 7½ Carretera Norte
Apartado 1909
Managua, Nicaragua
Phone: (505) 2-31-100
Fax: (505) 2-31-193

Julio Vigil
c/o Vigil y Caligaris
Apartado 202
Managua, Nicaragua
Phone: (505) 2-62-491

Taxes in Nicaragua

Exclusive of the tax incentives described as part of the economic reform program, the government has completely revamped the country's internal tax structure. In a move to streamline the filing system and broaden the tax base, the new tax reform package includes:

- A corporate income tax reduction from 45 percent to 35.5 percent
- A tax reduction on capital return from 20 percent to 5 percent

- The elimination of a 10 percent surtax on personal or corporate taxes of individuals considered "super earners" (obviously referring to high-income taxpayers)
- A property tax reduction from 3 percent to 2.5 percent

Certainly these moves help stimulate income accumulation and investment to some extent. However, as is true of so many developing nations unfamiliar with the forces that drive a market economy and create economic growth, Nicaragua's tax reforms have barely scratched the surface. To stimulate domestic growth, serious incentives must extend far beyond these meager improvements. Fortunately, foreign companies investing in free trade zone facilities enjoy a more liberal tax framework.

El Salvador: Washington's Pawn

Many of the troubles that ignited internecine conflict in El Salvador more than a decade ago remain unresolved today. The civil war that brought this nation of 5.3 million people to its knees also killed at least 75,000 of its citizens and drove another 2 million into exile.

To understand El Salvador in the mid-1990s, one must view the role played by this tiny, impoverished oligarchy in the context of what a highly regarded British journal called "the myopic paranoia" that existed in the halls of Washington during the latter stages of the Cold War.

Like its neighbor Nicaragua, El Salvador became a pawn in a great board game stretching from Afghanistan to Angola. Intent on supporting a government that was believed to be the antithesis of a Communist regime, regardless of the atrocities committed against its own people, the Reagan administration chose this unlikely place to "draw the line" against Communist encroachment in the Western Hemisphere. This policy put the U.S. Government smack in the middle of a domestic quarrel. The United States is still trying to extricate itself.

The quarrel began in 1980 when a group of Salvadoran landowners and coffee traders mounted a coup, convincing the miniscule army, the police, and judges, to defend the old ways that kept the landed aristocracy relatively rich while ensuring a life of poverty for the rest of the country. Opponents of the coup—including a few religious leaders—were swiftly killed, exiled, or driven into rebellion. The Soviet Union and its Cuban henchmen saw the opening, armed the rebels, and stood back to watch a ragged band of guerrillas take on the governments of El Salvador and the United States.

The United States Government trained a new army for El Salvador, adding 47,000 men to its previous 16,000. They proved as corrupt, idle, and reluctant to fight as the original forces. All told, the United States poured US$6 billion into this lost cause over a ten-year period.

The 1991 election has failed to change the situation. The old ruling class continues to thwart U.S. attempts at social change. Land reform has fizzled. The judiciary remains as corrupt as ever. Human rights abuses persist, even under a cease-fire.

It may be many years before El Salvador becomes a truly viable place in which to make an investment or to conduct serious trade. At a minimum, the United States will probably continue pouring billions down this sinkhole just to maintain the semblance of stability that Washington so hungers for.

Meanwhile, life goes on, and the Salvadoran government presses forward with economic reforms aimed at enticing foreign investment and, hopefully, encouraging increased exports. Among these reforms are:

- Removal of price controls on 240 classes of consumer goods
- Implementation of anti-inflationary monetary policies
- A purge of the monopoly buying and export authority of the national coffee, sugar, and cotton institutes
- Reduction of import duties to a range of 5 to 35 percent
- Gradual implementation of a free-market floating exchange rate system
- Legalization and licensing of foreign exchange trading houses
- Ten-year exemptions from income taxes and assets/equity taxes for companies exporting to non-Central American countries (applicable to both corporations and corporate shareholders)

Local Markets

With much of the country's industry destroyed by the civil war or abandoned by fleeing exiles, El Salvador must rely on imports of virtually all types of consumer goods to satisfy its citizens, and on imports of production equipment, machinery, technology, and capital goods to revitalize its industrial base.

On the consumer front, imports of health care products and supplies, household appliances, work and dress clothing for men and women, and, of course, foodstuffs are in very high demand by those with income or savings. Rural peasants face the same dire poverty as they do in neighboring Nicaragua, Honduras, and Guatemala.

There is the beginning of an upswing in commercial and industrial demand for telecommunications equipment, electric power generating and distribution equipment and supplies, textile and apparel machinery, woodworking equipment, and food processing equipment. Fertilizers are also desperately needed to rejuvenate the small agricultural sector.

Gradually, as the country stabilizes and additional workers are relocated from rural areas to urban factories, additional demand will arise for such product categories as:

- Automobiles, trucks, buses, and spare parts
- Computers, peripherals, and software (especially for business applications)
- Building materials and construction equipment
- Water treatment equipment
- Pollution control equipment, supplies, and engineering services
- Waste disposal equipment, vehicles, and services

With a population nearly double that of Nicaragua crammed into one half the land space, housing, hospitals, schools, and supporting products and services are currently in high demand and scarce supply.

The only way to sell anything in El Salvador is to be there. Foreign companies need to station at least one or two full-time bilingual employees in San Salvador to work with local agents and distributors. A joint venture partner isn't necessary except when bidding on construction or infrastructure projects.

Normal advertising techniques won't work here. As in Costa Rica, nearly all sales are made through personal contact and relationships.

Direct Investment Opportunities

The Salvadoran government offers a surprisingly wide range of incentives to attract foreign investment. The Foreign Investment Promotion and Guarantee Law includes such incentives as:

- Unrestricted remittances of all new profits (but only up to 50 percent of invested capital for services and commercial activities)
- Unrestricted management of foreign investment without interference of government or other local technocrats
- Unrestricted remittance of both principal and interest on external loans
- Guarantees of foreign currency account security

Within free trade zones, the Export Reactivization Law of 1990 grants ten-year exemptions on income tax and asset/equity taxes to companies that export 100 percent of production capacity outside Central America. The law also permits duty-free importing of machinery, equipment, tools, spare parts, lubricants, and fuels used in the production process.

The major free trade zone/industrial park, San Bartolo Free Zone, is located a mere twenty minutes from San Salvador. According to the zone's management, it offers easy access to domestic and international transportation centers and combines the features of a typical industrial park with:

- Proximity to local suppliers of raw materials and components
- Productive labor
- Government recruitment of labor and supervision
- Waste disposal facilities
- Extensive vocational and training programs for workers

A newly established 94.5 hectare free trade zone near Cuscatlan International Airport offers similar amenities.

El Salvador offers an abundant labor pool—especially in and around San Salvador—which seems to be remarkably trainable for a basically agrarian society. Traditionally, Salvadoran workers have been known to practice a work ethic not customarily found in many other Latin American nations. The ministry of economics estimates an underemployment rate of more than 40 percent.

Minimum wage rates for industrial workers run approximately 21 colones (US$2.85) per day—about US$0.45 per hour, including fringes. Agricultural workers get approximately 11.5 colones per day (US$1.30)—about US$0.21 per hour, including fringes. The rate for agricultural workers varies, however, depending on the season, the section of the country, and the agricultural commodity.

Shrimp farming, apparel assembly, and light manufacturing are the best prospects for investment projects. Of course, production will be for export, not local consumption.

Taxes in El Salvador

Apart from the ten-year tax exemption granted to exporting companies, El Salvador's tax system is on a par with most other countries in the region. The maximum corporate income tax rate is 30 percent, with branches paying 38 percent. Nondomiciled foreign companies pay 22 percent. An additional 2 percent tax is assessed against net worth. Withholding rates stand at 22 percent, although branch remittances remain tax free.

Additional corporate taxes include a sales tax of 5 percent and a tax of 0.9 to 2 percent on capital in excess of 500,000 colones. Social security taxes run 8.25 percent for the employer and 3.50 percent for the employee. The government also assesses a National Housing Fund tax on salaries up to a maximum of 700 colones, at rates of 5 percent for the employer and 0.5 percent for the employee.

Government approval is required for all foreign exchange transactions. No tax treaties have been concluded with any other jurisdiction.

Guatemala: Failure of Democracy

While armies and rebels in Nicaragua and El Salvador seem to have reached at least a temporary truce, human rights abuses and repression continue in Guatemala. No other Central American state has accomplished so little in preparation for rejoining the modern world. Worse, the powers-that-be show no inclination to change.

Although Washington would like to believe that all democratically elected governments work in a democratic way, Guatemala has proved that this is not always the case. War rages on between a belligerent, out-of-control military and roving bands of guerrillas. More political assassinations occurred in 1991 than at any time since the early 1980s. Yet an evangelical Protestant, Jorge Serrano Elias, was elected president after a five-year term by Christian Democrat Vinicio Cerezo, making for the longest unbroken period of civilian rule in Guatemala since 1954.

Civilian authority has never been strong in Guatemala. Nor is it now, with the army deliberately defeating Mr. Serrano's efforts to move the country forward. Although the president expresses a desire to find new markets for exports and to encourage foreign direct investment, the army and guerrilla bands appear intent on driving the nation ever deeper into obscurity.

As the U.S. State Department reported in 1992, the Guatemalan army and its auxiliaries have committed "extra-judicial killings, torture, and the disappearances of, among others, human-rights activists, unionists, indigenous people, and street children."

But even with the uncertainties associated with a country in a more or less constant state of insurgency and military repression, life goes on. The business community does its best to function, and in many ways Guatemala, with a population approaching ten million, offers more potential for profit to foreign companies willing to face such uncertainties than do either Nicaragua or El Salvador.

Local Market Demand

One surprising paradox of Guatemala is that even though the country is in the throes of insurgency, and battles among the army, guerrilla bands, and indigenous groups go on day and night, the country has a fairly well-developed infrastructure (in need of repair, of course) and industrial base. The country's "haves" represent a significant minority. They congregate in urban areas, primarily in Guatemala City and, to a lesser extent, in Antigua to the north. At US$11.1 billion, Guatemala's GDP is the largest in Central America.

The private sector dominates Guatemala's economy, generating nearly 90 percent of GDP. The government limits its involvement in productive activities to public utilities, a handful of development-oriented financial institutions, and a variety of regulatory agencies.

The best products for export to Guatemala comprise a longer list than might be suspected, given the wide gap between rich and poor. Such a list, by no means comprehensive, includes:

- Air conditioning and refrigeration equipment
- Agricultural machinery and equipment
- Agricultural chemicals, including fertilizer
- Building materials and products
- Computers, peripherals, and software
- Construction machinery, off-road and on-road
- Food processing and packaging equipment and supplies
- Hotel and restaurant supplies, furnishings, and equipment
- Machine tools and metalworking machinery
- Materials-handling equipment, mainly forklifts and conveyers
- Medical diagnostic and treatment equipment
- Medical supplies and pharmaceuticals
- Plastic materials and resins
- Printing and graphic arts equipment, machinery, and supplies
- Process instrumentation (measuring and controls)
- Railroad equipment and rolling stock
- Safety and security products and equipment
- Telecommunications products
- Trucks, trailers, buses, automobiles, and spare parts
- Yarns

It should be noted that a sizable number of the people living in the northern states, in the south along the Honduran border, and near the Rio Dulce and Puerto Barrios on the Caribbean coast, are very poor. The potential to develop export markets in these regions—other than for health care products and a small number of tourism goods—is practically nil. Foreign exporters do best, therefore, concentrating on products needed in urban areas or by government agencies.

In this country, more than any other in Central America, local partners are a must. A few years ago Exxon tried to build an oil exploration business here without local help. The result? Exxon was told to go home and never come back. United Fruit learned over many years of prospering in Guatemala that its success was due in no small way to a constant nurturing of bureaucrats and military strongmen.

To learn how to reach potential partners, it is best to work through the Guatemala Trade Council. Contact may be made through any of the following:

Embassy of Guatemala
Commercial Attaché
2220 R Street, NW
Washington, DC 20008
Phone: (202) 745-4952

Guatemalan-American
    Chamber of Commerce
7 Avenida 14-44, Zona 9
Guatemala 01009
Phone: 312-235

American Chamber of Com-
    merce
Attention: Spencer Manners
c/o Foodpro International,
    Inc.
12 Calle 1-25, No. 1114
P.O. Box 89-A, Zona 10
Guatemala City, Guatemala
Phone: 320-490

Environmental Opportunities

If Mexico City ranks near the top of the world's most polluted cities, Guatemala City is right behind it. Many of the same pollutants that make life untenable in Mexico City are causing air, noise, and water pollution in Guatemala City: autos, trucks, and buses without mufflers; the burning of leaded fuel; factories spewing forth unfiltered industrial gases and smoke; broken sewer pipes; and horrific public sanitation conditions.

Walking in Guatemala City without an air filter and ear plugs is extremely uncomfortable. Fresh fruits and vegetables are generally not safe to eat. The same goes for local meat. Of all the strange cities of the world I have visited on business, only Lagos, Nigeria, is a less desirable place to be than Guatemala City.

Whereas Mexico City recognized and started dealing with its pollution problems relatively early, Guatemala City has barely begun. With pressure from the International Monetary Fund and U.S. aid agencies to clean up their act, Guatemalans are beginning to look for help from foreign companies. This makes pollution control equipment, together with all the peripheral equipment and supplies necessary to clean up the mess, a wide open market. Trade officials predict that demand for these products will mushroom faster than any other.

Direct Investment Opportunities

Guatemala has traditionally welcomed foreign direct investment and continues to provide a business environment conducive to foreign ownership. Other than an inefficient bureaucracy that mirrors other developing countries in being corrupt and slow, there are few impediments to hinder foreign investors.

The government does not impose any restrictions on the repatriation of profits. Foreign investors may own any company wholly or partially and enjoy complete freedom in its management. Company officers may be either residents or nonresidents of Guatemala, and no requirements exist for minimum ownership by Guatemalan citizens.

Although statistics are not reliable, trade officials estimate that more than 300 midsize companies count on foreign capital to operate, which presumably means they are foreign owned. According to a government agency, the Guatemala Investor Services Center, foreign citizens and corporations are treated the same as Guatemalan citizens with respect to laws, courts, and "rights involved in acquiring land, the development of agricultural or industrial companies, mining, oil, and other subsoil concessions."

The fastest-growing industries for foreign investment involve nontraditional products, such as fresh and frozen vegetables and fruits, aquaculture (especially shrimp), and the light manufacturing of textiles and other assembly-type products. Excellent opportunities also exist in traditional agricultural products: green coffee, sugar, bananas, cardamon, beef, raw cotton, and petroleum exploration and production. As in other Central American countries, it makes a lot more sense for small and midsize companies to plan for exporting these products than to try to compete with local producers.

Direct investment facilities located outside the defined boundaries of Guatemala City enjoy special incentives, including:

- Financing by government institutions at favorable rates
- Free, preferential assistance from government institutions for studies involving technical requirements, economic feasibility, export markets, and marketing channels
- Priority in the utilization of industrial preinvestment studies performed by government institutions
- Preferential treatment in the utilization of industrial installations owned by the government (e.g., leasing government facilities)

Tourism is booming. The government would like to attract more foreign investment in this sector and has accordingly passed a new National Tourism Development Law. The law includes several incentives for foreign investment:

- Reduction of up to 50 percent of charter taxes and extensions of companies charters
- Exemption from all import taxes, duties, charges, and surcharges on raw materials, construction materials, equipment, appliances, vehicles or boats of any kind, utensils, furnishings and fixtures, and objects of entertainment, providing they are not produced in Guatemala
- Exemption from real estate taxes on new construction or on the value of expansions or modernizations
- Exemptions from all taxes on income generated through such investment, beginning two years after the start of operations

Wage rates are set by the Ministry of Employment. Minimum daily wage rates range from US$2 for agricultural workers to US$6 for operators of heavy construction equipment.

Free Trade Zones

The government operates a free trade zone called the Free Zone of Industry and Commerce (ZOLIC) on the Caribbean coast.

Several private zones have recently been started, including the Zeta Industrial Park Free Zone outside Guatemala City, Guatemala Woo Yang Development, and La Aurora International Free Zone. Standard free zone incentives include:

- Total exemption from import duties for materials, fuels, and equipment used in production
- Exemption from income taxes for twelve years
- Exemption from property taxes for five years

Taxes in Guatemala

Both resident and nonresident corporations are taxed only on Guatemalan source income. Income tax rates approximate those in neighboring countries with a maximum corporate rate of 34 percent. Capital gains are treated as ordinary income. Branches of foreign corporations are taxed at the same rates as corporations. While no branch remittance rate is charged, withholding tax rates are surprisingly high. For example:

For dividends:	12.5 percent
For interest:	25 percent
For royalties from patents, trademarks, copyrights, and so forth:	34 percent

In addition to income taxes, the following taxes apply to all companies doing business in Guatemala:

Value-added tax on nonpersonal services and the sale or transfer of merchandise:	7 percent
Sales tax on merchandise or services not subject to VAT:	3 percent

Payroll taxes for social secu-
   rity and other taxes on
   gross payroll (paid entirely
   by employer):   11.3 percent

Guatemala has no foreign exchange controls, although difficulties may be experienced when foreign exchange is in short supply. The exchange system is regulated through the banks, with the
quetzel pegged at Q3.45 = US$1.

PART IV
South America

CARIBBEAN SEA

PANAMA

Maracaibo
Caracas
VENEZUELA
Apure
Arauca
Orinoco
Caroni
GUYANA
Georgetown
Paramaribo
SURINAME
Cayenne
FRENCH
GUIANA
Cuca
Magdalena
Andes
Meta
Bogotá
Guaviare
Orinoco
Uraricoera
Coppename
Corentijn
Tapanahoni
Maroni
Oyapock
Branco
Negro
Jari
Pará
Belém
COLOMBIA
Quito
Caquetá
Vaupés
ECUADOR
Putumayo
Napo
Amazon
Tapajós
Iriri
Xingu
Itapicuru
Fortaleza
Natal
João Pessoa
Recife
Marañon
Javari
Juruá
Purus
Madeira
Arpuaná
BRAZIL
São Manuel
Araguaia
Tocantins
Parnaíba
São Francisco
PERU
Lima
Madre de Dios
Beni
Guaporé
San Miguel
Juruena
Teles Pires
Culuene
Mortes
Araguaia
Salvador
Lago Titicaca
La Paz
BOLIVIA
Mamoré
Cuiabá
Brasília
Jequitinhonha
PACIFIC OCEAN
PARAGUAY
Paraguay
Paranaíba
Grande
Tietê
Rio de Janeiro
Pilcomayo
Asunción
São Paulo
Bermejo
Paraná
Iguacu
Uruguai
Porto Alegre
Santiago
Saladо
URUGUAY
Colorado
Buenos Aires
Montevideo
CHILE
ARGENTINA
Andes
ATLANTIC OCEAN
Negro
Bahia Blanca
PATAGONIA
Chubut
Falkland Islands
(U.K.)
Punta
Arenas
TIERRA DEL FUEGO
Cape Horn

Chapter 16

South American Strategies

Whether exporting to South America, investing in a local facility to produce goods or services for domestic markets, making a direct investment to manufacture components or finished products for export, or exploiting valuable raw materials and skilled labor, conducting business in South America is substantially more complex than it is in Mexico, Central America, or the Caribbean.

The distances from the United States are much greater, shipping costs higher, linguistic dialects more varied, and cultures more dissimilar. The entire mode of conducting business, tricky at best for most Europeans, can seem especially incomprehensible to Americans. This is not a region for beginners. Companies without international experience and qualified, bilingual personnel should learn the ropes in the Caribbean or Mexico—definitely not in South America.

This advice is particularly true of South America's most established countries—Argentina, Brazil, Chile, and Colombia—and, to a lesser extent, Venezuela. These are not backwater cultures or newly emerging economies. They have a well-established business and political protocol, extensive experience with European trade and investment, sophisticated consumers, long-established industrial bases, and well-educated, tough-minded business managers. (If Argentina, Brazil, and Chile had not had decades of government mismanagement, their economies would today be substantially more developed than they are.) Table 16-1 compares the key trade statistics for South American markets.

The Impact of South American Trade Agreements

Something new is happening throughout the continent. Free trade agreements are being enacted between South American countries

Table 16-1. Key Trade Statistics for South American Markets ($US).

	Population (000,000)	GDP Per Capita	Imports From U.S. ($000,000,000)
MERCOSUR members			
Argentina	33	$3,108	$1.3
Brazil	152	3,134	5.9
Uruguay	3	2,984	0.1
Paraguay	5	1,297	0.1
Chile	14	2,110	1.4
Andean Pact members			
Venezuela	20	2,157	4.9
Colombia	33	1,285	1.8
Bolivia	7	760	0.2
Peru	23	1,457	0.9
Ecuador	11	1,011	0.6

and between these groups and the United States. These agreements will inevitably change U.S. and Canadian corporate strategies for doing business in this vast continent at least for the next twenty years—and probably for a lot longer.

To develop competitive strategies, it will be imperative to recognize the structure of these agreements and their potential implications for trade and investment within South America, as well as how they will affect trade with and from the United States, Europe, and East Asia. Because the Southern Cone Common Market, commonly referred to as MERCOSUR, is the largest and most important of the new trading blocs, that's a good place to begin.

Before beginning, however, I must reiterate that only those companies with bilingual executives experienced in international trade should contemplate competing for South America's vast natural resources, labor bases, or markets. For experienced foreign traders, however, South America may quickly become the only game in town. The following chapters should be read in the context of these caveats.

As newly elected South American administrations cleared away the last vestiges of the lost decade of the 1980s and fanned the fires of economic liberalization, the next logical step was to execute foreign trade alliances similar to those popularized in the north. One after another raced frantically to join the parade with their own versions of common markets, economic unions, and free trade areas.

The result was a carving-up of the continent into several trading regions:

- Argentina, Brazil, Uruguay, and Paraguay created a "common economic space" called the Southern Cone Common Market (MERCOSUR).
- Bolivia, Colombia, Ecuador, Peru, and Venezuela created a common market called the Andean Pact.
- Guyana and Suriname became participants in various trade pacts with Caribbean nations.
- Chile, which has progressed the fastest and farthest toward a free-market economy, elected to remain aloof, although it, too, has executed special trade arrangements with Mexico, Venezuela, Colombia and the United States, and has indicated a willingness to join MERCOSUR in 1995.
- French Guinea remains a department of France, with all the EC privileges that entails.

MERCOSUR

The relative importance of MERCOSUR far outshines that of the other trade groups, simply because the four member nations contribute more than half the region's aggregate GNP and 40 percent of its foreign trade.

The agreement is called a "common economic space" because in legal terms, it is a cross between a common market (which involves the free circulation of goods, capital, and labor among member countries) and an economic union (which harmonizes all member-country economic policies). Although common market aspects have been the driving force toward union, harmonization of economic policies must eventually be addressed to perpetuate the accord.

Spurred by the overnight transformation of political and social structures throughout Latin America, the four Southern Cone countries initiated MERCOSUR as a replacement for the 1960s' Latin American Free Trade Association (LAFTA) and its successor, the Latin American Integration Association (LAIA).

Argentina and Brazil started the ball rolling with a bilateral free trade agreement. In 1991, Paraguay and Uruguay joined their two neighbors under the Treaty for the Structuring of a Common Market (the "Asunción Treaty"), giving birth to MERCOSUR.

The treaty calls for the attainment of four objectives on or before December 31, 1995:

1. The free circulation of goods, services, and production factors within the four countries as the means toward achieving the elimination of all tariff and nontariff barriers
2. The establishment of a common external tariff, which will be the consequence of a common external trade policy
3. The coordination of macroeconomic policies
4. The harmonization of respective internal legislation as necessary

Given the wide economic variances between the countries and the overpowering position of Brazil (which still suffers a vicious hangover from its own lost decade), these objectives are necessarily more fuzzy than those of the Andean Pact and other free trade agreements. The treaty's one decisive act was the original bilateral agreement between Argentina and Brazil to effect a "systematic, general, linear and automatic elimination of tariffs" on or before December 31, 1994.

On the first anniversary of the Enterprise for the Americas Initiative, June 19, 1991, representatives from the four MERCOSUR countries and the United States signed a document called the "Rose Garden Agreement." This agreement provided the basis for further negotiations on trade and investment policies aimed at converting the two Americas into the world's largest free trade area.

Whether MERCOSUR is finalized on the target date or later is really immaterial to foreign traders. The mere fact that the largest and most industrialized nations in South America are even talking about free trade among themselves and plan to implement common external tariffs has had a major impact on trade and investment strategies. Ultimately that impact will not only be felt in Latin American markets and resources, but in Europe and Asia as well. An economic power bloc of MERCOSUR members and NAFTA should give European and Asian competitors more than a little to worry about.

Strategy Scenarios

The major economies of South America have never been united—have never seen eye to eye on economic policies, political institutions, fiscal or monetary policies, language, or their role in the global community. But then, neither have the European nations. Now a combination of world, regional, and national forces are driving administrations and business leaders in Argentina, Brazil, Chile—and in fact in nearly every South American nation—to face the reality of radically changing trading patterns.

Without the unification of the European Community it seems doubtful that U.S. trade officials would bother with South America, or that South American administrations would make much of an effort toward strengthening their bargaining position by combining forces. But Europe 1992 is a fact. The consequent decreasing reliance on the GATT and increased emphasis on bilateral trade agreements has materially affected Western Hemisphere trading strategies.

U.S. corporate strategies must now deal with trade policies of powerful groups of countries rather than those of weakened nations, while at the same time trying to gain competitive advantage by logistic positioning of company resources and markets, primarily in the Western Hemisphere. Making the right decisions will not only affect giants like IBM, AT&T, and GE but determine the global destiny of second- and third-tier companies as well.

For example, what if MERCOSUR, with its total population of 200 million and its GDP of more than US$500 billion, struck a free trade agreement with the EC that erected external tariffs and quotas specifically designed to keep out U.S. imports? Or made a deal to give the EC a monopoly on the region's natural resources in exchange for financial aid? Such developments would place U.S. companies at a severe competitive disadvantage, both in terms of global markets and in terms of global resources.

What if, after bringing in Chile, which has access to the Pacific and close ties to both Arab Middle East financial resources and East Asian cultures, MERCOSUR enacted a trade agreement with Japan (and/or Japan and the booming economies of Singapore, Hong Kong, Taiwan, and South Korea) barring American imports in favor of those from East Asia? Or banning U.S. companies from exploiting the region's natural resources but permitting East Asian firms ready access? The results would be just as devastating as agreements with the EC.

What if, for reasons unfathomable at this time, MERCOSUR developed its industrial, agricultural, and mining bases and then turned isolationist, erecting barriers similar to those being considered by the European Community? Clearly this would leave U.S. companies struggling for natural resources and significantly increase U.S. production costs.

On the other hand, if MERCOSUR were to execute trade agreements with the United States, enormous advantages would flow to U.S. companies. This would be especially true for those companies which had had the foresight to establish a base of operations there.

The inherent advantages of lower production and shipping costs, and hence of lower prices, should enable U.S. companies to compete on a level playing field with their European and Japanese counterparts—not only on the world stage but even more effectively in the Western Hemisphere and in their home markets.

Clearly, developments in MERCOSUR bear close scrutiny by corporate strategists over succeeding years. But now is the time to position their companies within MERCOSUR to take advantage of radically changing trade patterns.

Chapter 17

Argentina: Reformed Peronism

Even more than Mexico, the Argentine Republic's rejuvenation must be regarded as the greatest success story in modern-day Latin America. Led by the resourceful President Carlos Menem, a team of market-oriented technocrats has in three short years brought order and progress to a chaotic economy that for sixty years was headed steadily downhill.

Long regarded as Latin America's worst basket case, with rampant inflation (hitting 20,000 percent in 1990), chronic budget deficits, obstreperous trade unions, and an overregulated economy, the nation appeared headed for economic anarchy. A country that was regarded as one of the world's richest in 1930 had descended to approximately seventieth place by 1990.

Now, in the mid-1990s, President Menem has achieved as if by magic what few other Latin American leaders dared to dream: a 180-degree turnaround making Argentina one of the world's more viable locations for foreign investment and trade.

The Domestic Market Potential for Foreign Exports

Current import tariffs, as reformed by the Menem administration, average out at 9 percent; however, local industry is still protected by a three-tier tariff schedule:

For finished goods with domestic competition:	22 percent
For intermediary goods with domestic competition:	11 percent

> *For primary goods without do-*
> *mestic competition:*   no tariffs

Other barriers have also fallen. Special protection laws for electronic equipment and computer imports have been significantly liberalized. Argentine producers have seen the last of the dreaded import licenses. Although relatively high port fees still need improvement, they are lower than before reforms were enacted.

Although early trade liberalization policies created a trade surplus of US$8.2 billion, a subsequent recession slowed consumer buying. Since 1992, however, the wave of preference by Argentine consumers for imported goods has built to a crescendo, dissolving the trade surplus.

Annual growth rates in five Argentine industrial sectors are expected to meet or exceed 10 percent through the year 2000:

1. *Telecommunications equipment markets,* now totaling US$145 million, will experience an annual growth rate in excess of 27 percent. Privatization of the nation's telephone systems is a prelude to a massive refurbishing effort, which will entail significant demand for state-of-the-art switching gear and components, transmission stations and lines, satellite equipment, and related receivers and transmitters. Demand for cordless and cellular phones and related systems is accelerating.

2. *Oil and gas field equipment markets* are expected to increase 13 percent per year, although market size statistics are sketchy. New offshore exploration calls for drilling rigs, along with all support gear, transport facilities, refining capacity, and distribution equipment and materials.

3. *Electronic components market* estimates offer conflicting information, but official projections call for an annual growth of between 11 and 13 percent. After years of deprivation, the Argentine citizenry is calling for state-of-the-art electronic appliances. Government agencies and industrial firms need specialized monitoring and control instrumentation, measuring devices, and electronic security systems.

4. *Computer and peripheral markets* totaling US$105 million will experience a 10 percent annual growth rate. Both government and

Print media is most frequently used to reach a large market segment. The major national newspapers are *La Nacion* and *La Prensa*. Picture magazines are a very popular advertising medium. In addition, a plethora of technical, professional, and trade magazines carry advertisements.

The Buenos Aires market can also be reached by television and radio commercials. Radio Rivadavia is the leading Buenos Aires station, with 40 percent of the radio market. Four television channels service the country, all headquartered in Buenos Aires.

Trade shows are gaining favor for promoting new industrial products and financial services.

Further information about trade or investment opportunities can be obtained from:

The Argentine Trade Office
900 Third Avenue, 4th Floor
New York, NY 10022
Phone: (212) 759-6477

Economic Reforms

The Menem administration has enacted a lengthy list of economic reforms to attract foreign trade and direct investment. Some have been imminently successful, while others are still on the drawing boards.

One of the most import reforms was the wholesale privatization of state-owned businesses. Not only is this getting the government out of the private sector, it is creating an entire new industrial and commercial base against which foreign companies must compete for market share, labor, and natural resources.

Foreign firms interested in investigating direct investment through the privatization process should contact the executive director of the government privatization administration:

Juan Carlos Sanchez Arnau
Hipolito Yrigoyen 250, Piso 9
Buenos Aires, Argentina
Phone: (54-1) 331-2823 or 331-6423
Fax: (54-1) 331-5653

Privatization is not the only dramatic reform. Equally impressive incentives have been initiated to bring private industry into a competitive mold. Furthermore, foreign investment is welcome once again for the first time in more than sixty years.

By 1992, the economy was feeling the full impact of deregulation. A few of the more radical reforms were:

- Elimination of all restrictions on prices
- Removal of all constraints on business opening hours
- Elimination of controls over professional fees
- Abolishment of all barriers to entry into markets
- Decentralization of wage bargaining, allowing firms to negotiate at a local level instead of with a national union
- Elimination of all export taxes

Based on GATT objectives, these reform measures have given a country with one of the most closed economic systems in Latin America (and the world) one of the most open.

Foreign Investment Liberalization and Deterrents

President Menem wasted no time in executing the Bilateral Investment Treaty, the first investment protection treaty between the United States and a Latin or Caribbean country since President Bush announced his Enterprise for the Americas Initiative.

The treaty guarantees U.S. companies the right to invest in the Argentine private sector on terms no less favorable than those accorded domestic or third-country investors. It also guarantees:

- Free transfer of capital
- Freedom from performance requirements of any kind
- Access to international arbitration
- Internationally recognized standards of compensation for expropriation of private property

In effect, internal economic reforms ratified by treaty with a major world power like the United States make Argentina the most liberal country in Latin America for foreign direct investment. As

Deputy U.S. Trade Representative Julius Katz remarked, the treaty "signals that Argentina is a good and suitable place for U.S. investment and will further strengthen economic links between our countries."

Deterrents to Foreign Investment

Several important deterrents remain, however, that will dissuade inexperienced foreign companies from investing in Argentina. Although the government continues to move aggressively to open the economy, it has not been able to break the tight grip that special-interest business and financial groups have on their respective sectors. Three of the more serious examples are these:

1. Local banks will only open accounts for people who own property.
2. Corrupt favoritism still persists between state bureaucrats and private companies.
3. Industry cartels are as much in evidence today as before deregulation, although the completion of the privatization program should help cleanse the air.

On the Plus Side

The Menem regime's most dramatic reform was a presidential order to end industrywide bargaining agreements.

Many of the horrors suffered by the Argentine people over the last sixty years, and probably the strongest factor in the deterioration of a once-strong economy, was the extraordinary, far-reaching power of the country's labor unions. United Nations observers attribute the overriding force behind the depletion of Argentina's gold reserves, industrial base, and financial institutions to the control exercised by organized labor over politicians, trade policies, the business community, and social programs. Labor unions, in effect, built an impenetrable wall to keep foreigners out, Argentinians in, and militant dictators in power.

Now that businesses are allowed to negotiate wages, benefits, and conditions directly with employees instead of through national unions, labor bosses are up in arms. The long-term results won't be known for several years, but as Jose Pedraza, a spokesman for the 2 million-member General Workers Confederation commented, "It undoubtedly is going to have an impact on a whole range of social, political, economic, and cultural activities."

Clearly, foreign companies considering Argentina as a viable trading partner or as a logical site for direct investment must bear in mind the turbulent history of the nation's militant trade union movement. The economy is not yet out of the woods, and the unions have not been completely defused.

Repatriation of capital by foreign investors is now permitted. The peso (once the austral) is fully convertible to the U.S. dollar in a free foreign exchange market. No limitations are placed on dollar deposits within or outside of Argentina. Investment registration is required only for statistical purposes. Foreign firms have free access to local capital markets.

U.S. companies will find the Overseas Private Investment Corporation (OPIC) open to insurance guarantees for any investment approved by the Argentine Ministry of Economy. In turn, the Argentine government has established semiautomatic ministry approval of OPIC investment coverage applications.

On balance, economic reforms have been positive, and the few obstacles remaining should not deter serious foreign investors from exploiting Argentine markets and resources. If for no other reason than to position a company in the most vibrant economy in MERCOSUR, direct investing in Argentina makes sense.

An economy as established as that of Argentina doesn't possess any one or two industries that cry out for foreign investment any more than the U.S. economy does. However, companies entering a few specialized sectors will find less competition and better reception from the minister of the economy.

On the consumer side, financial services (especially banks) and specialty retail stores look like the best prospects. In the commercial and industrial sectors, oil and gas exploration, food processing, apparel and textiles, and semifinished agricultural products head the list, along with wholesale distribution centers. The tourist industry is also growing rapidly, and foreign investment in new hotels, resorts, and restaurants is more than welcome.

Argentine companies export approximately US$6.5 billion annually, mostly in a narrow product range: grains, oilseeds, sugar, tobacco, fruit, cotton, meat, crude oil and petroleum products, aluminum, and steel plates, sheets, pipe tubes, and fittings. As MERCOSUR begins to function, this export band will certainly widen. For now, however, this listing gives a good indication of Argentina's major industries and where the bulk of the large corporate competitors reside.

Social Features

This country of 33.3 million people offers a diversified industrial base and a skilled labor force (unionized, of course). Of the total number of 12.5 million workers, 57 percent are in service jobs, 31 percent in manufacturing, and 12 percent work in the agricultural sector. The country also boasts a substantial cadre of upper- and middle-level managers who are more than capable of competing at the international level.

The risk of stringent economic reforms causing social unrest is much less in Argentina than in any other Latin American country, mainly because income inequalities are much less pronounced there than elsewhere. The income differential between the top 20 percent of the population and the lowest 20 percent is only one third what it is in Mexico, Brazil, and Venezuela. Unemployment runs about 6 to 6.5 percent.

The country also boasts the most highly educated population in Latin America. Adult illiteracy is a mere 5 percent, compared with Brazil's 22 percent. Some would argue that 5 percent is also substantially less than in the United States, although U.S. statistics are incomplete and contradictory.

Forty percent of a population of 33 million live in Buenos Aires. Other regional centers offering major consumer markets include Córdoba, Rosario, Santa Fe, Mendoza, Tucuman, and La Plata.

Free Trade Zones

The use of Argentine free trade zones is highly restricted—not as to who can use them, but as to where the goods will be shipped. Three free trade zones may be used to assemble and ship goods exclusively for local consumption: Tierra del Fuego, the South Sandwich Islands, and the South Shetland Islands.

Table 17-1. Free Trade Zones in Argentina.

	Applicable Export Destinations
Barranqueras	Bolivia
Buenos Aires	Bolivia, Paraguay, Chile
Concordia	Brazil, Paraguay, Uruguay
Empedrado	Brazil
Jujuy	Bolivia, Chile
La Quiaca	Bolivia
Mendoza	Bolivia, Chile
Monte Caseros	Brazil, Paraguay
Paso de los Libres	Brazil
Pocitis	Bolivia
Rosario	Bolivia, Paraguay, Chile
Salto	Bolivia, Chile
San Juan	Bolivia, Chile

Source: Official Export Guide.

Thirteen free trade zones are maintained throughout the country, exclusively to store and assemble transshipments. There is a catch, however. The zones apply only to goods transshipped to Brazil, Bolivia, Chile, Paraguay, or Uruguay. Furthermore, each zone has its own designated country of destination. The applicable destinations for each zone are shown in Table 17-1.

Further information about using Argentina's free trade zones can be obtained from:

Administración Nacional de Advanas
Azopardo 35
Buenos Aires, Argentina

Taxes in Argentina

Corporate tax rates in Argentina are reasonable relative to other Latin countries, but are certainly not low. The income tax rate is 20 percent; the capital gains rate runs 20 to 36 percent; the branch tax rate stands at 36 percent. Withholding taxes on dividend income run 10 percent for residents and 20 percent for nonresidents;

on interest income, 14.4 percent; and on royalties, 28.8 percent. There is no branch remittance tax.

A value-added tax of 15.6 percent and various local taxes are also in effect. The social security tax remains totally unreasonable at 33 percent—all of it to be paid by the employer. Plans are in the works to privatize the social security system, so changes in the tax rate appear imminent. Only Argentine source-income is taxable. Since all foreign exchange controls have been eliminated, transactions are conducted at free-market prices set by supply and demand.

Financial Markets

Foreign confidence in Argentina's progress has been restored, and flight capital as well as new foreign portfolio investment is flooding the market.

Capital flight had plagued Argentina for decades. A widely publicized estimate puts the total capital removed from the country by citizens seeking to avoid runaway inflation and tax collectors at more than US$40 billion in the years since the 1970s. The newly appointed president of the government's National Securities Commission (NSC), Martin Redrado, was given the task of luring this capital home with the promise of a new, emerging capital market and rich profit opportunities.

Coincidence being the handmaiden of success, the new president of the NSC took over just as the Buenos Aires stock market experienced its first wave of several boom periods. Stock prices soared 60 percent in one month. Trading volume topped US$40 million, up from the usual US$4 million. Foreign companies and investors beat a path to a market with price/earnings ratios running at three to four times multiples.

The Buenos Aires Stock Exchange continues to be one of the fastest-growing in Latin America (including Mexico). Lower taxes, new financial innovations, and quicker approval for new stock and bond issues have stimulated domestic and foreign companies to use the capital markets as an alternate financing tool for expansion and business acquisition. Portfolio investments have also done very well.

Without question, the Menem administration and its agency chiefs have worked miracles on the Argentine economy. A 5 percent growth in 1991 and an estimated 5 to 7 percent growth in 1992 represent a success story. But for several reasons, it does seem improbable that such momentum can be sustained for very long. The most important reason is that, with the peso pegged to the dollar, Argentina's inflation must coincide with U.S. inflation to prevent the peso from becoming overvalued. This has not happened. The Argentine inflation rate hit approximately 10 percent in 1992 while the United States came in at just over 5 percent.

Second, imports have risen sharply, while exports have stagnated. If this continues, foreign reserves will plummet and the government must either let the money supply shrink and risk economic contraction or print more money, thus destroying public confidence. Either path risks a return to capital flight.

Despite these risks, Argentine opportunities for foreign traders and investors should continue to be viewed in a favorable light. The same cannot be said of its northern neighbor, Brazil.

Chapter 18

Brazil:
A Reeling Giant

When viewing the potential of Brazil's vast wealth of natural resources, enormous labor base, and diversified markets, it is difficult not to place this nation at the top of the list for both trade and investment opportunities. Certainly, with a population of 152 million and a well-developed manufacturing base, the nation should be a prime target for foreign traders and investors.

Such is not the case, however. While it is certainly true that several large multinationals from the United States and Europe are beginning to venture in again, too many obstacles still remain to make the nation an attractive market for any but very well-endowed companies.

Furthermore, while Brazil's wealth of natural resources—minerals of virtually all types used in production processes, and timber (two thirds of the nation is woodland)—could supplement dwindling reserves in the United States, Europe, and Japan, the Brazilian government is not eager to open its doors to foreign exploitation.

The third major attraction, a large, diversified labor base, is difficult to tap. Nearly 50 percent of the nation's 152 million people are under 20 years of age and therefore not economically active. By the year 2000, an additional 5 percent will fall into this group. About three fourths of the remaining 75 million are economically active; this is a small number, however, for a country with nearly 50 percent of its GDP in the manufacturing sector.

Statistics are helpful, but what they really boil down to is the fact that, although the Brazilian labor base may be large by Latin American standards, competition for skills is fierce. A newly established facility will not find it easy to staff up with skilled labor.

Despite these obvious drawbacks, Brazil cannot be totally ignored in corporate strategies. It has too much future potential to
allow short-term deterrents to interfere with long-term strategic
positioning. Companies inclined to look seriously at Brazil should,
however, learn from the experience of the Fortune 500 companies
that have been active in this country for decades: Don't bank on
exports to establish a beachhead; competition is too keen. Long-
term positioning should be viewed from the perspective of a direct
investment to tap the nation's natural resources—when and if government regulations permit.

Historical and Political Perspectives

Prior to the lost decade of the 1980s, the Federal Republic of Brazil
enjoyed what was probably the most vibrant economy in the world:
forty years of practically unbroken expansion, averaging 7 percent
per year. It was a remarkable feat by anyone's standards. Real
GDP, according to the World Bank, grew about 4 percent per year—
exceeding that of the United States.

By 1980 the economy was well-balanced and responsive. It
boasted hundreds of thousands of successful entrepreneurial businesses, as well as many world-class corporations. Even today, 60
percent of Brazil's exports are manufactured products. The nation's
US$32 billion in foreign direct investment is the largest accumulated
amount in the developing world.

It is hard to understand why a nation that was once a keen
competitor in world trade and economic growth now reels like a
drunken giant. Nor do official government statistics tell the
whole story.

The failure to control inflation and all its related side-effects
has spawned an enormous underground economy. Some estimates
place it at as much as 50 percent of official GDP. This is not an
underground economy that provides goods and services to rural
peasants or nefarious street bankers. It is the principal means of
livelihood and the major source of goods and services for a large,
healthy, well-to-do middle class.

Visiting homes away from Rio, São Paulo, and Brasília, one

is reminded of the affluence enjoyed by middle-class American suburbanites. In stark contrast to this well-off segment of the population is Brazil's large underclass of indigenous groups, small farmers, and urban poor. The agonies of these social outcasts match the suffering of those with similar standing in the United States.

The Reasons for Brazil's Fall From Grace

Brazil's decline can only be attributed to inept federal management. A steady parade of administrations has, over the years, enacted policies that increase the wealth of privileged bureaucrats and private-sector special interest groups, while ignoring the long-term well-being of the majority of Brazilian citizens.

Over a five-year period, political divisiveness produced ten finance ministers, ten central bank governors, five separate shock-therapy economic reform packages, and four currencies.

Inflation rates so high as to be virtually unmeasurable have eaten away at Brazil's economic base. Today's cruzeiro equates to 1 million cruzeiros in 1986. From 1960 through 1989, world price levels multiplied eleven times, the worst global inflation ever recorded over a thirty-year period. In all of Latin America during the same period, prices multiplied 244,000 times. In Brazil, prices multiplied 29 million times! The stumbling giant's chronic inflation problem has succeeded in separating Brazil from the rest of the world.

Attempts to bring triple-digit inflation under control and thereby revive the economy focus primarily on maintaining very high real interest rates—5 to 7 percent per month. The government has also tightened its fiscal belt and reduced spending. Although the country did not experience any economic growth in 1991 and none is in sight for 1992, the Brazilian congress passed legislation to raise US$12 billion in extra taxes to help balance the budget by the end of 1993 (this in itself would be a miracle if achieved). Such efforts are not without reward: a trickle of flight capital is returning.

Most outsiders would agree that Brazil's problems are deep-seated and far-reaching—not susceptible to the quick fix. Part of the blame rests with an unwieldy political structure, which foreign companies must learn to deal with if they have any plans to do business here.

Brazil is a federation of twenty-six states, with some 4,300 municipalities operating under highly decentralized authority. Less than 50 percent of total government expenditures are controlled by the federal government. Even worse, only 8 percent of all federal revenues collected remain under federal control. The balance passes to state governments.

Although major trade and investment policies are established at the federal level, states and municipalities exercise substantial authority over permits, licenses, and other regulations. Compliance with state and local requirements can often be as cumbersome for foreign investors as compliance with federal regulations. Also, bureaucratic delays and "satisfaction" payments increase under such a decentralized structure.

This decentralized structure, which is not dissimilar to the U.S. federal system, creates myriad problems for foreign companies trying to tap local markets either with imports or local production. The sheer volume of paperwork can be overwhelming. The number of government bureaucrats and conflicting laws for permits and licenses create a labyrinth few foreign companies are willing to tackle.

Still, positive signs can be seen on the horizon. Many multinationals have stayed the course and others are rediscovering Brazil's potential. DuPont, for instance, recently started up a sizing and packaging facility for titanium-dioxide pigment in Uberada. The plant receives semifinished white pigment (used in a variety of products) from DuPont's U.S. and Canadian plants and performs the final processing steps in Brazil. Perhaps optimistically, DuPont designed the facility to expand into a full manufacturing plant.

IBM, Hewlett-Packard, Digital Equipment, and NEC recently jumped at the chance to take 49 percent shares in computer manufacturing joint ventures. Acquiescing to consumer demand for computers that not only worked but sold for a reasonable price, the government opened the import door a crack. It now permits computers and peripherals to be imported, provided that the importing company is a joint venture with a Brazilian partner. In addition, the equipment must be labeled with the Brazilian partner's name and logo.

Direct Investment Considerations

Brazil has the fifth-largest landmass in the world (it is about the same size as the United States). Its gross domestic product of more than US$385 billion makes it the world's ninth-largest economy. The country is blessed with an abundance of natural resources, including timber, energy, a wide variety of minerals, agricultural land, and fresh water. It also boasts a broad manufacturing base with a good supply of management talent.

Brazil's low-wage work force of 57 million is split between agriculture (35 percent), manufacturing (25 percent), and services (40 percent). Unemployment in urban areas hovers around 5 percent. The number of underemployed in rural areas is much higher, although precise statistics are not available. Urban areas account for the greatest concentration of people, with 90 percent of the population living on 10 percent of the land.

Brazil's infrastructure is fairly well developed by South American standards. It has diverse, widespread domestic markets. Most raw materials necessary for the production of goods are readily accessible within the country.

Foreign dividend remittances remain unfettered as long as the total does not exceed the amount of capital employed. This works fine for capital-intensive companies but not for service firms with a small capital base.

Foreign firms are subject to the same company laws as national firms, except in oil exploration, drilling, and refining; domestic transport; all media industries; and mineral extraction. These industries remain off-limits to all foreign investment.

Although state and municipal laws affect trade, raw material acquisition, land use, and worker's right, the federal government sets company organization regulations and corporate laws.

Despite many obstacles, the country has some interesting advantages for foreign investors, such as:

- A substantial export-oriented agricultural base with 90 percent of available land not yet under cultivation
- A huge reservoir of untapped mineral resources
- A well-established, functioning, and growing industrial base
- Plenty of available, low-cost energy provided by massive

hydroelectric facilities, as well as alternative energy sources like alcohol
- A large urban population with more than adequate disposable income
- Serviceable overseas transport through several ports and air terminals

Even though the government's privatization program will affect the landscape of private-sector opportunities, Brazil's well-established companies in its major industries—steel, chemicals, petrochemicals, machinery of various kinds, motor vehicles, consumer durables, cement, lumber, and shipbuilding—will probably retain significant competitive edge over foreign intruders.

Free Trade Zones

Brazil does not yet enjoy the benefits of a network of free trade zones. There is only one of any significance, operating near the city of Manaus in the state of Amazonas. Typical free trade zone rules apply to transshipments and to the processing of goods for export. Sales from the Manaus zone to domestic customers get hit with the same licensing and duties as do imports from outside the country.

Several new export processing zones (ZPE) are being developed, however, in various parts of the country. Once up and running, ZPE companies must export 90 percent of their production capacity. Ten percent may be sold domestically, subject to the normal import licensing and duty restrictions.

Taxes in Brazil

All companies domiciled in Brazil, together with all subsidiaries, divisions, branch offices, agencies, or representative offices of companies domiciled abroad, are subject to a corporate income tax of 30 percent, plus a surtax of 5 percent on profits that exceed the government inflation index (BTN) by approximately US$115,000. Withholding tax rates for dividends, interest, and royalties stand at 25 percent.

In addition, all entities pay a social contribution tax of 10 percent (15 percent for financial institutions). A federal net with-holding tax of 8 percent and a state income tax of 5 percent of the federal tax are levied on profit remittances.

State-assessed value-added taxes range from 7 to 25 percent; the federal VAT runs from zero to 365 percent. On top of this, social security contributions on all wages run 25.2 percent for em-ployers and 8 to 10 percent for employees. Several other state and federal taxes apply under various circumstances.

The entire Brazilian tax structure is subject to change as part of economic reforms currently under way. The best way to stay abreast of developments is to get competent tax advice from Ernst & Young or other major accounting firms with branches in Brazil.

The Potential for Privatization

The privatization of government-owned companies has proved a major revenue raiser for Argentina, Mexico, and Chile, among others. Brazil could potentially achieve similar results.

Unlike its rejuvenated neighbors, however, Brazil's cumber-some political structure, nonworking economic reforms, and the pure complexity of getting anything accomplished in such a large, diverse country, have combined to stall all but preliminary efforts. Still, hope springs eternal, and the government placed twenty-two of its 600-plus federally owned companies on the block in 1992. In addition, many states have their own programs for disposing of public-sector businesses.

Foreign investors looking for a quick entry into Brazilian mar-kets might do well to keep an eye on developments in the privatiza-tion program. In time, bargains are bound to spring up—assuming, of course, that government privatization procedures get ironed out.

The biggest complaints from bidders so far have been that restrictions prohibit access to company records and business prac-tices and deter meaningful evaluations of the management team. Nothing has been proposed to alleviate these problems.

As a further obstacle, the government forbids foreign owner-ship of more than 40 percent in a privatized company; foreign capital tendered must remain in Brazil for twelve years; and invest-ments cannot be sold for a period of two years. Plans are afoot to modify the latter two conditions to six years with no holding period.

It is not surprising that foreign companies have not jumped on the privatization bandwagon.

Domestic Markets

Brazil boasts the largest foreign trade base in South America. Yet of all the South American industrialized nations, its progression toward a free-market economy has been the slowest. A nation with a population of 155 million people (two thirds the size of the U.S. population and five times the size of Argentina's), controlling half the landmass of the South American continent, Brazil presents foreign firms with enormous market and resource opportunities. It also offers immense challenges.

Although economic reforms have been successfully inaugurated, they are meager compared to other Latin American countries, and they barely open the door to improved foreign trade and direct investment. One reform measure that did help was the abandonment of the onerous "law of similars," which effectively blocked imports of products similar to those produced in Brazil.

Other, less profound reforms include:

- The elimination or reduction of company and sectoral import quotas
- The abolishment of the complete list of prohibited imports and import subsidies
- A new tariff schedule with average rates of between 15 and 45 percent

Import licensing is still very much in evidence, however. Foreign exporters are responsible for ensuring that an import license is obtained prior to shipping the merchandise. Customs confiscation will be the result for failure to do so. Licenses covering most products are valid from 60 to 180 days and can be obtained from the Departmento Nacional de Comercio Exterior (DENCEX).

As a general rule, the government discourages imports of any consumer goods, although they still represent about 14 percent of total imports. Of the nation's US$15 billion annual imports, crude oil comprises 21 percent, capital goods 25 percent, and raw materials 26 percent.

Companies located in a member country of the Latin American Integration Association (ALADI)—formerly the Latin American Free Trade Association—pay substantially reduced duties. Of course, for members of MERCOSUR, tariffs are being eliminated on most goods and services. This being the case, most foreign companies will find it easier, cheaper, and less competitive to set up facilities in Argentina, either to produce goods for export to Brazil or as a stopover point for shipments from the United States that can then be moved to Brazil duty-free.

Short of going through the underground economy, the best markets for foreign exports are in the commercial and industrial sectors and in the tourism industry. Indeed, foreign exporters, especially those from the United States, are not flocking to Brazilian markets. Those who are giving it a try find the following to be the best prospects:

- Electronic components
- Test equipment
- Medical instruments and supplies
- Process-control instrumentation
- Analytic and scientific instruments
- Education supplies and equipment
- Tourism-related products
- Printing and graphic arts equipment
- Organic chemicals
- Aircraft and aircraft parts
- Coal
- Machine tools

In addition, subject to the previously discussed restrictions, computers, computer parts, and software present growing markets, as do all types of machinery and equipment in textiles, telecommunications, electric power generation and distribution, oil and gas field development, and irrigation.

Competition is fierce, however. What local manufacturers can't supply, foreign multinationals can and very often do. The business community is accustomed to dealing with large European and

Japanese suppliers, and new entrants from the United States and Canada must offer something different and unique—new, high-tech products, spare parts service, free training, and so on—to make a serious dent.

Environmental Products

The 1992 Rio de Janeiro Worldwide Earth Summit sponsored by the United Nations and the simultaneous trade fair in São Paulo stimulated a high level of interest in environmental products and services. This was the prelude to a new era of environmental concern in Brazil and throughout Latin America.

The United States is taking the lead with experimental projects conducted by the Environmental Protection Agency in Puerto Rico. If successful, the program will be expanded throughout the region.

Brazil is already leading Latin American nations with automobiles and buses that run on nonfossil fuel. But the nation has a long way to go, as is evident to anyone flying to Rio recently. Peering down as the plane begins its approach, one can't miss the mat of waste discharge glaring up from Guanabara Bay. As reported in Rio's *Jornal do Brasil*, a mountain's worth of sewage is dumped daily into the bay.

The greeting upon landing is equally repulsive: open-air sewers in the Mare shantytown, the Joatinga canal, and the Tijuca and Jacarepagua lagoons, which receive sewage from some 600,000 people. As environmental consultant Guido Gelli remarked while attending the Earth Summit, "We have here a typical case of total lack of sanitation—the most common type of pollution in the city—with refuse and discharge coming in from all sides."

It seems inevitable that within the next few years, demand will accelerate for all types of products and services related to waste management, air quality, reforestation, water purification, and other environmental protection and clean-up. Brazilian firms will certainly be in the forefront of development and production. Nevertheless, opportunities for foreign products as well as for direct investment to manufacture them locally will inevitably mushroom. Be prepared for fierce opposition, however. Brazilian firms won't take foreign competition in this vital new market lightly.

The seriousness with which foreign companies and local firms treat environmental hazards was demonstrated when twenty-four major companies in Brazil launched a pioneering foundation to promote sustainable development and green business ideas, including the preservation of the rainforest.

President Israel Klabin of the newly founded Brazilian Foundation for Sustainable Development reported that the foundation was established with US$100,000 in donations from its initial members, which included subsidiaries of Mannesmann, Royal Dutch/Shell Group, C. Itoh, and St. Gobain, and nearly all of the major Brazilian construction, steel, paper, and oil companies. (One would think that such an array of industrial giants could do better than US$100,000.)

Another example of foreign pressure in the environmental area occurred when the Washington-based Nature Conservancy, an environmental group, used US$850,000 of private donations to purchase US$2.2 million of discounted Brazilian government debt in the secondary market. The debt was then donated to a private Brazilian conservation group, Fundacao Pro-Natureza (FPN). FPN then exchanged the debt with the Brazilian government for US$2.2 million in long-term Brazilian "Environmental Government Bonds" that pay 6 percent interest. This interest income will help fund activist efforts to preserve a national park in northern Brazil.

The Need for Intermediaries

Even the large multinationals advise newcomers not to attempt penetration in any market without help from a Brazilian intermediary. Complex trading protocol and a convoluted legal system, coupled with constantly changing import tariffs, quotas, and currency modifications, make intermediaries a prerequisite to success.

The most popular choices are attorneys and CPA firms for pure advice, and trading companies (very popular in Brazil and modeled on the German and Japanese versions) for local partners. A Brazilian partner is almost a necessity to cut through port and inland transport red tape. It appears unlikely that this will change in the foreseeable future, regardless of new government reforms. The discreet income to port officials is too great to assume that they will willingly give it up.

Also, with the scarcity of hard currency, local importers normally try to pay in cruzeiros. Even with the new convertibility law, this can be a dangerous road. It is far better to demand a letter of credit payable in U.S. dollars at a U.S., European, or Japanese bank.

Advertising in Brazil

The Brazilian advertising industry isn't as sophisticated as that in Argentina, but it is expanding rapidly. Literally hundreds of local and multinational agencies have offices in all major cities. The agencies have direct access to research institutes, film companies, printing houses, sound-recording studios, and direct-mail firms, all of which are used extensively for private-sector advertising.

Foreign companies seriously considering Brazilian markets are advised to keep the following in mind when developing trade and expansion strategies:

1. Smaller foreign companies frequently find the tightly knit Brazilian business community and bureaucratic red tape difficult to manage.
2. Environmental products and services, computer hardware and software, and medical and scientific instrumentation are the best long-term markets for foreign participation.
3. A great many state and municipal laws differ from federal regulations (even more than is the case in the United States).
4. The underground economy is the best place to make business contacts.
5. Direct investments should be viewed as long-term commitments that exploit opportunities to tap Brazil's neighbors through duty-free MERCOSUR preferences.

Further information about trade or direct investment can be gathered from:

Brazilian Government Trade Bureau
551 Fifth Avenue, Suite 210
New York, NY 10176
Phone: (212) 916-3200

Chapter 19

Chile:
The First to Fly

For foreign traders or investors looking for a small but vibrant economy with consumer and industrial markets eager for imported products, a government pushing hard for increased foreign trade and direct investment, and a strategic location convenient to Pacific Basin export markets, Chile could well be the best answer. Conditions there have improved immeasurably since the days of Augusto Pinochet's military dictatorship, when human rights abuses and drug trafficking were the norm. For foreign businesses, the present administration is also a vast improvement over that of the previous president, Socialist Salvador Allende, who nationalized most foreign holdings in the country. Today, say those who have tried Chile, the nation's only major disadvantages are its remote location and its far-flung geography.

Two key factors should be noted by corporations that are encouraged by Chile's recent economic reforms and are contemplating operations in the country:

1. The Chilean business community has increasingly close trading ties with Taiwan, Japan, Australia, New Zealand, and several nations in Southeast Asia.
2. The Chilean government has developed very close financial ties with Saudi Arabia.

The reasons for Chile's ties with East Asia are obvious: a prime location on the Pacific ocean for shipments to and from the Pacific Basin and a willingness on the part of Japan and others to finance infrastructure development.

The reasons for Chile's close ties with Saudi Arabia are not as self-evident. In the early stages of economic reforms, the Chilean government was in default on its external bank debt. The Saudi National Commercial Bank (NCB), owned and managed by the Mahfouz family, came to the rescue by joining forces with a company called Asset Chile to swap its debt holdings for controlling interest in a flock of companies engaged in fishing, forestry, and fruit packing. NCB expanded its investment to own the third-largest privately held firm in Chile.

Although these trade and investment ties may be of only passing interest to historians, their immediate impact on U.S. and other foreign companies is that the door has been opened to East Asian trade on one hand, and to potential additional financial support from the Arab community on the other—both key elements in developing corporate strategies for companies seeking to enter South America.

Political and Business Changes

The Republic of Chile has moved farther and faster toward a free-market economy than any South American country. In 1990, after seventeen years of General Augusto Pinochet's military rule, Chile returned to its 150-year-old tradition of elected civilian government. The administration of President Patricio Aylwin Azocar quickly announced objectives to promote economic stability, improve conditions for poor and working-class Chileans, rectify human rights abuses committed by the Pinochet regime, further democratize Chile's political institutions, and rejoin the international community.

The proclamation sounded remarkably similar to those emanating from newly elected leaders in Argentina, Brazil, Colombia, Peru, Bolivia, Mexico, and the rest of Latin America. The big difference was that Aylwin, who inherited a near-free-market economy from the former administration, is closer to making his economic goals a reality than any of the others.

President Aylwin has not been as successful in achieving social reform. Since his inauguration, the conservative opposition has stymied virtually all his major social reform initiatives, from labor reforms to the restoration of a fair legal system.

Despite holdovers from Allende and Pinochet, Chile has shown substantial progress toward integration into the international business community. The fiscal deficit has been significantly reduced, the financial sector liberalized, and large-scale privatizations completed. Inflation is gradually coming under control, although the government predicts a 20 to 30 percent rate for the next couple of years.

President Aylwin has firmly established Chile's future in foreign trade by enticing consumers with a steady stream of foreign goods, thereby successfully silencing a vociferous protectionist business class. The next major step is to build on this market base to silence the remaining populists, money launderers, and revolutionaries. And it appears that government leaders are doing just that. All import tariffs now stand at 11 percent, down from an already low 15 percent. Business leaders want the government to go further.

The signing of a free-trade framework agreement with the United States as part of the Enterprise for the Americas Initiative let the rest of Latin America know that Chile plans to be the first nation to actively participate in any trade and investment benefits that evolve. This establishes the country as a strategic location for North American, European, and Asian firms to be among the first to reap U.S.–South American free trade benefits.

Although no one can accuse the Aylwin administration of not making an honest effort to reform the economy, new incentives for economic growth and for a broadening of the entrepreneurial base are obviously needed. As President Aylwin has admitted, the best way to achieve growth is through increased foreign trade. And the most effective way to broaden the business base is with foreign direct investment.

The Direct Investment Bonanza

As part of its efforts to expand the country's manufacturing base, both for domestic consumption and for export, the government has, over the past five years, encouraged private industry participation in several megaprojects to the tune of US$7 billion. Mining, forestry/pulp, and telecommunications have attracted the most interest.

The Chilean government has long viewed foreign investment as a partnership venture that produces benefits for all economic sectors. It is no longer fashionable to tell the "Yankee imperialists" to go home. On the contrary, both the Chilean government and the private sector welcome foreign investors from all countries— including, and most especially, the United States.

The Chilean-American Chamber of Commerce in Santiago reports that over the last fifteen years 3,000 contracts have been signed with companies from fifty-three different countries. The chamber also reports that over one third of foreign companies have recapitalized their original investment or renegotiated new deals for further ventures.

The government does not discriminate against foreign companies. Foreign firms enjoy the same rights and privileges as local companies and fall under identical company laws. Compared with the bureaucratic delays in other Latin American countries, government red tape is minimal and customs delays short. Chile does not restrict the remittance of profits, although capital cannot be taken out of the country for three years.

U.S. companies—most of them the Fortune 500 corporations— represent the largest segment of foreign investment, accumulating more than US$1.2 billion in invested capital. Many have had a presence in Chile for years. Some of the biggest include Exxon, Phelps Dodge, Scott Paper, W. R. Grace, General Motors, and St. Joe Minerals. Both Citibank and Bankers Trust maintain active branches. However, although enormous opportunities exist for smaller companies, few have taken the plunge.

Major Products and Industries for Direct Investment

Copper continues to be the major Chilean export, accounting for about 43 percent of the total. More than US$8 billion worth of copper exports leaves the country each year. Fish products, cellulose and pulp, fruit, and nuts account for another 30 percent. Although the full list of export products totals more than 1,500 items, the majority of the 27 percent balance is comprised of gold, other minerals, women's apparel, frozen foods, selected industrial machinery, and even a small amount of biotechnology products. These are the industries in which the major Chilean and large foreign companies have concentrated their investment. Quite obviously, these industries are also the most competitive.

Mining remains the most important industry in Chile, and the production of support equipment and supplies offers the greatest potential. Chile owns approximately 20 percent of the world's copper reserves as well as significant deposits of molybdenum, rhenium, sodium nitrate, lithium, and coal.

Forestry and related pulp and paper manufacturing comprise one of Chile's most dynamic sectors. The nation has more than 1.1 million hectares of radiata pine forests.

Commercial fishing and fish processing is another hot industry. Expanding at a rate of 10 percent per year, it has been the fastest-growing export segment for the past decade. Fish products account for 13 percent of Chilean exports.

Copper and lumber continue to be favorite industries for foreign investors, accounting for more than half of all investment. Generous government incentives tempt companies to invest in reforestation and selective tree harvesting. A lumber derivative, cellulose, is also a good choice. According to a recent study by the World Bank, other good opportunities for foreign investment to produce exportable products exist in textiles, packaging, explosives, and plastics.

Chilean domestic markets are far from saturated; foreign investors who don't mind a little friendly competition can still find good opportunities. One word of caution: Since local capital goods industries are in their infancy, most new manufacturing investments require additional imports of equipment and technology to round out local production and service capabilities.

Other areas with good potential for both exportable products and domestic consumption include:

- Telecommunications equipment, supplies, and services
- Food processing and packaging (enjoying an 8 to 10 percent annual growth)
- Agribusiness, especially fruit products (growing at 32 percent per year)

- Shipbuilding
- Woodworking equipment and wood products
- Medical and scientific instruments and equipment
- Safety and security products (for which markets have quad-
  rupled over the last three years in Santiago alone)

Hotels, office buildings, shopping malls, and medical and dental clinics are shooting up like spring flowers in and around Santiago. These private-sector developments desperately need such diverse products as furniture and fixtures, elevators, security systems,
building cleaning and maintenance supplies, and restaurant and
bar supplies.

A wide variety of opportunities also exist for foreign participation in the service sector, currently representing 45 percent of the
nation's GDP. Management consulting, computer services, pension
funds, private health services, banking, and insurance products are
a few of the booming industries in this segment. Ernst & Young
is the most prominently represented multinational accounting firm.

The Chilean Labor Force

More than 60 percent of Chile's population resides within 100
miles of Santiago, the capital city, with a population of 4.3 million.
Unemployment runs close to 6 percent (compared with more than
7 percent in the United States during 1992). Urban workers possess
a fairly high level of skills. Minimum wages run about US$85 per
month. A small but technically capable management pool exists.
Best of all, literacy approaches 96 percent, which speaks volumes
for the Chilean emphasis on education.

Assistance for Foreign Companies

Formed in 1977 by a group of Chilean, American, and Canadian
business executives to improve trade and commerce between the
three countries, the North American–Chilean Chamber of Commerce (New York) (not to be confused with the Chilean-American
Chamber of Commerce in Santiago) has been a major force behind
the steady stream of foreign investment flowing into Chile. The
chamber's officials proudly point out that North American invest-

ment during 1990 hit US$1.1 billion, an 11 percent growth from the previous year. Since then, additional U.S. and Canadian companies have joined the race to tap Chile's small (14 million people) but burgeoning markets and natural resources. For more trade and investment information, contact:

North American–Chilean
   Chamber of Commerce
220 East 81st Street
New York, NY 10028
Phone: (212) 288-5691

Free Trade Zones

Like Brazil, its neighbor across the continent, Chile has not yet caught on to the benefits of a network of free trade zones. Only two zones are active: Iquique in the northern province of Tarapacá, and Punta Arenas in the southern province of Magallanes. The rules governing transshipments are similar to those in other countries. Domestic sales from these zones carry the same tariff duties as those imported from abroad.

Taxes in Chile

The corporate income and capital gains tax rates at 15 percent are about the lowest anywhere in Latin America. Branches of foreign corporations also pay 15 percent. While resident corporations are taxed on worldwide income, foreign corporations pay on Chilean-source income only. Special provisions may apply to foreign companies that reinvest profits in Chile.

Withholding taxes are much worse: 20 percent on dividends paid to nonresidents and branch remittances and 40 percent on royalties and license fees, thereby discouraging technology transfer. Interest income, on the other hand, is taxed at only 10 percent (35 percent less 15 percent corporate income tax).

A value-added tax (VAT) is assessed on the sale price of all goods and services, including real estate. Social security taxes run 0.9 percent of wages for employers but 20 percent for employees.

Personal income taxes are a different matter entirely, with a progressive scale hitting 50 percent for income over approximately

US$30,000 (adjusted monthly according to a consumer price index). Residents pay tax on worldwide income, except that expatriates pay on Chilean-source income for the first three years of residence. Residence is defined as physical presence in the country for more than six months in one calendar year or more than six months in two consecutive assessment years. Furthermore, all employee benefits are taxable, including employer-paid or reimbursed entertainment expense. Employers are required to withhold the tax. Expatriates working in Chile for periods of less than six months may elect to be taxed as residents or at a flat 20 percent on total income without any deductions.

Financing Options

The availability of trade finance as well as long-term project financing is plentiful and relatively easy to arrange. The two largest Chilean banks are Banco de Santiago and Banco de Chile. Bankers Trust has an active Santiago office.

In addition, Citibank has maintained a very active operation in Santiago since 1916. The bank participates in a variety of corporate finance areas: mergers and acquisitions, advisories, and local and international fund raising. It is also active in project financing and corporate retail banking. Special departments handle mutual funds and stock brokerage activities. Small and midsize U.S. companies will find this Chilean branch much easier to deal with than the New York operation. For more information, contact:

Citibank
Ahumada 48, Piso 9
Santiago, Chile
Phone: (56-2) 690-8000
Fax: (56-2) 672-2325

Privatization Program

Chile's privatization program began shortly after Pinochet wrested power from President Allende in 1974. Allende's nationalization efforts involved—among other industries—85 percent of the nation's mining industry. Anaconda and Kennecott, which owned the biggest companies, ended up seeking their just compensation in a court of law.

Since 1974, various privatization programs have promoted the sell-off, merger, or liquidation of all but twenty-three of 524 state-owned enterprises. Further efforts are still being made to sell off 49 percent interests in a few of the remaining businesses. These minority interests apply only to new projects.

The Best Foreign Trade Markets and Products

It's always dangerous to guess which import markets will do better than others, especially in a country as ethnically mixed as Chile, which is made up of indigenous groups in the north, in the mountains, and in the south; enclaves of northern European descendants in Patagonia; and a mixture of Hispanic and Asian cultures in the metropolitan areas.

However, certain imports are currently in greater demand than others. Basic, non-high-tech goods make up the bulk of the best prospects. For commercial and industrial markets they are:

- Machine tools
- Power and hand tools
- Transportation equipment and parts
- Chemicals and lubricants
- Telecommunications equipment
- A wide range of earthmoving and other off-road equipment
- Mining machinery
- Food processing and packaging equipment
- Fish-farming services and technology (principally for salmon and turbot)
- Woodworking equipment
- Computer hardware and software
- Air-conditioning and refrigeration equipment
- Textile machinery

The best products for consumer markets include:

- Women's work and dress clothes
- Leather goods

- Dried and frozen foods
- Low-priced toys
- Basic furniture
- Medical instruments and disposable supplies
- Security and safety products

Statistics that show U.S. companies accounting for only 20 percent of the nation's imports bear out the fact that Pacific Basin companies as well as those from Europe have already discovered Chile.

Market Quirks

The fact that the current administration actively solicits the rather long list of import products given above does not mean that attracting customers or managing the bureaucratic tangle is easy. It is not. Chile is no different from the other South American countries; local contacts are essential for a successful export program. Foreign suppliers have an excellent chance of failing miserably by not following local marketing rules and customs, and local agents make the difference.

A further complication arises in defining market parameters. The biggest markets are in and around Santiago, where 60 percent of the population lives. On the other hand, the nation's geography— a narrow strip of land bordered by the Andes mountains on the east and stretching from a latitude of 20 degrees in the north to the very tip of the continent at Tierra del Fuego in the south— makes reaching the other 40 percent extremely awkward and costly.

Yet sizable market demand for both consumer and agricultural products exists in Patagonia to the south. When Chile joins MERCO-SUR it might make more sense to sell to the Patagonian region from Buenos Aires than from Chile. Meanwhile, the only satisfactory way to distribute goods to this market is by ship (overland passage is nearly impossible). This means working with a local agent—or preferably a partner—who has the wherewithal to arrange ocean transport within Chile.

Also, in a country whose length stretches a distance equivalent to that from Winnipeg, Canada, to well south of Texas, traditional advertising and promotion methods are insufficient. Fortunately, the nation's four largest cities other than Santiago are all grouped to the north or the south of the capital: Viña del Mar and Valparaiso to the north, Talcahuano and Concepción to the south. A competent local agent can be a welcome help in structuring advertising and promotions to hit these markets. At least that takes care of close to 60 percent of the consumer base.

Sparked by the active encouragement of the government, tariffs at a low 11 percent, and no licensing requirements, imports are expected to grow 40 percent a year for the next two to three years. This bodes well for U.S. or Canadian companies willing to undertake a marketing program in this, one of the most distant and geographically complex markets in South America.

Chile has signed free trade agreements with Venezuela and other Andean Pact nations, has negotiated a limited trade agreement with Mexico, and has plans to join MERCOSUR after 1995. With borders opening to markets within South America and the United States, Chile could easily become one of the most strategic locations for U.S. companies. Chile's geographic location gives it access to the Western Hemisphere and to shipping routes that lead directly to the South Pacific and the rest of the Pacific Basin as well.

Environmental Opportunities

Santiago sits in a valley between high mountains. Thermal inversions, well known to residents of Los Angeles, Cincinnati, and Mexico City, trap warmer air, with all its pollutants, close to the ground. Wind currents do little to diffuse contaminants, and the result is suffocating, dirty air. Air pollution is so bad in Santiago that asthma and chronic pneumonia force school children and adults alike to wear gas masks when outside.

The greatest sources of pollution are Santiago's 14,000 smoke-belching buses, 8,000 taxis, and 285,000 private cars—all emitting large doses of carbon monoxide and sulphur, and all operating on low-grade diesel fuel and old replacement parts imported from abroad. Chilean environmentalists admit that the country's vehicle-inspection system is "riddled with fraud."

About 3,000 factories, located throughout the city in residential areas and monitored by only five city inspectors, add to the pollution by spewing out very high levels of carbon, sulphur dioxide, nitrogen dioxide, and other gases. Traffic kicks up clouds of dirt and dust from unpaved roads. The arid climate prevents plants from growing in many parts of Santiago, thereby contributing to the dust storm.

When stepping outside the international arrivals exit at the airport terminal, it's a good idea to have one or two clean handkerchiefs ready as a makeshift gas mask.

Although the city's pollution problems make it a bad place to live and work, they are a bonanza to foreign investors with the wherewithal to design and/or sell pollution control products and supplies. As the 1993 general election approaches, it seems certain that government programs will be initiated to attract substantial foreign assistance to clean up this mess. Several U.S. firms are already at the door, but the magnitude of the problem offers markets for any company wishing to participate.

Some government programs are already under way. A recent spending spree was initiated to acquire environmental protection systems, filtration systems, engineering know-how, and new environmental cleanup technology. Catalytic converters are likely to be required before the 1993 election. Lead-free gasoline has already been introduced. Relatively strict automobile maintenance requirements have recently been enacted (but enforcement remains lax).

Aside from government programs, the private sector in and around Santiago already experiences difficulty in attracting qualified workers and managers. Inevitably, private companies will take it upon themselves to bring in appropriate pollution remedies.

The administration faces several municipal and national battles during the upcoming presidential and congressional elections. The parties of the governing coalition, the Concertación, are already jockeying for position, demanding that more money be spent for social improvements to give voters more than a "warm democratic feeling."

That's encouraging news for foreign investors and traders, not only ready to sell environmental products but also to rebuild crumbling infrastructures. The country desperately needs massive government spending in both areas. In addition, the government will spend huge amounts to bring in the myriad products, equipment, and services necessary to operate social programs. Foreign investors and traders can participate in all of these projects.

In addition to a recently announced US$1.6 billion expenditure for an irrigation project to double the acreage available for cultivation, a few of the items on President Aylwin's US$2.35 billion public spending program include:

- New roads
- Refurbished ports
- A rehabilitated and expanded rail system
- Water pumping and purification systems
- Sewage drainage and sanitizing
- Primary and secondary schools
- Health care
- Worker training programs
- Low-income housing
- Shopping malls

Chapter 20

The Andean Pact and Venezuela

Long before NAFTA or MERCOSUR were conceived, a commercial relationship existed between the five contiguous Andean countries of Venezuela, Colombia, Ecuador, Bolivia, and Peru. Now referred to as the Andean Pact, this multilateral commercial structure was formalized under the Cartegena Agreement in 1969. Since then, Andean Pact nations have abided by common guidelines and policies with respect to foreign investments made in their countries and various commercial activities involving each other. Chile was an original signatory but withdrew in 1974.

Administered by a commission comprised of representatives from each member country, the Andean Pact set out investment and commercial guidelines as minimum standards for each country to use as a base in drafting its own legislation.

Prior to the 1990s, Andean Pact countries were primarily concerned with protecting and promoting local investment. As in the rest of South America, foreign companies could not hold majority interest in local businesses, remit payments abroad either by means of dividends or licensing arrangements, or protect intellectual property.

Now, with liberalism flourishing throughout the hemisphere, these countries have decided to join the throng. The signing of the Caracas Act officially created free trade among the five countries beginning January 1, 1992. The Act stipulates:

- The abolishment of tariffs on trade between member countries

- A common set of minimum external tariffs for trade with nonmember countries
- An effort by member countries to work toward harmonization of exchange regulations, tax laws, and labor and financial matters

Bolivia, Colombia, and Venezuela abolished intracountry tariffs in 1991; Peru and Ecuador, in 1992. However, all members still enforce tariffs to protect their agricultural and automobile industries.

In 1992, Colombia and Venezuela implemented the following common external tariffs for the period 1992 through 1994:

Capital goods and raw materials:	5 percent
Intermediate goods not produced within the region:	10 percent
Intermediate goods available from producers within the region:	15 percent
Finished products:	20 percent

Bolivia, Ecuador, and Peru have also reduced external tariffs, but not to these levels. After 1994, external tariffs for all five nations will be fixed at 15 percent.

In addition to Andean Pact arrangements, Venezuela and Colombia executed a free trade agreement with Mexico (called the Group of Three or G3 agreement) calling for the removal of all intracountry tariffs by 1996.

Table 20-1 provides the key trade statistics for each of the five Andean Pact members.

Venezuela's Advantages—And Its Dilemma

In many respects, Venezuela offers greater opportunities to small and midsize American firms or those with little experience in inter-

Table 20-1. Andean Pact Profile as of 1990.

	Population (000,000)	GDP Per Capita	Imports From the United States ($000,000,000)
Bolivia	7	$ 760	$2.0
Colombia	33	1,285	1.8
Ecuador	11	1,011	0.6
Peru	23	1,457	0.9
Venezuela	20	2,157	4.9

Source: U.S. Department of Commerce.

national trade than any other South American country. Located on the northern rim of the continent, Venezuela's unhurried culture and history of laissez faire business practices (except when it comes to oil) are closer to those of the Caribbean Basin than to those of Brazil, Argentina, or other major South American nations.

A decidedly international flavor permeates sections of the country, especially Caracas, Maracaibo, and the Caribbean harbor towns. During the oil rush of the 1970s, Venezuela drew foreign companies and expatriates like flypaper. Many stayed on, preferring the cosmopolitan tropical setting to their native lands. Of course the longtime foreign presence increases the competition in some markets, but it also provides a trained expatriate supervisory base (with North American and European consumer tastes) that is lacking in most of South America.

Finally, Venezuela has traditionally been an import trading partner with the United States, taking nearly three times the amount of U.S. imports as its Andean neighbor Colombia. Although certain political differences remain unresolved, Venezuela has a long history of trade with U.S. companies and direct investment from them.

Notwithstanding Venezuela's obvious pluses, its future as a viable market for foreign products and a profitable location for foreign direct investment remains in doubt. Foreign companies interested in tapping Venezuela's potential markets, vast mineral resources, and extensive labor and management base must first make a careful assessment of the problems facing the nation and the economic reforms being implemented to reduce or eliminate them. In this nation more than others, it is wise to take the country's economic and political temperature before deciding which markets to tap or how to develop a direct investment.

King Oil

If two words can characterize a country, *oil* and *corruption* fit Venezuela: *oil* because it gives the country the potential for being a major trading power, *corruption* because until it is brought under control, the Republic of Venezuela will remain a piranha in foreign trade circles.

Venezuela fairly oozes oil. Its proven reserves of 60 billion barrels are greater than those of any country outside the Middle East. But there is more. Beneath a patch of land no bigger than Portugal, along the Orinoco River, lie 1.2 *trillion* barrels of tar and pitch—more than the world's entire oil reserves. Even if only one fifth of the sticky goo could be extracted economically, Venezuela would easily replace Saudi Arabia as the world's oil kingpin.

Of course tar is too thick to refine or burn, so billions of dollars will have to be spent to turn it into salable oil. And that is exactly what the state oil company, Petroleos de Venezuela (PDV), is doing. Estimates place the cost of extracting this muck at a mere US$3 a barrel, compared with US$9 a barrel in Canada and Russia, the only other two countries with substantial tar sands and oil shale.

PDV's first attempt at a commercial venture turned the tar into an emulsion containing 70 percent oil and 30 percent water. The company already has six contracts to supply power generators in Europe, the United States, and Japan with ten million tons of *orimulsion*, as it calls the fuel. Another twenty-six deals are under discussion.

PDV pumps approximately 2.318 million barrels of crude oil per day. Excluding revenues from tar extraction, oil sales account for 24 percent of the country's GDP, 83 percent of its tax revenues, and 86 percent of its foreign exchange.

Why, then, with industrial nations crying for more oil and willing to pay virtually any price, hasn't Venezuela advanced further in its economic development? One reason is that PDV has become a world-class oil company needing world-class investment. Venezuela, however, is still only a developing country struggling to control inflation and public spending and at the same time improve the lot of its impoverished masses. The nation has very little left over to invest in oil. Why, then, one might ask, doesn't the government bring in private capital?

As in Mexico, the mere thought of privatizing the state-owned oil giant sends cold chills through the country's citizens. Oil is considered part of their national heritage; foreigners are definitely not welcome.

The U.S. General Accounting Office (GAO) surveyed twenty-two American oil companies to determine their views on investing in Venezuela. Responses were overwhelmingly similar. Nearly all companies cited a series of conditions making such investment unpalatable, including:

- The absence of any clear guidelines explaining the nature of activities in which foreign companies may engage
- A lack of rules stipulating the contractual terms that companies must abide by when participating in these activities
- The requirement that foreign investments have Venezuelan congressional authorization
- The high tax rate on petroleum-related activities
- The lack of a U.S.–Venezuelan tax treaty
- Concerns over the security of foreign assets in Venezuela's petroleum sector
- The absence of effective judicial protection against actions taken by the Venezuelan government (e.g., the unavailability of international arbitration for settling disputes between foreign investors and the government)

Nearly all respondents also stated that when and if these deterrents are rectified, they would jump at the opportunity to invest. The reasons most cited were abundant oil reserves, an established petroleum infrastructure, a favorable location, a reliable source of oil (operating wells), and a democratic government.

Quite clearly, the ball is in Venezuela's court.

Corruption and Poverty

Another source of problems for Venezuela is the continued corruption in government, military, and business sectors that prevents the filtering down of oil wealth to average citizens. While elite classes enjoy all the amenities of an industrialized country, the masses live in abject poverty. The corrugated metal shacks blanketing the hills around Caracas remind a visitor of the garbage pit suburbs of Cairo, the airless shacks around Jakarta, or the tar paper hovels of Mississippi.

While the country remains painfully divided between wealth and poverty, Venezuelans are not happy with the austerity measures brought in by President Carlos Andres Perez's economic reforms. In 1992, raging throngs and belligerent, military-led coup attempts forced embattled President Perez to back down from some of his more serious market-price reforms: a temporary freezing of electricity prices; a cap on prices for medicines, flour, cooking oils, pasta, rice, and milk; and a freeze on gasoline prices, abandoning the highly unpopular monthly increases begun in 1990 under pressure from the International Monetary Fund. A special presidential advisory committee subsequently recommended constitutional changes, including sweeping legal reforms and the creation of the post of prime minister.

Economic Reforms in Venezuela

The government's reform efforts, begun in 1989 shortly after Perez took office, were similar to those enacted with such resounding success in Chile and Mexico, although the timetable for full implementation was substantially longer.

The restructuring of Venezuela's external debt under the Brady Plan started the reforms rolling and was coincident with forecasts of rising oil prices from the Persian Gulf war. As prices climbed, the economy looked sounder. Many bank creditors opted to retain their claims rather than go for discounted repayment, further strengthening the nation's position in world financial markets.

The government's reform package included several other measures: slashing import tariffs to a maximum of 20 percent by the end of 1993, eliminating import quotas on all but 192 products, joining GATT negotiations, floating the bolivar exchange rate, reducing the central government's deficit, slicing subsidies of public services, and eliminating price controls on most goods and services.

Inflation peaked at 81 percent in 1989, dropped to 45 percent in 1990, hit 30 percent in 1991, and leveled out in the 25 to 30 percent range in 1992.

Direct investment laws were revamped, allowing foreign companies to invest in most sectors of the economy (with the investment limited, in most cases, to a minority interest). Cumbersome approval procedures were changed to allow foreign companies entrance merely by registering with the government. Limits on profit repatriation were removed. Foreign investors are now permitted to borrow from local banks and participate in the Caracas stock market. The overvalued bolivar has been set afloat.

Although many reforms have been put in place, much remains to be done. The Venezuelan bureaucracy remains horrendously cumbersome. Corruption in and outside of government circles continues to be a problem for foreigners doing business in the country. Although growing, the private sector is still relatively small compared to that in Chile and Mexico. In addition, many companies have been protected by decades of cartels and government favoritism.

Foreign Trade Attractions

Venezuela has several features that attract foreign traders. Its convenient Caribbean location provides a strategic site from which to develop a full Latin American trading base. Since 1958, a bipartite political system has functioned reasonably well. Its vast oil reserves make Venezuela one of the richest countries in South America, with per capita income reaching US$2,200. Inflation remains too high, but as reforms take hold it continues to trend downward.

In addition to oil, the country has a developed industrial sector, primarily in mining (bauxite, aluminum, and iron ore) and automobiles. Local firms export crude oil, aluminum, steel products, ore, coffee, fish, cement, and gold, primarily to the United States. Agricultural products also contribute. The agricultural and manufacturing sectors have received the greatest boost from the government's economic reforms. A skilled, low-cost work force is split between service companies (56 percent), the industrial sector (28 percent, including mining), and agriculture (16 percent).

Government forecasts indicate that Venezuela will be one of the top three world aluminum producers by the end of this century, with projected output to increase fivefold to 2 million metric tons per year. Steel capacity is forecasted to double by the year 2000 to 10 million metric tons: coal will grow thirteen times to 6.5 metric tons; and 1987 gold exports totaling US$300 million are expected to increase sixfold. One fallout from such an intense concentration on mining is a rapidly growing need to import mining machinery, equipment, supplies, and services of all types, mostly from the United States.

The agricultural sector also shows expanding potential as new growing techniques are introduced. To meet demand, imports of a wide range of agricultural equipment will be needed, especially dairy machinery, harvesting and haying equipment, dryers, and silage.

Foreign exporters will also find ready markets in virtually all types of automobile parts and accessories, including engine parts, gear box components, torque converters, carburetors, ignition systems, and the whole gamut of diagnostic and repair equipment and tools to service cars.

Other excellent markets exist for the following imports:

- Foodstuffs
- Chemicals
- A wide range of consumer and industrial manufactured products
- Food processing and packaging equipment
- Machine tools
- Transport equipment
- Telecommunications equipment
- Computers, peripherals, and software
- Medical diagnostic and treatment equipment
- Chemical processing machinery
- Safety and security products
- Oil and gas field products (primarily pumps, taps, cocks, valves, turbine pumps, and drilling equipment)

Venezuelan companies have maintained close trading ties with

U.S. companies for decades, with U.S. suppliers accounting for 45 percent of all Venezuelan imports.

Maximum tariffs have been reduced from 40 percent to 20 percent and are now set at four levels: 5 percent, 10 percent, 15 percent, and 20 percent—still much too high, but at least heading in the right direction.

But what the government giveth, the government taketh away. As an offset to the benefits of reduced tariffs, all imports are now subject to an ad valorem customs handling charge which varies with the product and shipment value.

Agents and Distributors

Marketing in Venezuela can be a nightmare for U.S. and Canadian companies. Actual market conditions and business protocol are seldom as advertised. Corrupt customs officials, obstreperous bureaucrats, at-times-unfathomable trade laws, cagey hustlers posing as import agents, and substantial competition from well-established foreign corporations like GE, Ford, Siemens, and Mitsubishi (not to mention competent and well-accepted local producers) can easily frustrate the most determined foreign exporter.

As an example of the kind of problem that can arise, U.S. exporters have reported difficulties with sight-draft payment transactions. Venezuelan buyers either delay or refuse to claim merchandise from the receiving port. Products are then impounded by customs officials, shippers are charged large fines, and the goods are sold at auction—many times to the original buyers. Although other countries are home to similar practices, those countries are usually far less developed and progressive than Venezuela.

If sight drafts against document delivery must be used, it's important to recognize that Venezuelan law does *not* require an importing company to pay its bank before obtaining the original documents in order to obtain the merchandise. Customs may release the goods merely upon presentation of a copy of the bill of lading by the importer and the posting of a bond for duties.

Local import agents/distributors can help circumvent this problem (as well as most others). However, it's a good idea to check them out before executing a contract. Some pull the same stunts as unscrupulous buyers.

When Is an Agent an Agent?

Foreign companies unfamiliar with the peculiarities of Venezuelan distribution channels frequently have trouble defining the buyer. Distinctions between forms of representation are much less well defined than they are in the United States, Canada, or Europe.

A local company can act as a manufacturer's representative, import-distributor, dealer, wholesaler, *and* retailer—all at the same time. The company may act as a sales agent that takes orders on commission, maintain an inventory stock for distribution to other companies, and also have a retail store. Many retailers who import directly order through agents and buy direct from exporters, jobbers, or dealers.

The government does not require import licensing; neither does it publish a list of importers—making it difficult to find out who is actually doing the importing. According to Venezuelan law, anyone can import.

Venezuela has practically no "general merchandise" importers, except for department stores. Rarely do agents or distributors take on competing lines.

The best way to learn the ropes is to go to Venezuela and start talking to people. Overseas telephone calls and correspondence just don't get the job done.

Confusing Laws

It's also important to grasp the key elements in the country's commercial code before executing an agent or distributor agreement. To be valid, any contract must meet the following criteria:

- Be written in Spanish
- Use metric measurements
- State all monetary values in local currency
- Be signed by an attorney
- Be notarized

Venezuela does not have laws to protect agents or distributors. No indemnification is required upon contract cancellation. Companies that set up a facility in Venezuela and then put an agent or distributor on the payroll must abide by labor laws that entitle employees to profit sharing, bonuses, social security, time of service, and separation allowances. The normal commission rates for agents or distributors run from 5 to 30 percent.

Selling to the government is another matter entirely. The extent and complexity of procedures and laws is far too elaborate to discuss here. However, those companies with an interest in going this route must register in Venezuela with the National Register of Contractors, which is maintained by the Central Office of Statistics and Information.

The best place to get additional information about exporting regulations and protocol as well as about procedures for selling to the government is:

Latin America/Caribbean Business Development Office
U.S. Department of Commerce
14th Street and Constitution Avenue NW
Washington, DC 20230
Phone: (202) 377-0703

The Potential for Foreign Investment

It seems unlikely that the Venezuelan government will enforce another round of nationalization. This administration can't run a business any better than could the previous ones and the majority of the working population knows it. With economic reforms taking hold and austerity measures proving effective in controlling inflation, the cries for nationalization by populists become ever dimmer.

On the contrary, long-term prospects for major intraregional growth, at least over the next twenty years, appear very good. Liberalized foreign investment laws, a working banking system, strengthened capital markets, one of the better infrastructures in the region, and an avowed desire on the part of the government to broaden the country's manufacturing sector make Venezuela a viable location to establish a South American foothold.

Venezuela could be an especially attractive location to produce goods for export to other Andean Pact nations. With most trade barriers eliminated, it's much less costly to export from Venezuela to these countries than it is from the United States. Similarly, the Group of Three agreement makes Mexico a very viable Venezuelan export market.

Several other advantages also beckon foreign investors:

1. A strategic location for trade with the Caribbean and Central America
2. Easy access by air and sea from U.S. ports on the Gulf of Mexico and the East Coast
3. Some of the best shipping and air facilities in South America
4. A nucleus of technically qualified supervisors made up of expatriates who have lived in Venezuela since its oil heyday
5. A highly trainable work force whose literacy rate tops 85 percent

Although peripheral petroleum products and services offer the most visible opportunities, other sectors also need foreign technology and products and possess excellent potential for local production. Among the major industries to explore are:

- Computers and software
- Health care services and products
- Processed food
- Automobile parts
- Mining services and peripheral equipment
- Tourist facilities
- Pleasure boats
- Seafood farming
- Private aircraft, services, and parts
- Ground and ocean transport equipment and services

Company Law

Foreign investors need to understand the different categories of company ownership under Venezuelan law. A *national company*

is one in which foreign ownership does not exceed 19.99 percent.
A *mixed company* is one in which foreign ownership is limited to
49 percent. If foreign ownership exceeds 49 percent, the company
is deemed a *foreign company*. Investment in the following business
sectors is strictly limited to national companies: banking, insurance,
guard and security services, television, radio, Spanish-language
newspapers, and professional services.

Intellectual piracy is as pronounced in Venezuela as it is elsewhere in South America. However, foreign companies should, at
a minimum, protect their trademarks, logos, brand names, and
patents by registering them with the Ministry of Development
(FOMENTO) in Caracas.

Privatization

The 1990 privatization program to sell off over 400 state-owned
companies is moving forward, albeit at a snail's pace. In contrast
to Argentina and Brazil, which are selling state-owned companies
as is without fixing them up, Venezuela has taken an alternative
course. U.S. and Canadian companies looking at privatization as
a means of establishing a Venezuelan facility will probably applaud
the slow approach even though it takes longer to close a deal.

Financing privatized acquisitions is also very restricted. As a
general rule, the government does not allow foreign buyers to use
local financing. Government debt/equity swaps are also forbidden.
Each purchase must be for cash.

Free Trade Zones

The Venezuelan government has not seen fit to establish any
free trade zones. This presents a major barrier to foreign companies
wishing to use the nation as a transshipment location for either
Caribbean or Latin American destinations. Economic pressures in
the near term will probably force the opening of at least one,
however.

The country does have one free trade port: the Island of Margarita off the Caribbean coast. Margarita is a yacht haven and provi-
sioning center for private boaters. It is also a thriving mecca for
Venezuelans and cruise ships. Duty-free luxury goods of all types
are plentiful. Rules for transshipments to other countries follow

normal free trade zone protocol, and shipments to the mainland are subject to the same barriers as are imports from abroad.

Advertising and Market Research

The mass media advertising structure is similar to that found in the United States: newspapers, magazines, radio, television, and billboards. Compared with the citizens of most other Andean Pact nations, Venezuelans are relatively sophisticated consumers.

Newspaper and magazine advertising predominates, simply because it reaches a broader audience. The two tabloids, *Ultimas Noticias* and *El Mundo*, boast circulations of 200,000 each. The more influential dailies, *El Nacional* and *El Universal*, each reach 150,000 readers.

Market research sources remain very sketchy. As the nation develops, however, the need for more professional service is escalating. New firms enter the field monthly. Check out the Caracas telephone directory for listings of the better-established ones or get help from the American Chamber of Commerce. Contact:

American Chamber of Commerce
c/o Donald H. Veach
Carton de Venezuela, S.A.
Apartado 609
Caracas 1010, Venezuela

Obtaining Visas

Tourists do not need a visa to enter the country. A simple passport or similar identification is sufficient. Theoretically, business travelers need a *transient visa* which is good for sixty days and can be obtained from any Venezuelan Consul office. In practical terms, most short-term business visitors simply enter under the tourist umbrella.

Further information on trade or investment in Venezuela may be obtained from:

Embassy of Venezuela
1099 30th Street, NW
Washington, DC 20007
Phone: (202) 342-2214

Overall, the outlook for future trade and investment with Venezuela looks promising. The nation boasts five conditions that could conceivably make it a major force in Western Hemisphere trade:

1. Vast mineral wealth, especially oil
2. An abundance of hydroelectric power
3. A large pool of national and expatriate management talent
4. A highly literate population and a trainable labor force
5. A strategic location and a favorable climate

Recent trade agreements will enhance the nation's strategic position.

Whether the Perez administration can control dissident forces and continue moving the country toward a free-market economy remains uncertain, although 1992 developments look positive. The IMF and the U.S. government are both optimistic and continue to support the country's reform programs. Unscathed by the drug cartels and guerrilla warfare so prominent in other Andean countries, democratic Venezuela appears to be on the right track. To foreign companies willing and able to tough it out during the conversion period, Venezuela's future prospects as a growth market and natural resource supplier look promising.

Chapter 21

Colombia
and Its Neighbors

Foreign traders and investors, and especially U.S. companies, should not be misled into believing that the doors to trade with Andean Pact nations have been thrown open. Contrary to the media hype coming out of Bolivia, Peru, and, to a lesser extent, Colombia, opportunities for U.S. businesses in these nations remain very limited. Even if all barriers were broken, traditional trading ties with U.S. and Canadian companies would remain negligible.

Imports from U.S. companies to the largest nation of the group, Colombia, average a meager US$1.8 billion per year. Exports to Peru (US$0.9 billion), Ecuador (US$0.6 billion), Bolivia (US$0.2 billion) reflect even smaller markets. To put it in perspective, compare these figures with an average of US$4.9 billion exported to Venezuela.

On the direct investment side, continuing drug trafficking from Colombia and coca plant farming in Peru and Bolivia, together with guerrilla violence and street crime, tend to dissuade even the most astute foreign investors. Efforts are currently being made by the administrations of these countries to stem the tide of illicit drugs and clean up the criminal elements, but so far, at least, with minimal success. Ecuador, of course, remains locked in medieval, semi-isolationist policies, even with its newly elected administration.

Notwithstanding these negatives, Colombia, Bolivia, and Peru do have two major attractions for foreign investment:

1. A substantial, very low-cost supply of labor
2. A wealth of natural resources

For these reasons, the three countries deserve consideration as

267

potential sites for production facilities—if not immediately, then in the years to come. One very attractive feature that can be exploited by U.S. companies with the determination to risk a direct investment here is the twin-plant benefits resulting from President Bush's Andean Trade Initiative.

The Andean Trade Initiative

The best news to hit the Andean nations in more than twenty years (at least with respect to foreign trade) was the late-1991 announcement from Washington that President Bush had signed the Andean Trade Preference Act (ATPA), creating the Andean Trade Initiative (ATI). This fulfilled a commitment made by the President at the Cartegena Drug Summit in early 1990 to expand economic activities to those countries that were fighting to eliminate the production, processing, and shipment of illegal narcotics. ATPA named Bolivia, Colombia, Ecuador, and Peru as beneficiaries of the initiative. (Since Venezuela was not considered a primary narcotics haven, it was excluded.)

The Andean Trade Initiative is patterned after the Caribbean Basin Initiative. The same duty-free benefits granted CBI countries are now extended to the four Andean Pact nations. Like CBI, the Andean Trade Initiative specifically excludes textiles, footwear, canned tuna, and petroleum, and reduces duties for leather goods excluding footwear. It also excludes rum.

The Andean Trade Initiative is not as broad as CBI in other areas, however. Whereas CBI is permanent, ATI will remain in force for only ten years. Section 936 funding is not available for investment in Andean Pact nations. The Guaranteed Access Levels (GALS) for textile products and the waiver of the "Buy America" Act for government procurement contracts are not included either. At current levels, approximately 5 percent of those products now entering the United States from Andean countries will benefit by ATI, outside of those already coming in under the Generalized System of Preferences (GSP).

Demanding their day in court, the U.S. Department of Agriculture and the Environmental Protection Agency exacted additional exclusions for certain agricultural products that would normally qualify under the initiative. However, negotiations with Colombia, and, to a lesser extent, with the other countries, are under way to find alternatives.

According to the International Trade Administration, imports of the following products from the respective countries benefit most from ATI:

Colombia: Cut flowers, one of the nation's most important exports—especially roses and chrysanthemums; fresh tuna and skipjack; glazed ceramic products; raspberries; grapes; tropical fruits such as passion fruit and mangos; and melons

Bolivia: Cereals (including rice); cut flowers; wood products; and spices

Ecuador: Cut flowers; fresh tuna and skipjack; pineapple and grape juice; iron and steel wire; limes; tropical fruits; and melons

Peru: Rope; zinc; copper wire; lead; precious metals (including gold); asparagus; seafood (including yellowtail, mackerel, and sardines); and dried potatoes

Although the Andean Trade Initiative is not expected to have a major impact on the economic growth of any of these countries, the symbolism attached to a trade preference treaty with the United States cannot be ignored. Furthermore, the ATI opens new possibilities for U.S. companies to use Andean nations as twin-plant locations, exporting subassemblies or components back to the United States.

In addition to trade incentives under ATI, the Andean nations have made internal efforts to spur foreign trade and investment, albeit with varying degrees of success. The liberalization of tariff and regulatory barriers is having a favorable impact on decisions by foreign companies—especially U.S. and Canadian companies— to look again at opportunities in the area. The ATI gives assurance that the U.S. government backs such efforts, and that Eximbank, the Overseas Private Investment Corporation (OPIC), and other support agencies will look favorably on requests for financial and other assistance.

Colombia and Bolivia have already made considerable strides in improving their respective business climates. Many tariff and nontariff barriers have been reduced or eliminated. Bolivia, for instance, has reduced tariffs to 5 percent for capital goods and 10 percent for all other imports, giving it the lowest tariffs in the region. Colombia's tariffs now average 14.8 percent. Colombia has also taken important steps to open all sectors of the economy to direct investment, guaranteeing foreign investors the same treatment as local companies.

Peru and Ecuador have been slower to liberalize, but both are heading in that direction. Unfortunately, when Peru's President Fujimori abandoned the democratic process in 1992, implementation of economic reforms temporarily ground to a halt.

On a regional level, according to the International Trade Administration, the best prospects for U.S. exports to all four countries are:

- Agricultural machinery and equipment
- Food processing and packaging equipment
- Commercial fishing equipment and products
- Computers, peripherals, and software
- Telecommunications equipment
- Biotechnology products
- Mining equipment

Detailed information about provisions and applications under the Andean Trade Initiative can be obtained directly from the ITA's Latin America/Caribbean Business Development Center at:

International Trade Administration
U.S. Department of Commerce, Room H-3203
14th Street and Constitution Avenue, NW
Washington, DC 20230
Phone: (202) 377-0703/0841

Be sure to ask for the *ATPA Guidebook*. Telephone calls are accepted by desk officers at the following numbers:

Bolivia and Peru:	(202) 377-2521
Colombia and Ecuador:	(202) 377-1659

Colombia: On the Edge

Colombia's strategic location is unique on the South American continent, adjoining Panama in Central America, and both the Pacific Ocean and Caribbean Sea. It has a wealth of natural resources, including hydrocarbons, coal, oil, nickel, emeralds, gold, and platinum, as well as abundant forests and fertile agricultural land.

While all other Latin American countries suffered to varying degrees from the lost decade of the 1980s, Colombia's economy enjoyed an average sustained growth of 4 percent, while incurring a relatively modest amount of external debt. To its credit, debt service payments have been made regularly.

It is indeed unfortunate that Colombia presents such a dark image to potential investors. But it does. Newly arrived visitors to Bogotá are soon aware of three rather frightening factors:

1. An armed-camp atmosphere
2. A prevailing sense of doom among articulate, well-educated Colombians
3. A collapsing infrastructure

The drug cartels, decades-long guerrilla warfare, excessive street crime, and, in 1992, prolonged, power-dissipating drought have combined to render the citizens of Bogotá, Medellín, Cali, and other urban areas disconsolate about the future.

Such an image is sufficient to keep many foreign companies away from Colombia. In fact, however, substantial opportunities do exist in this country of 33 million—for those with foresight and courage.

The Beginning of Reforms

President Cesar Gaviria Trujillo's political and economic reforms—aimed at permitting Colombia to rejoin the world community—point to a light at the end of the tunnel. But so far, it remains only a light.

In less than a year Mr. Gaviria defused a murderous drug war, coaxed some of his country's top cocaine dealers into jail (including Pablo Escobar, the most violent of the Medellín drug czars, who later escaped), and oversaw the writing of a new constitution. Smaller guerrilla groups were persuaded to lay down their arms, form a political party, and elect representatives to the national assembly.

On the economic front, import tariffs have been slashed. The stock market is gradually being opened to foreigners. Exchange controls have been relaxed. A rapidly growing middle class now earns enough income to own cars and moderate housing. A federal court system has been redesigned. Constitutional rights are being observed, though there is considerable lawlessness among street gangs and drug dealers. A unicameral Congress is being set up.

Although these gains are impressive, three issues still frustrate private-sector attempts to rejuvenate the economy:

1. The lack of a peace accord with major guerrilla bands
2. The absence of a treaty with the now-rising Cali drug cartel
3. An unmanageable inflation rate

Inflation ran about 30 percent in both 1991 and 1992 while the economy grew a measly 2 percent in both years. With oil, gas, coal, coffee, and a plethora of new exports, Colombia probably could achieve a noninflationary growth rate of more than 8 percent—but not until the government quiets the countryside.

Privatizations

The privatization leg of the Gaviria Administration's reform package is proceeding at a snail's pace. A few state-owned banks have been sold. A minimal number of businesses in other sectors have also been sold: a shipyard, a silk manufacturer, an automobile producer, and a paper company. The government plans to sell the telephone company and the electric company (which is currently about US$4 billion in debt). It also plans to grant concessions for toll highways, ports, and railways.

Direct Investment Opportunities

Despite the government's renewed emphasis on developing an international trade presence, Colombian output, exclusive of coffee and certain minerals, remains focused inward. The total industrial sector is 30 percent smaller than that of Venezuela.

Colombia's main industries are coffee, bananas, cut flowers, exotic fruit, textiles, chemicals, light manufactured products, and, more recently, automobiles and spare parts.

Competition from foreign players is not as pronounced as it is in Venezuela, Chile, or Argentina. Local producers are a different story. Colombia boasts a well-developed, deeply entrenched business community. Regardless of efforts by the government to open domestic markets to foreign competition, few outsiders have successfully bridged the pricing structures and distribution channels managed by local businesses.

Furthermore, foreign companies that plan to invest in Colombia to produce export goods in product lines considered the domain of home-grown companies—specifically coffee, flowers, textiles, food, and leather goods—will find head-on competition for skilled labor, local financing, facilities and equipment acquisition, and licenses and permits.

A better strategy might be to forget about competing in major export markets and to concentrate on three areas:

1. Penetration of domestic markets, those industries not controlled by Colombian producers that the government is pushing for development, such as capital goods for agribusiness, forestry, the exploitation of sea products, and the conservation and dehydration of agricultural products and fruit
2. Utilization of raw materials and low-cost labor for assemblies or components to be shipped back to the United States in a twin-plant arrangement duty free under the provisions of the API
3. The exporting to other Andean Pact nations of basic consumer goods such as low-tech mining equipment and spare parts, insecticides, and machined parts for construction vehicles, automobiles, and basic food processing equipment

Doing Business in Colombia

With the exception of the mining and petroleum industries, which caught the attention of large multinationals, foreign direct investment has historically been meager, averaging a mere US$59.4 million per year throughout the 1980s. Colombia followed the same line as other Andean Pact nations during the lost decade, deliberately shutting out foreign investment in an effort to protect local companies. Prohibitions against imports of products that compete with Colombian producers were vigorously enforced.

New laws have now been adopted to include both direct and portfolio foreign investments. According to trade ministry announcements, these laws are based on the following three principles:

1. *Equal treatment:* Foreign companies will be "treated the same as Colombian nationals, except for fiscal and exchange issues."
2. *Universality:* Foreign investment is allowed in "all sectors except those affecting national security, defense, and disposal and elimination of toxic, dangerous, or radioactive waste not produced in the country."
3. *Automaticity:* A general authorization will be granted to foreign companies for all commercial activities "except in the financial sector, hydrocarbons and mining, activities related to the supply of public services, and those covered by insurance mechanisms for noncommercial risks."

To begin doing business in Colombia, foreign companies need only register at the exchange office of the Central Bank and comply with the same laws and regulations as are followed by local companies. Temporary work visas can be easily obtained for six months. Beyond that, ordinary visas are sufficient for two years. Profits, capital, and gains on the liquidation of investments, may be repatriated. An additional incentive has reduced the remittance tax from 20 to 12 percent. No taxes are imposed in free trade zones.

Six free trade zones operate in various sections of the country: Cartagena, Cúcuta, Cali, Buenaventura, Santa Marta, and Barranquilla, Colombia's main FTZ, located on the Caribbean coast. Facilities located in these zones follow standard transshipment and domestic sales regulations.

In addition, three free trade ports offer duty-free sales to tourists and Colombians: Leticia (on the Amazon River), and the islands of San Andros and Providencia in the Caribbean.

Colombia subscribes to the United Nations Multilateral Investment Guarantee Agency (MIGA) and has enacted several bilateral investment and trade agreements with neighboring countries.

Foreign Trade

U.S. exports to Colombia have been very meager, in part due to the relatively small size of Colombian companies and their concentration on internal markets. Large corporations—General Electric, the auto companies, the Bells, metals companies, and so on—have been the prime exporters. Very few smaller companies have ventured in.

As previously described, domestic markets are tough to crack, and with so many other locations offering more lucrative opportunities, most corporate strategists have ignored Colombia. For those companies that do have an interest, here is some basic information about import markets.

Most administrative restrictions on imports have been dismantled. Import tariffs are being reduced over several years. On the commercial and industrial side, telecommunications equipment and accessories are one of the fastest growing import markets, especially electronic switching gear. Good markets also exist for:

- Computers, peripherals, and software
- Earthmoving and mining equipment
- Electronic components and test gear
- Safety and security products
- Oil and gas field equipment
- Aircraft and avionics
- Medical diagnostic and treatment equipment and products
- Food processing and packaging equipment
- Agricultural machinery
- Electrical-power generating equipment
- Printing and graphic arts products

- Auto parts and accessories
- Waste management and disposal products and equipment
- Water purification systems

The consumer market beyond the urban areas is not worth bothering with. Disposable income is too low for people to buy imported goods. Within the urban centers the hot import markets are:

- Telephones
- Data sets
- Teleprinters
- Microwave equipment
- Mobil radios for aviation, marine, public safety, industrial and individual use

Some of the items needed in the resort area of Cartagena are produced locally; most, however, must be imported. For example:

- Hotel and restaurant supplies
- Processed food
- Air-conditioning and refrigeration equipment
- Maintenance supplies
- Hotel furniture and appointments

Demographically, 65 percent of the population live in the urban areas of Bogotá, Cali, Medellín, Barranquilla, Bucaramanga, Cartagena, Cúcuta, Pereira, and Manizales.

One caveat about marketing in Colombia: As in so many other South American countries, trying to do it without a local partner is impossible. The best source of information about which local companies can be trusted in a partnership may be obtained from:

American Chamber of Commerce
c/o William Wide
Fiberglass Colombia, S.A.
Apartado Aereo 9192
Bogotá, Colombia
Phone: 225-7920

Although Colombia has definite potential, neither the government nor local business leaders have completely thrown off the yoke of protectionism. While neighboring countries are actively soliciting trade with the United States, Canada, and Europe, Colombia seems content just to slowly feel its way through the maze of international free-market development.

No doubt unresolved guerrilla activity and the pervasive power of the drug cartels color the country's foreign trade policies. However, an underlying distrust of foreigners and monopolistic favoritism toward local business cartels have not been eliminated. Until business leaders genuinely want open trade with the rest of the world, Colombia seems doomed to remain a second-class trading partner.

Those interested in exploring Colombian opportunities should contact:

Embassy of Colombia
2118 Leroy Place NW
Washington, DC 20008
Phone: (202) 387-8338

Bolivia: Against All Odds

Of the three very poor Andean countries, Bolivia probably has the most to offer. The probability of armed revolt or government expropriation is also less than it is in either Peru or Ecuador. Except for the adventurous, however, foreigners will generally do better elsewhere.

Nevertheless, some positives do exist, at least in Bolivia and Peru. Governments of both countries are working diligently to bring their horrendous drug-trafficking problems under control. Both have implemented a series of severe economic reforms to convert their economies to the free market. And both are struggling toward democratic administrations—although the outcome of Peru's current political situation remains in doubt.

Ecuador, on the other hand, remains a semisocialist state, discouraging most foreign trade, and locked into outmoded policies of self-sufficiency. Whether a new center-right president can coerce an opposition congress to sustain new economic and political reforms is anyone's guess.

Even though internal political and economic problems plague landlocked Bolivia with a tiny population of 7 million, the government of President Jaime Paz Zamora has made remarkable strides toward rejoining the world community.

For the first time in over a decade, Bolivia's economy has begun to grow faster than its population. Although statistics are skimpy, growth for 1992 should be in the 3.5 to 4 percent range. Inflation, which hit a world high of 24,000 percent in 1982, appears to be stabilizing at 10 to 12 percent. Interest rates are the lowest in five years.

New investment laws have jump-started mining exploration after thirty years of stagnation. Of the sixty-plus state-owned companies in the privatization program, only six or so are going concerns, but at least their losses have been reduced. Flight capital is returning from Miami; deposits in the Bolivian banking system have tripled since 1989.

On the downside, private investment remains a paltry 3 percent of GDP and is not likely to increase much in the near future. Imports exceed exports by a wide margin.

Demographics and Social Ills

One of the biggest problems facing President Jaime Paz is the sharp class demarcation in Bolivia's social strata. About 1 million of Bolivia's citizens live as comfortably as many Americans, with adequate health care and educational opportunities. Below them come 3 million urban dwellers who also enjoy reasonable Bolivian living standards. Then the problems start.

Bolivia's 2 million or so urban poor barely scrape together enough to eat. At the bottom of the heap, at least 1 million rural dwellers live in abject poverty, with living standards and occupational tools reminiscent of the eighteenth century. Although literacy for the country at large has reached 63 percent, in the bottom two classes it's closer to 2 percent. Overall per capital income for 1990 was a startlingly meager US$760.

It is the plight of the bottom two classes that the president must address if Bolivia is to regain status as a viable trading partner in the world community. Voters are growing cynical about the administration's austere economic reforms, even as politicians busily accuse each other of drug dealing and even murder.

A 1992 poll indicated that only 13 to 18 percent of the voters have any faith in the political parties, the trade unions, or the army. A meager 60 percent of those polled drew confidence from the Catholic church, a sure sign of despair in a country that is nearly 100 percent Catholic.

Foreign Investment and Trade

The government's ambitious economic reform programs started as early as 1985. Progress to date includes abolishing foreign exchange restrictions; dropping tariff rates to the lowest in the Andean group of nations; eliminating most import restrictions; and making significant fiscal reforms through massive government austerity programs. A bilateral free trade framework agreement was signed with the United States in 1991.

The nation's infrastructure remains in serious disrepair. Potable water supplies, electricity, and telephones are a luxury when they function. Roads, schools, and hospitals are in terrible shape.

The Bolivian government considers agriculture to be its most important sector. Primary commodities are soybeans, lumber, coffee, and fruits. Its major export markets are Argentina, Chile, and Brazil. Mining and hydrocarbons represent approximately 70 percent of the country's official exports. Primary metals include tin, lead, zinc, silver, cadmium, and gold. Bolivia's manufacturing sector is very small and consists mainly of artisan jewelry, wood furniture, textiles, beer and liquor, ceramics, leather goods, alpaca, llama wool products, and wood handicrafts.

Special tax incentives have been enacted to encourage foreign investment in joint ventures with the state-owned oil company YPFB. Although most petroleum exports go to neighboring Argentina, Bolivia is soliciting U.S. companies for drilling equipment, seismic drilling services and studies, duct equipment and other products to help develop potentially large oil and natural gas reserves.

The country has one free trade zone, operating in the northern border town of Cobija. Additional zones have been approved in Oruro, Tarija, and the Beni area, but are not yet fully operable.

As a land-locked country, Bolivia has no major ocean ports of its own. However, port privileges are available at the Argentine port of Rosario and the Chilean port of Antofagasta. Puerto Quijarro in the southeast corner of Bolivia on the Paraguay River also has accommodations for smaller shipments.

Peru: A Nation in Turmoil

On April 13, 1992, President Alberto Fujimori grew impatient with democracy, fired a stalemated Congress, suspended the constitution, and began ruling the war-torn country with the help of an incompetent, corrupt army. Naturally, the United States and the Organization of American States (OAS) were furious, cutting aid and preparing to embargo Peru from the hemispheric community. Fujimori begged off, promised a plebiscite within six months, and bought time by meeting with OAS leaders in the Bahamas to explain his motives.

It's hard to find fault with Mr. Fujimori when one understands what a mess Peru has been for so long and the nature of its completely unworkable constitution. The president has in fact tried hard to stabilize his country in the face of a more serious narcotics problem than is faced by either Colombia or Bolivia.

Economic Reforms

Shortly after Mr. Fujimori was elected president, taking over a country rife with corruption and fraud from former president Alan Garcia, he unleashed a set of more than one hundred draconian reforms aimed at correcting years of mismanagement in a few months. His primary goal was to implement structural adjustments designed to achieve a massive conversion from state control to free markets, and thus to gain support from the IMF and World Bank in the form of desperately needed financial aid. This he achieved.

Foreign and local investors alike are now protected by investment guarantees from the Overseas Private Investment Corporation (for American investors) and the Multilateral Investment Guarantee

Agency with full permission to repatriate earnings and access necessary foreign currency. A far-reaching privatization program was enacted to sell state-owned companies in mining, oil, fishing, telecommunications, air, sea, and rail transport, electricity generation and distribution, water systems, and, of course, the cholera-infested sewage system. All these businesses were in such terrible shape, however, that few buyers lined up. Fujimori's liberalization of the Lima Stock Exchange was more successful, bringing in a flood of foreign capital, especially from neighboring Chile.

In a sense it seems grossly unfair that Fujimori's dismantling of the country's protectionist and statist economic policies has been largely stymied by forces beyond his jurisdiction: an out-of-control drug war initiated by Colombia drug czars and fed by Peru's coca farmers; and a ferocious guerrilla war waged by the bloodthirsty Shining Path.

Meanwhile the Peruvian people suffer, with a minimum legal wage of US$35 a month, one eighth what the United Nations judges necessary to sustain a family.

Foreign Trade and Investment

Foreign companies wishing to export to Peru should find plenty of hard currency flooding in from a surprising rash of investments from East Asian companies.

According to the Peruvian economy ministry, import products in highest demand are:

- Oil and gas products
- Mining equipment
- Machine parts
- Food processing equipment
- Vegetable oil
- Insecticides
- Medical supplies and equipment
- Fertilizers
- Plastic consumer products
- Construction equipment

In the face of an unpredictable political environment, positive reforms to encourage foreign direct investment were laid down by the Framework Law of Private Investment in December 1991. This law guarantees foreign investors the following rights:

- Freedom to invest in any sector of the economy
- Protection of private property
- Notice of any taxes due at least five days before they are due to be paid

Under the law, the government must now fulfill the following commitments:

- Inform foreign investors of all required administrative procedures when asked, including time limits and associated fees.
- Desist from setting prices for anything outside the public sector.
- Stop using foreign exchange rates, prices, tariffs, or other taxes to discriminate between foreign investors.
- Accept international arbitration in the event of disputes.

Certainly, Peru offers many favorable conditions not found in most of Latin America. The unresolved question, however, is whether the Fujimori administration can enforce its own laws.

The best source of information about market or investment opportunities in Peru is from:

Latin American/Caribbean Business Development Center
U.S. Department of Commerce, Room H–3202
14th Street and Constitution Avenue, NW
Washington, DC 20230
Phone: (202) 377-0703
Fax: (202) 377-2218

forget that, they can very quickly become persona non grata. Many years ago, when Japanese construction crews first came to Central America and the islands, they made just such a mistake. In parts of the Caribbean at least, it took them decades to learn the ropes and earn a welcome.

Interestingly, a very different situation exists for Asians working elsewhere in Latin America. In Brazil, Chile, Peru, Ecuador, and Panama, for example, Chinese, Japanese, and other Asian nationals benefit from close traditional ties with the rest of the population. These ties go back several generations, to the days when Asian laborers first emigrated to work in these developing countries. Today the president of Peru is of Japanese ancestry. Children of the Mexican president attend Japanese schools. In Trinidad and Tobago, at least 40 percent of the population traces its heritage back to East Indian ancestors.

Although the West Indian culture derives from that of African slaves, shared ancestry does not win a foreigner approval as "one of the family." Skin color has scant bearing on the success or failure of business deals or community acceptance. Here, as elsewhere in the region, only the manners and mind-set of a courteous visitor will make one welcome and open opportunity's doors.

Personal Survival Tactics

Beyond cultural differences, first-time travelers may find it difficult to cope with local practices and institutions that are substantially different from those found at home. Personal safety, health care, living accommodations, and transport arrangements seem to cause the greatest problems.

Compared with conditions that prevailed there in the 1970s and early 1980s, most Latin American and Caribbean countries are today perfectly safe for foreigners, provided they follow the same prudent rules that a stranger would practice in New York, Chicago, Toronto, Los Angeles, or Houston:

- Don't walk alone on city streets at night.
- Don't drive alone on unlighted streets or backcountry roads.
- Don't get intoxicated in public.

- Don't be rude.
- Don't flaunt jewelry or other expensive accessories.
- Stay away from decrepit neighborhoods, broken-down bars, and out-of-the-way restaurants.

One precaution many of us have used for years is to carry a clearly written document bearing our name, local address, and local American contact (chamber of commerce or embassy); the name, address, and local telephone number of persons to notify in case of accident or incarceration; blood type; and any medication we may need or are allergic to. It can be a frightening experience to be left to the devices of local doctors or, worse yet, to those of the local police. It pays, therefore, to carry this document at all times and in all countries. It's also a good idea to carry your passport with you wherever you go—in a safe (and hidden) place, of course.

Health Precautions

As in any developing country, health hazards and the absence of good health care are common throughout the region (except in Puerto Rico and the U.S. Virgin Islands). In most cities, potable water and food are generally safe, especially in first- or second-class hotels and restaurants. (Stay away from anything below second-class.) Still, it can't hurt to avoid tap water (many countries have excellent local wine or beer as substitutes). It's always wise to avoid local meat until one gets to know the source; and stay away from milk.

Although most countries are free of serious communicable diseases, outbreaks of cholera in some areas have caused health authorities to tighten immigration regulations. Experienced travelers carry the International Certificate of Vaccinations approved by the World Health Organization showing the dates and types of their latest vaccinations. Malaria and typhoid shots are a must if traveling off the beaten track.

With the exception of Mexico City, Buenos Aires, Rio de Janeiro, Santiago, and Puerto Rico, professional health care is generally not reliable. Most hospitals are government-run, with doctors and nurses on the government payroll. Basic pharmaceuticals are generally available; forget about special prescription drugs.

Health Insurance

Except for some of the more advanced hospitals in large cities, most health care facilities will not accept standard U.S. health insurance (such as Blue Cross) in lieu of payment. Therefore, before leaving home, it's necessary to make provision for transferring funds via American Express, bank wire transfers, or other means in case of emergency. It's also a good idea to verify that your group or individual policy covers overseas health care so that, at a minimum, you can be reimbursed when returning home.

Many experienced travelers have had difficulty getting overseas coverage from employee group policies and prefer to take out separate coverage. In many cases, special policies issued specifically for international travelers are accepted in local hospitals when a Blue Cross or other group policy isn't. They also cover evacuation costs if it becomes necessary to fly home for treatment. Two of the best policies are Travel Assistance International, provided by Europ Assistance Worldwide Services, Inc., (202) 347-7113, and Global Plus, obtained through Clements & Company, (202) 872-0060.

Accommodations and Transport

As for living accommodations, nearly all locations have adequate housing at substantially lower cost than in the United States. Major cities boast suburban living that matches U.S. or Canadian standards. Even on the smaller Caribbean islands, modest-to-elaborate homes owned by foreigners can be rented on short- or long-term leases.

Transportation can easily be arranged through car rental agencies, although the rates are high. An international driver's license isn't essential; it doesn't hurt to carry one, however, just for emergencies. All countries have a bus service of one type or another that is inexpensive and convenient, however dirty, crowded, and, in some locations, downright decrepit it may be. Argentina, Brazil, Mexico, and a few other countries have extensive rail systems.

Climate and Geography

Unless your destination is Patagonia or the higher altitudes, such as Lake Titicaca, leave woolen apparel at home. Most of the region is warmer than the United States (except southern Florida) and warm weather clothing is the norm.

For those unfamiliar with South American geography, the Argentine section of Patagonia is a vast windswept plateau, very arid and sparsely settled, rising to about 5,000 feet above sea level (similar to Denver's elevation) at the highest point, and resembling Wyoming or Montana. It stretches 1,000 miles south from the Rio Negro to the Strait of Magellan, comprising 300,000 square miles of Argentina in the southern part of South America. Chile's section includes a heavily wooded strip of land falling westward from the Andes, and now called Magellanes.

Lake Titicaca, at an elevation of 12,500 feet, straddles the Andean border of Peru and Bolivia. Stretching 110 miles from end to end, it is the highest inland navigable body of water in the world and a major transportation artery between the two countries.

Other Tips for First-Time Travelers

- Always dress in business attire when conducting business.
- If you are a woman, leave your slacks at home and restrict shorts and tops to the beach or pool.
- If you are a man, never wear shorts other than for leisure activities (except in Bermuda).
- Register with the local American Chamber of Commerce upon arrival.
- For extended stays, register with the local police department.
- Try to learn some Spanish—it's only common courtesy and will help you get around—especially in South and Central America and Mexico. A few Portuguese words and phrases can work wonders in Brazil. A smattering of French opens doors in the French islands.

The Influence of Religion

Except in the English-speaking Caribbean islands (mainly Anglican) and the Netherlands Antilles, Catholicism is the predominant religion throughout the region—a heritage of the sixteenth- and seventeenth-century Spanish Conquistadors and Jesuit missionaries. In recent years, however, a wave of Pentecostal Evangelism has swept across much of the Caribbean, Central America, and parts of South America and Mexico.

In Guatemala, for instance, it is estimated that a quarter of the population has left the Catholic Church in favor of the Evangelicals. Barbados, Trinidad and Tobago, the U.S. Virgin Islands, Chile, and others are seeing similar shifts. To most Americans, the idea that religion has a bearing on business conduct may seem farfetched. To Latin Americans and Caribbean islanders, however, it makes perfect sense. Americans traveling in the region need to be aware that the battle being waged there by two (and sometimes three) very different faiths for people's hearts and souls is an indication of the powerful role that religion still plays in everyday life there.

Throughout Latin America and the Caribbean, religion has always had a powerful influence in the realms of politics and economics. Anglicanism carries overtones of English social and political assumptions. Catholicism, led by liberal Jesuit missionaries, is a "people's" church, advocating the rights of peasants and a basic allegiance to Rome. Pentecostal charismatics, on the other hand, preach acquiescence to secular authority, along with abstinence from such modern-day "sins" as alcohol, adultery, and social dancing.

Conflicting religious doctrines have had a major impact on the rise of Latin American and Caribbean dictators and on their later overthrow. They have also had an impact on market conditions, financial institutions, and government regulations on foreign investment.

It would be foolhardy to choose sides or to generalize about the specific influence these opposing forces exert on foreign trade and investment. However, prudent foreign investors and serious traders certainly need to understand the impact of each side on consumer choice, profit motives, and government influence peddling.

Macho Males and Businesswomen

On numerous occasions, women friends and business associates have asked me about acceptable protocol in Latin America and the

Caribbean and sought my suggestions for dealing with discriminatory practices. Since I am only slightly braver about assessing the role and status of women in the region than I am about discussing its conflicting religious beliefs, the following comments should be taken as general observations only, and applied to specific situations only as the occasion warrants.

During the 1950s, 1960s, and 1970s, machismo dominated social, political, and business life in both Latin and West Indian cultures. While still evident, this attitude toward women had materially changed by the end of the 1980s. It would be a gross exaggeration, however, to assume that women have achieved as much in their battle against sexist prejudice in Latin America or the Caribbean as they have in the United States and Europe.

Women are certainly accepted in the business community, in social organizations, and increasingly in government circles. Still, many people continue to treat the sexes differently. For that reason, businesswomen may want to keep the following guidelines in mind:

- Don't venture out alone until you thoroughly understand the country's culture, language, and social protocol.
- Leave jewelry at home.
- Be gracious and accept a traditionally feminine role.
- Be firm but polite, reserved but pleasant, to stay in command of the situation, especially with the police or military.
- Forget about social drinking (except wine) unless you know your hosts well.

All Caribbean and Latin American cultures are class-conscious. Each differentiates strongly between the business and government elite, the workers, and the peasants. The biggest faux pas that foreign business travelers tend to make is not to recognize these distinctions. This is especially true in the case of foreign businesswomen. In Latin America and the Caribbean, a "lady" is judged by the company she keeps and the distance she maintains between herself and men whose social and economic class is deemed lower than her own. However "undemocratic" this view may be, it remains a standard of behavior that must be borne in mind while traveling in the region.

Since 1987, I have been involved in several business transactions in which the active participation of one or more women has sealed the deal. Had they been absent, many opportunities would have been lost. The role of women in Latin American and Caribbean business may be more muted than it is in developed economies, but in many situations women can be far more effective than men. Go for it! Don't let the Latin and West Indian macho men intimidate you. Again, be firm but polite, reserved but cooperative, to achieve your goals.

Corruption at the Border

Most of us like to believe that people are basically honest. In developed nations this belief is more often than not well-founded. In most situations, if we treat one another fairly and honestly, our actions will be reciprocated. In so-called First World countries, this modus operandi is just as true when passing through customs and immigration as it is in any other aspect of our lives. But in many of the countries of the globe that are still striving for the lofty status of "First World," customs and immigration is a realm apart, a world where anything goes. Africa is far and away the worst, with the Middle East close behind; some of the South and Southeast Asian countries can also present serious problems in this area.

Compared to these regions, the corruption experienced by travelers at Latin American borders is minimal (I have never had or even heard of problems in the Caribbean island states). Still, the situation can be difficult without adequate preparation. It is not unheard-of to offer uniformed customs and immigration officials something to get through customs without harassment. The traveler's demeanor can also make a big difference.

Here are a few tricks of the trade that stand experienced travelers in good stead:

- As often as possible claim to be a tourist rather than a business traveler.
- Carry some loose change and dollar bills with you.
- Avoid wearing jewelry of any kind until safely in the country.

- Learn a few Spanish words of greeting (or Portuguese or French, depending on the location).
- Be cheerful and businesslike.
- Create an air of being in command.
- Know the telephone number of the local American embassy or consulate.

One final tip on personal survival: Invariably, after clearing customs and immigration, you will be approached by swarms of hawkers clamoring, in broken English or in their own native tongues, to offer you a taxi ride. Businesspeople are put upon the most. Don't get flustered. Look for a dispatcher. If one isn't available, pick out the taxi driver who looks the most presentable, not the one who is the most persistent.

Since metered cabs are hardly ever available, be very certain to negotiate a fare *before* entering the taxi. When going to a new country, always ask airline personnel, police officials, or fellow business travelers about taxi rates to your hotel of choice. Without that information, negotiating a reasonable fare is impossible. Above all, don't panic. Stay in command.

The Importance of Insurance

Although few companies have difficulty protecting their assets and employees at home, the problems and questions seem to multiply when those employees are faced with the peculiarities of foreign practices. The problem arises partly from a lack of understanding of local laws and regulations and partly from an inability to adjust quickly to different cultural practices. But in Latin America and the Caribbean (and in most developing regions, for that matter), the major hurdles seem to be the kind of hazards not encountered at home: an inadequate infrastructure, the corruption of minor bureaucrats, government-owned businesses, powerful labor organizations, and so on. One of the best ways a company can compensate for these hazards is to design a comprehensive insurance program.

Companies experienced in global trade generally find comprehensive insurance coverage a relatively inexpensive way to avoid monetary losses and the voluminous bureaucratic paperwork that invariably follows an accident or other mishap. This is especially true in the developing nations of Latin America and the Caribbean. Because business insurance is not as popular overseas as it is in the United States, far fewer local insurers are available to choose from.

Most companies find that it is generally easier and less expensive to place insurance with home-country carriers than to sort out options in a foreign environment. Many poorer or smaller nations do not have any insurance companies. In others, the few small carriers frequently shun foreign customers, or charge prohibitive premiums.

Types of Coverage

The Foreign Credit Insurance Association (FCIA), a branch of Eximbank, is the most prominent insurer of export credit risk. American International Group (AIG) is the largest private sector insurer, although CIGNA and Lloyds also offer good coverage.

The best American coverage for political risk comes from the Overseas Private Investment Corporation (OPIC). Similar government agencies in other developed nations provide it for their companies.

In addition to credit and political risk, both exporters and investors should include product liability, property protection, and lost-income reimbursement coverage. Most domestic policies do not extend to overseas property or activities. However, major carriers will issue riders or additional policies for an increased premium.

Comprehensive employee health and accident coverage is a must, and should be designed to cover traveling employees as well as those permanently stationed overseas. Very frequently, U.S. policies do not cover personnel on overseas assignment, and in such cases special riders should be obtained. In those cases where the cost of bringing ill or injured personnel home for treatment is not included, separate repatriation coverage can make employees feel more comfortable working overseas. In addition, those companies with overseas branches should obtain voluntary workers' compensation policies to cover overseas personnel.

When leasing a car, positive proof of automobile insurance is essential to avoid a hassle. Also, even if auto insurance can be purchased locally (impossible in many countries), it is substantially more expensive than it is in the United States and Canada.

The risk of damage to or complete loss of shipments going to poorer countries such as Peru, Bolivia, or Guyana is very real. Chapter 20 describes reports of intentional usurpation of cargo at Venezuelan ports. Inland transit to rural areas in Mexico, Guatemala, and Colombia frequently results in broken containers and damaged or lost goods. The solution lies in a good cargo-in-transit policy from a home-country carrier.

Cargo-in-transit coverage, which protects against loss or damage of shipments between point of embarkation and point of debarkation, is a requirement of Eximbank and most commercial banks involved in trade finance. Full-package policies can be purchased from AIG, CIGNA, Continental Insurance, and several other major business insurers. In addition to standard coverage, it's a good idea to include coverage for four special occurrences:

1. Refused or returned shipments
2. Concealed damage
3. Brand and label removal
4. Control of damaged goods

Most companies prefer to go through a qualified insurance broker who knows which carriers offer the best deals. Two of the biggest and most reliable are Alexander & Alexander and Frank B. Hall & Co.

Captive Insurers

Wholly owned insurance subsidiaries, or "captives," are the self-insurance wave of the future. With premiums skyrocketing and large competitors able to charge lower product prices by self-insuring, smaller companies have no choice but to do the same. Captives are usually set up to self-insure a portion of property, liability, and marine exposure. Some companies even include portions of employee coverages.

In its simplest form, a captive agrees to take back a portion of the normal coverage from the major insurer, perhaps assuming the first US$250,000 of annual losses. This reduces the premium and permits a company to invest the savings until needed to pay for losses. Rather than paying high premiums to outsiders for predictable, noncatastrophic losses, the cash stays in-house and earns income.

Latin America and the Caribbean offer some unique tax-haven locations for captive subsidiaries. Panama, the Cayman Islands, and the Turks and Caicos Islands are the most popular. Bermuda, the Bahamas, and Puerto Rico are also good choices. Income earned by captive investments is then tax free, multiplying the advantage.

Advertising to Fit the Market

Companies that advertise extensively in their home country frequently make one of two mistakes (sometimes both) when structuring a campaign to reach Latin America or Caribbean markets. They forget to take into consideration the vast differences in various countries' competition, advertising media, and cultural tastes, and the intense national pride that, in many countries, creates a resistance to products "not invented here." Elaborate television commercials won't work in nations like Colombia or Bolivia that have few TV sets or erratic reception. Trade journal advertisements won't reach consumers in Costa Rica, where most selling is done through personal relationships. Extensive newspaper spreads will be ineffective in most of the small Eastern Caribbean nations that, at best, have three-page weeklies, or in Peru, where barely half of the population can read.

To be effective, advertising must be carefully designed to fit the particular country and market. Global campaigns just won't work in a region of fifty-one countries and many more cultures.

Trade shows are an excellent way to reach specific audiences for commercial and industrial products. A variety of exhibitions for a range of industries are held throughout the year in most major cities. Buyers from the small Caribbean states frequent shows in Puerto Rico. Mexico City draws potential buyers from Central America. Buenos Aires, São Paulo, Caracas, Bogotá, and Santiago draw from their respective regions. Of increasing importance are the trade shows in Miami specifically designed to attract Latin

American and Caribbean buyers and those in Houston designed to draw Mexican buyers.

The annual Miami Conference on the Caribbean, including Mexico, Venezuela, and Colombia, sponsored by Caribbean/Latin America Action out of Washington, is a premier trade exhibition and conference. It attracts government and business leaders from the entire Latin/Caribbean region, many with checkbook in hand. Trade fairs are also very popular in less-populated countries. Business groups from several Caribbean states hold annual trade fairs that attract displays of consumer products and services as well as commercial lines.

Virtually all Caribbean and Central American states promote tourism. Flyers, pamphlets, and other printed advertising to attract visitors as well as local consumers, proliferate in hotels, resorts, and airport terminals. In the Caribbean, weekly island newspapers, advertising circulars, and commercial tabloids reach both consumer and tourist audiences. Cable TV also reaches most island states and channels from San Juan, Caracas, and other peripheral cities are used to tap Caribbean Basin markets.

The main thrust should be to target market groups in specific countries, research appropriate advertising media available in each country, and then tailor a campaign to fit that media and audience.

Franchising: Boon or Boondoggle?

As regional consumers develop free-market tastes, local entrepreneurs are turning to their northern brethren for management advice and technology. This has led to a virtual explosion in the demand for franchises, considered by many to be the easiest way to start a small business. Although technology licensing has always been in demand, business format franchising is the hot new market.

From tiny Caribbean islands like Montserrat and St. Vincent to giant economies like Brazil, consumers are developing tastes along the same lines as Americans, Canadians, or Europeans. The business format franchise, such as that pioneered by McDonalds, fits perfectly into the Latin America/Caribbean mold.

This type of franchise not only includes the licensing of a trademark, product, or technology, but of a complete system for operating a business, and it is the operating know-how that small businesses in this region desperately need.

Franchising is not only for multinationals. In Brazil, for instance, according to the Associacao Brasileira de Franchising census, the number of franchises more than doubled in the three years to 1989, generating over US$15 billion in sales and employing 300,000 people. Mexico, Argentina, Panama, and Jamaica, and of course Puerto Rico and the U.S. Virgin Islands, are other red-hot locations for franchising.

On the downside, several countries lack adequate bank financing or government aid programs for starting or expanding a local business. This means that the franchiser must either provide funding or assist in locating the necessary capital.

A variety of issues need to be addressed to protect franchisers, especially in Latin American countries. (Most Caribbean nations are fairly secure already). Chief among these is adequate trademark and patent protection. Intellectual piracy is still prevalent in many countries and adequate safeguards must be built into their legal systems to enforce protection laws currently being implemented.

In addition, many countries in Central and South America have inadequate definitions of royalties. This results in discriminatory taxing laws, difficulties in obtaining trademark or patent registrations, and questions concerning the repatriation of the full amount of royalties earned. Mexico has made the most progress in enacting legislation to protect intellectual property, but even here, in one of the most advanced countries in the region, enforcement is lax and piracy remains a very real risk.

What to Do About Bank Financing

As a result of their dismal lending records during the 1970s and early 1980s and a protracted absence of global vision, few American banks are willing to finance either trade or investment in Latin America without ironclad, U.S. government guarantees.

According to a group of bankers attending the 1992 annual convention of the Bankers Association for Foreign Trade, most of the nation's 12,000 or so commercial banks don't even know the meaning of trade finance. Of those that do, only 15 to 20 percent are willing to consider financing trade to Latin America, regardless of the country involved.

According to Darin P. Narayana, the international executive vice-president of Norwest Corporation (one of the few regional banks actively promoting trade finance), "fear of foreign risk really concerns banks in this country." Such an attitude jeopardizes the long-term competitiveness of American companies, regardless of opportunities to tap new Latin American resources and markets.

Fortunately, a small number of banks—mainly the ten or so money center banks and the twenty-plus large regional banks—are very committed to financing Latin American trade and investment. Chase and Citicorp have branches throughout Latin America and are especially dominant in the Caribbean Basin. Regional banks— Norwest, NationBank, First Interstate, First Chicago, and so on— will handle trade finance from the United States but are not eager to fund foreign investments.

Meanwhile, banks from those Latin American and Caribbean countries that have a working financial system are stepping up to the challenge. Mexican banks are especially active in promoting both trade finance and investment funding. Banks in Argentina and Brazil are also becoming more aggressive in attracting foreign business. Appendix H lists the addresses and telephone numbers of major Latin American banks with a New York presence.

Multinational Canadian and European banks are far more sophisticated in international trade than their American counterparts and offer a viable alternative. Many have been active in the Latin/ Caribbean market for decades. Mr. Narayana put it succinctly: "There isn't much competition, and most of it is from Dutch, German, British, Swiss, and French banks." He should have added "Canadian, too."

Barclays already has a Latin American regional headquarters in Miami and is rapidly expanding trade finance activities in Mexico and other Latin American/Caribbean countries. Baden-Wuerttembergische Bank of Germany, Lloyds, Midland, and Westminster banks from Britain, Bank of Nova Scotia and Royal Bank from Canada, and several Dutch and Swiss banks are all increasing their regional business. British and Canadian banks are especially active throughout the Caribbean. Given the cold shoulder they are receiving from their regular banking connections, American companies would do well to investigate one or more of these as an alternative.

Managing Corruption

The twenty-year-old U.S. Foreign Corrupt Practices Act, among other provisions, prohibits U.S. companies or employees from accepting or giving bribes, payoffs, kickbacks, or other favors in exchange for favored treatment from foreign government officials relating to any contract, financing, or assistance that:

- Affects the U.S. government or its agencies (including Eximbank, OPIC, and USAID) in any way
- Could be detrimental to the security of the United States
- Is against U.S. public policy

Strict adherence to this law puts U.S. companies at an extreme competitive disadvantage in world markets, including those in Latin America, and, to a lesser extent, those in the Caribbean. Companies from Europe and Asia are far less shackled, recognizing that such payments are a normal part of doing business in many developing nations, as well as in many industrialized countries.

Since U.S. multinationals have been successfully competing in global markets for decades, they must have found a way to compensate. They have. The answer lies in using intermediaries. All multinationals do so; small and midsize companies must join in if they wish to compete.

Middlemen or intermediaries flourish in every Latin American/Caribbean country. They go by different titles: labor brokers, import houses, commissioned agents, consultants, trading companies, audit firms, and attorneys. Since many practices forbidden to U.S. firms are perfectly legal, or at least acceptable, under local laws, intermediaries are more than willing to help foreign companies find their way through the bureaucratic maze—many times the corrupt bureaucratic maze.

APPENDIXES

Appendix A

Multilateral, Bilateral, and U.S. Government Assistance Programs

A wide variety of public institutions and private organizations stand ready to provide assistance to any company, large or small, wishing to do business in the Latin American/Caribbean region. Such assistance may take the form of:

- Information about demographic trends and product demand
- Competition listings and pricing surveys
- Raw material and labor availability statistics
- Identification of joint-venture partners
- Names and addresses of host-country government agencies
- Sources of trade finance and investment capital

Some agencies are more helpful than others, and an agency's local office in one city may be more helpful than the same agency's office in another. Unfortunately, the size and strength of the company seeking assistance often determines the amount of cooperation it will receive from various public institutions. (Not surprisingly, the larger the company, the more assistance it is likely to be offered.) Smaller companies can also get help; it just takes more persistence.

Space limits the coverage of institutions providing trade finance or direct investment funding. Interested readers can get further information from my book, *The McGraw-Hill Handbook of Global Trade and Investment Financing.*

United Nations/World Bank Programs

International Finance Corporation (IFC)

The International Finance Corporation's mission is "to assist, in association with private investors, productive private enterprises that contribute to the development of its member countries." A private company making an investment can turn to the IFC for direct managerial and technical assistance, as well as for help in identifying and structuring the project and guidance in making equity contributions and providing long-term loans without government guarantees.

In addition, fee-based IFC advisory engagements include help in developing new project proposals, advice on the choice of technical partners, and assistance in structuring appropriate financing.

International Finance Corporation
1818 H Street, NW
Washington, DC 20433
Phone: (202) 477-1234
Fax: (202) 477-6391

Multilateral Investment Guarantee Agency (MIGA)

MIGA's primary mission is to encourage foreign investment in developing countries by providing:

- Investment guarantees against the risks of currency transfer, expropriation of property, war and civil disturbance, and breach of contract by host-country government bureaus; equity investments, stockholder loans, and loan guarantees are all covered
- Advisory services to developing member countries on the ways and means by which they can improve their attractiveness to foreign investment

Multilateral Investment Guarantee Agency
Vice President, Guarantees
1818 H Street, NW

Washington, DC 20433
Phone: (202) 473-6168
Fax: (202) 477-9886

Investment Development Office for Program Policy and Evaluation

This facility provides short-term, low-cost financing of between $15,000 and $100,000 per project for feasibility studies of potential investment projects in the poorest developing nations. Applications must come from a national, regional, or multilateral sponsoring financial institution.

Investment Development Office for Program
  Policy and Evaluation
United Nations Development Program
One UN Plaza
New York, NY 10017
Phone: (212) 906-5060

Caribbean and Central America Business Advisory Service

This is a special program within the International Finance Corporation designed to assist companies making direct investments in Caribbean and Central American nations. The Business Advisory Service (BAS) acts as a bridge between private enterprises and lenders and investors from around the world for direct investment projects costing at least US$500,000. (It has also assisted companies with projects costing much less in the smaller island states.)

Although not a direct lender or investor in private-sector projects, BAS helps companies structure and appraise new investments or expansion projects for presentation to prospective lenders and investors. Such assistance may include helping a company hire technical and marketing consultants, advising it on alternate sources of financing, and helping it negotiate with financial institutions. Not infrequently, the addition of BAS to a company's negotiating team assures lenders that the project is economically sound

and worthy of funding. Guarantees or external security are generally not required by lenders when BAS backs the project.

Caribbean and Central America
  Business Advisory Service
1818 H Street, NW
Washington, DC 20433
Phone: (202) 473-0900
Fax: (202) 334-8855

Bilateral Aid Programs

Inter-American Investment Corporation (IIC)

This is the merchant banking arm of the Inter-American Development Bank. It is specifically charged with the task of encouraging
private enterprise in the Latin American/Caribbean region by helping foreign companies in the small and midsize range. Its assistance
takes the form of:

* Technical counseling for the preparation of pre-investment
  and feasibility studies
* Advisory services aimed at restoring the operating and financial capacity of companies requiring such assistance
* Advice on structuring privatization deals
* Help in identifying investment projects and potential joint-
  venture partners
* Coordination with financial institutions for additional financing
* Technical and financial aid to start new companies and develop projects

A qualifying project must meet at least one of the following criteria:

* Use material and human resources from the host country (or
  other member country) and create new jobs in the region.
* Create local management skills.

- Encourage exports from the region.
- Transfer technology.
- Promote the savings and use of investment capital.
- Generate and/or save foreign exchange.
- Promote broad ownership structures.

For information, contact:

Inter-American Investment Corporation
1300 New York Avenue, NW
Washington, DC 20577
Phone: (202) 623-3900
Fax: (202) 623-2360

Canadian-Caribbean Business Cooperation Office

This facility helps Canadian companies identify business opportunities, locate joint-venture partners, negotiate joint-venture
contracts, and start up businesses in Caribbean and Central American countries. For information, contact:

Canadian-Caribbean Business Cooperation Office
99 Bank Street, Suite 250
Ottawa, Ontario K1P 6B9
Phone: (613) 238-8888
Fax: (613) 563-9218

Canadian International Development Agency

This agency provides financing assistance to Canadian companies interested in making direct investments in offshore facilities
or projects. For information, contact:

Canadian International Development Agency
Industrial Development Program
Industrial Cooperation Division
200 Promenade du Portage
Hull, Quebec, K1A OG4
Phone: (819) 997-7901

Commonwealth Development Corporation (CDC)

This British agency provides long-term financing, management expertise, and technical assistance for projects involving agriculture and aquaculture, telecommunications, power and water projects, tourism, manufacturing, and financial service investments. It also helps train local managers for senior management positions.

For Anguilla, Antigua, Barbados, British Virgin Islands, Dominica, Grenada, Guyana, Montserrat, St. Kitts-Nevis, St. Lucia, St. Vincent, and Trinidad and Tobago:

The Commonwealth Development Corporation
East Caribbean Office
P.O. Box 1392
Culloden Office Complex, Ground Floor
Lower Collymore Rock
St. Michael, Barbados, West Indies
Phone: (809) 436-9890
Fax: (809) 436-1504

For the Cayman Islands, Jamaica, and the Turks and Caicos Islands:

The Commonwealth Development
   Corporation
West Caribbean Office
P.O. Box 23
17 Barbados Avenue
Kingston, Jamaica, West Indies
Phone: (809) 926-1164
Fax: (809) 926-1166

For Belize, Honduras, Nicaragua, Costa Rica, and Ecuador:

The Commonwealth Development Corporation
Latin America Office
Apartado 721-1000
3er Piso, Edificio San Jorge
Calle 40, Paseo Colón

San José, Costa Rica
Phone: 220969/220932
Fax: 220890

European Investment Bank (EIB)

The European Investment Bank provides long-term financing for productive direct investments in the Caribbean, Africa, and Pacific regions with loans of $300,000 to $30 million. For information, contact:

European Investment Bank
100 Boulevard Konrad Adenauer
Luxembourg L-2950
Phone: 352-43-791

German Finance Company for Investments in Developing Countries (DEG)

The DEG provides long-term loans, equity contributions, and guarantees. The equity involvement of a German or European Community partner in a joint venture is usually required, although exceptions are sometimes made. For information, contact:

German Finance Company for
  Investments in Developing Countries
Belvederstrasse 40
P.O. Box 45 03 40
D5000 Cologne 41, Germany
Phone: (02 21) 49 86-1

Netherlands Development Finance Company (FMO)

Jointly owned by the government of the Netherlands and Dutch private-sector businesses and industrial organizations, the FMO provides feasibility study financing and technical assistance. The FMO has no requirement that there be Dutch participation in a project. For information, contact:

Netherlands Development Finance Company
62 Bezuidenhoutseweg
P.O. Box 93060
2509 AB The Hague, Netherlands
Phone: (31) (70) 419641

Industrialization Fund for Developing Countries (IFU)

A wholly owned agency of the Danish government, the IFU
provides loans, guarantees, and equity capital, and also finances
feasibility studies, technology transfer activities, and training
grants. The IFU prefers to finance joint ventures with participation
by a Danish private-sector partner.

Industrialization Fund for Developing Countries
Bremerholm 4
P.O. Box 2155
DK-1069, Copenhagen, Denmark
Phone: 45-33-14 25 75

United States Government and Affiliated Agencies

U.S. Department of Commerce

The U.S. Department of Commerce does not directly assist
U.S. exporting companies or those making foreign direct investments. Two divisions, the International Trade Administration (ITA)
and the United States & Foreign Commercial Service agency
(US&FCS) do, however, maintain the most voluminous, comprehensive collection of foreign trade and investment data of any
single organization in the world. For a small fee (and, in some
cases, no fee), the forty-eight district offices and nineteen branch
offices of US&FCS provide reports, periodicals, computer data
banks, books, and other reference material covering:

- Exporting and direct investment opportunities
- Foreign markets for U.S. products and services
- Services to locate and evaluate overseas buyers and represen-
  tatives

- Financing sources
- International trade exhibitions
- Export documentation requirements
- Macroeconomic statistics by country
- U.S. export licensing rules
- Host-country import licensing requirements
- Foreign trade seminars and conferences

For information, contact:

U.S. Department of Commerce
14th Street and Constitution Avenue, NW
Washington, DC 20230

Appendix B lists the city locations and telephone numbers of the US&FCS district and branch offices. If one of them can't help, try calling a country desk officer in Washington with responsibility for Caribbean and Latin American countries.

For the Caribbean Basin and Mexico:	(202) 377-5327
For South America:	(202) 377-2436

Export-Import Bank of the United States (Eximbank)

Eximbank's main mission is to provide trade finance for U.S. exports to world markets by granting direct loans, loan guarantees, and buyer credit through a variety of programs. The toll-free number to a government hotline counseling service specifically designed to answer questions from smaller businesses about financing and other export matters is (800) 424-5201. For more information, contact:

Export-Import Bank of the United States
811 Vermont Avenue, NW
Washington, DC 20571
Phone: (202) 566-8111 or (800) 424-5201

Foreign Credit Insurance Association (FCIA)

The FCIA provides U.S. exporters insurance coverage against both commercial and political risk of export orders, including expropriation, bad debts, and currency fluctuations. For information, contact:

Foreign Credit Insurance Association
40 Rector Street, 11th Floor
New York, NY 10006
Phone: (212) 306-5000

Overseas Private Investment Corporation (OPIC)

OPIC's mission is to promote private-sector economic growth in developing countries by helping small U.S. businesses as follows:

• Obtain information about investment opportunities in foreign lands.
• Source joint venture partners.
• Arrange financing for direct investments.
• Insure long-term investments in foreign facilities.

This assistance is administered through several programs: the Investor Advisory Services, Investment Missions, Preinvestment Services, and Outreach Services (seminars and conferences). In addition, OPIC offers risk insurance and several types of financing for foreign direct investments, including direct loans and loan guarantees. For information, contact:

Overseas Private Investment Corporation
1615 M Street, NW, Fourth Floor
Washington, DC 20527
Phone: (202) 457-7010 or (800) 424-6742

Appendix B

U.S. and Foreign Commercial Service Offices

State	City Location(s)	Telephone number(s)
Alabama	Birmingham	(205) 731-1331
Alaska	Anchorage	(907) 271-5041
Arizona	Phoenix	(602) 261-3285
Arkansas	Little Rock	(501) 378-5793
California	Los Angeles	(213) 209-6707
	Santa Ana	(714) 836-2461
	San Diego	(619) 557-5395
	San Francisco	(415) 556-5860
Colorado	Denver	(303) 844-3246
Connecticut	Hartford	(203) 240-3530
Delaware	(Served by Philadelphia)	(215) 962-4980
District of Columbia		(202) 377-3181
Florida	Miami	(305) 536-5267
	Clearwater	(813) 461-0011
	Jacksonville	(904) 791-2796
	Orlando	(407) 648-1608
	Tallahassee	(904) 488-6469
Georgia	Atlanta	(404) 347-7000
	Savannah	(912) 944-4204
Hawaii	Honolulu	(808) 541-1782
Idaho	Boise	(208) 334-3857
Illinois	Chicago	(312) 353-4450
	Palatine	(312) 397-3000
	Rockford	(815) 987-8123
Indiana	Indianapolis	(317) 269-6214

State	City Location(s)	Telephone number(s)
Iowa	Des Moines	(515) 284-4222
Kansas	Wichita	(316) 269-6160
Kentucky	Louisville	(502) 582-5066
Louisiana	New Orleans	(504) 589-6546
Maine	Augusta	(207) 622-8249
Maryland	Baltimore	(410) 962-3560
Massachusetts	Boston	(617) 565-8563
Michigan	Detroit	(313) 226-3650
	Grand Rapids	(616) 456-2411
Minnesota	Minneapolis	(612) 348-1638
Mississippi	Jackson	(601) 965-4388
Missouri	St. Louis	(314) 425-3302
	Kansas City	(816) 426-3141
Montana	(Served by Denver)	(303) 844-3246
Nebraska	Omaha	(402) 221-3664
Nevada	Reno	(702) 784-5203
New Hampshire	(Served by Boston)	(617) 565-8563
New Jersey	Trenton	(609) 989-2100
New Mexico	Santa Fe	(505) 827-0264
	Albuquerque	(505) 766-2386
New York	New York	(212) 264-0634
	Buffalo	(716) 846-4191
	Rochester	(716) 263-6480
North Carolina	Greensboro	(919) 333-5345
North Dakota	(Served by Omaha)	(402) 221-3664
Ohio	Cincinnati	(513) 684-2944
	Cleveland	(216) 522-4750
Oklahoma	Oklahoma City	(405) 231-5302
	Tulsa	(918) 581-7650
Oregon	Portland	(503) 221-3001
Pennsylvania	Philadelphia	(215) 962-4980
	Pittsburgh	(412) 644-2850
Puerto Rico	San Juan	(809) 766-5555
Rhode Island	Providence	(401) 528-5104
South Carolina	Columbia	(803) 765-5345
	Charleston	(803) 724-4361
South Dakota	(Served by Omaha)	(402) 221-3664
Tennessee	Nashville	(615) 736-5161
	Memphis	(901) 521-4137

State	City Location(s)	Telephone number(s)
Texas	Dallas	(214) 767-0542
	Austin	(512) 482-5939
	Houston	(713) 229-2578
Utah	Salt Lake City	(801) 524-5116
Vermont	(Served by Boston)	(617) 565-8563
Virginia	Richmond	(804) 771-2246
Washington	Seattle	(206) 442-5616
	Spokane	(509) 456-4557
West Virginia	Charleston	(304) 347-5123
Wisconsin	Milwaukee	(414) 291-3473
Wyoming	(Served by Denver)	(303) 844-3246

Appendix C
American Chamber of Commerce Offices

Regional Headquarters

David A. Wicker, President
Association of American Chambers
  of Commerce in Latin America
National Distillers do Brazil
Av. Brig. Faria Lima, 4 e 5 Andar
01451 São Paolo, SP-Brazil
Phone: 813-4133

Argentina

Federico Dodds, President
Union Carbide Argentina
SAICS
Virrey Loreto 2477/81
1426 Buenos Aires, Argentina
Phone: 782-6016

Bolivia

Charles Bruce, President
The Anschutz Corporation
P.O. Box 160
La Paz, Bolivia
Phone: 35-55-74

Brazil: Rio de Janeiro

John P. Polychron, Director
  President
R. J. Reynolds Tobacos do Brazil
Raia de Botafogo, 440/25

P.O. Box 3588
22.250 Rio de Janeiro, RJ-Brazil
Phone: 286-6162

Brazil: São Paulo

Enrique Sosa, Director President
Empresas Dowda.
Caixa Postal 30037
01051, São Paolo, SP-Brazil
Phone: 212-1122

Chile

M. Wayne Sandvig, Director
Fundación Chile
Casilla 773
Santiago, Chile
Phone: 28-16-46

Colombia: Bogotá

William Wide, Chairman of the
  Board
Fiberglass Colombia S.A.
Apartado Aereo 9192
Bogotá, Colombia
Phone: 255-7900

Colombia: Cali

Richard Lee, General Manager
Goodyear de Colombia

Apartado Aereo 142
Cali, Valle, Colombia
Phone: 686-141, 689-868

Costa Rica

Federico A. Golcher, Managing
Partner
Peat, Marwick, Mitchell & Co.
Apartado 10208
1000 San José, Costa Rica
Phone: 21-52-22

Dominican Republic

Jack R. Rannik, President
Baez & Rannik, S.A.
P.O. Box 1221
Santo Domingo, Dominican
Republic
Phone: 565-6661

Ecuador: Quito

Robert L. Rice, General Manager
Xerox del Ecuador, S.A.
P.O. Box 174-A
Quito, Ecuador
Phone: 245-229, 451-614

Ecuador: Guayaquil

Carson Watson, Managing Director
Johnson & Johnson del Ecuador
Casilla 7206
Guayaquil, Ecuador
Phone: 39-96-00

El Salvador

Ramsey L. Moore, President
Moore Commercial S.A. de C.V.
29 Avenida Sur 817
P.O. Box 480
San Salvador, El Salvador
Phone: 71-1200

Guatemala

Spencer Manners, Vice President,
Latin American Operations
Foodpro International, Inc.
12 Calle 1-25, No. 1114
P.O. Box 89-A, Zona 10
Guatemala City, Guatemala
Phone: 320-490

Haiti

Robert L. Burgess, General
Manager
Sylvania Overseas Trading Corp.
P.O. Box 1005
Port-au-Prince, Haiti
Phone: 6-0037, 6-3859

Honduras

J. Mark Werner, Attorney-at-Law
21 Ave. S.O. 9 y 10
C. #88 Coloia Trejo
P.O. Box 500
San Pedro Sula, Honduras
Phone: 54-27-43, 54-42-58

Mexico

Purdy C. Jordan, Director
Embotelledora Tarahumara S.A. de
C.V.
Rio Amazonas No. 43
06500 Mexico City, Mexico
Phone: 591-0066
(Branch offices also in Monterrey
and Guadalajara)

Nicaragua

Julio Vigil, President
Vigil y Caligaris
Apartado 202
Managua, Nicaragua
Phone: 262-491

Panama

Robert M. Cooney, Vice President
Citibank, N.A.
Apartado 555
Panama 9A, Republica de Panama
Phone: 64-4044, 64-1255

Paraguay

Desiderio Enciso, Director
Petroleos Paraguayos
Chile y Olivia, Piso 4
Asunción, Paraguay

Peru

Miguel J. Godoy, President
M. J. Godoy & Co., S.A.

P.O. Box 5661
Lima 100, Peru
Phone: 28-7006, 28-7515

Uruguay

John Dale, Financial Director
General Motors Uruguay, S.A.
Sayago 1385
Casilla de Correo 234
Montevideo, Uruguay
Phone: 38-16-21/28

Venezuela

Donald H. Veach, Executive
    Director and General Manager
Carton de Venezuela, S.A.
Apartado 609
Caracas 1010, Venezuela

Appendix D

Inter-American Development Bank Offices

Argentina

Calle Esmeralda 130, Pisos 19y20
Casilla de Correo No. 181,
  Sucursal 1
Buenos Aires, Argentina

Bahamas

IBM Building, 4th Floor
P.O. Box N 3743
Nassau, Bahamas

Barbados

Maple Manor, Hastings
P.O. Box 402
Christ Church, Barbados

Bolivia

Edificio "BISA," 5 Piso
Avenida 16 de Julio No. 1628
La Paz, Bolivia

Brazil

Praia do Flamengo N 200, 21
  Andar
Caixa Postal 16209, Z0-01
22210 Rio de Janeiro, Brazil

Chile

Avenida Pedro de Valdivia 0193,
  11 Piso
Casilla No. 16611, Correo 9
  Providencia
Santiago, Chile

Colombia

Avenida 40 A No. 13-09, 8 Piso
Apartado Aereo 12037
Bogotá, Colombia

Costa Rica

Edificio Centro Colón, Piso 12
Paseo Colón entre Calles 38y40
San José, Costa Rica

Dominican Republic

Avenida Winston Churchill
  Esquina
Calle Luis F. Thomen, Torre BHD
Apartado Postal No. 1386
Santo Domingo, Dominican
  Republic

Ecuador

Avenida Amazonas 477 y Roca
Edificio Banco de los Andes, 9o,
  Piso

Apartado Postal 9041-Suc. 7
Quito, Ecuador

El Salvador

Condominio Torres del Bosque
Colonia La Moascota-10 Piso
Apartado Postal No. (01) 199
San Salvador, El Salvador

Guatemala

Edificio Geminis 10
12 Calle 1-25, Zona 10, Nivel 19
Apartado Postal 935
Guatemala City, Guatemala

Guyana

47 High Street, Kingston
P.O. Box 10867
Georgetown, Guyana

Haiti

Bâtiment de la Banque Nationale
  de Paris
Angle de la Rue Lemarre et Calve
Boîte Postale 1321
Port-au-Prince, Haiti

Honduras

Edificio Los Castanos, Pisos 5y6
Colonia Los Castanos
Apartado Postal No. C-73
Tegucigalpa, Honduras

Jamaica

40-46 Knutsford Boulevard, 6th
  Floor
P.O. Box 429
Kingston 10, Jamaica

Mexico

Paseo de la Reforma 379, 7 Piso
Col. Cuauhtemoc
Delegacíon Cuauhtemoc
06500 Mexico, DF, Mexico

Nicaragua

Edificio BID
Kilometro 4-1/2 Carretera a
  Masaya
Apartado Postal 2512
Managua, Nicaragua

Panama

Avenida Samuel Lewis
Edificio Banco Union, Piso 14
Apartado Postal 7297
Panama 5, Panama

Paraguay

Edificio Aurora I
Calle Caballero Esquina
Eligio Ayala, Pisos 2y3
Cailla 1209, Asunción, Paraguay

Peru

Paseo de la Republica, 3245, 14
  Piso
Apartado Postal No. 3778
San Isidro
Lima 27, Peru

Suriname

Zwartenhovewn Brugstraat
32 Boven
Paramaribo, Suriname

Trinidad and Tobago

Tatil Building, 11 Maravel Road
P.O. Box 68
Port of Spain, Trinidad

Uruguay

Andes 1365, 13 Piso
Casilla de Correo 5029, Sucursal 1
Montevideo, Uruguay

Venezuela

Nucleo A, Piso 16
Conjunto Miranda
Multicentro Empresarial del Este
Avenida Liberador, Chacao
Caracas 1060, Venezuela

Appendix E

Major Latin American Export Credit Insurers

Argentina

Compañia Argentina de Seguros
de Credito, S.A. (CASC)
Sarmiento 440, 4o Piso
1347 Buenos Aires, Argentina

Brazil

Instituto de Resseguros do Brazil
(IRB)
Avenida Marechal Camara, 171
Rio de Janeiro, GB Brazil

Mexico

Banco de Mexico SA
Fondo de las Exportaciónes de
Productos Manufacturados
(Fondo)
Avenida 5 de Mayo No. 2
Mexico DF, Mexico

Source: Caribbean/Central American Action.

Appendix F

Caribbean Regional Organizations

Caribbean Association of Industry
and Commerce
P.O. Box 259
Musson Building, 2nd Floor
Hincks Street
Bridgetown, Barbados
Phone: (809) 436-6385

Caribbean Community and
Common Market (CARICOM)
Bank of Guyana Building
P.O. Box 10827
Georgetown, Guyana
Phone: (02) 69285

Caribbean Congress of Labor
Bridgetown, Barbados
(Phone: unavailable)

Caribbean Development Bank
P.O. Box 408 Wildey
St. Michael, Barbados
Phone: (809) 429-7216

Caribbean Employers'
Confederation
Port of Spain, Trinidad
Phone: (809) 625-4723

Caribbean Food and Nutrition
Institute
Port of Spain, Trinidad
Phone: (809) 662-7025

Caribbean Hotel Association
18 Marseilles Street, Suite 1-A
Santurce, Puerto Rico 00907-1672
Phone: (809) 725-9139
Fax: (809) 725-9108

Caribbean Tourism Organization
Mer Vue, Marine Gardens
Christ Church, Barbados
Phone: (809) 427-5242
Fax: (809) 697-4258

East Caribbean Common Market
Antigua Sugar Factory
Gunthrop, Antigua
Phone: (809) 463-3500

East Caribbean Central Bank
P.O. Box 89
Basseterre, St. Kitts
Phone: (809) 253-7138

Organization of Eastern Caribbean
States
Bridge Street
Castries, St. Lucia
Phone: (809) 462-3500

Sugar Association of the Caribbean
P.O. Box 230
80 Abercromby Street
Port of Spain, Trinidad
(Phone: unavailable)

Appendix G

Caribbean and Central American Trade Promotion Organizations

Caribbean Association of Industry
and Commerce
P.O. Box 259
Musson Building, 2nd Floor
Lower Hincks Street
Bridgetown, Barbados
Phone: (809) 436-6385
Fax: (809) 436-9937

Costa Rican Coalition of
Development Initiatives
(CINDE)
P.O. Box 7170-1000
San José, Costa Rica
Phone: (506) 20-00-36
Fax: (506) 20-47-54

Eastern Caribbean Investment
Promotion Service
1730 M Street, NW, Suite 901
Washington, DC 20036
Phone: (202) 659-8689
Fax: (202) 659-9127

Economic Development
Administration (FOMENTO)
355 F.D. Roosevelt Avenue
G.P.O. Box 2350
Hato Rey, Puerto Rico 00918

Phone: (809) 765-0358
Fax: (809) 754-9645

Entrepreneurial Chamber of
Commerce
Edificio de Industria
9 Nivel, Ruta 6. 9-21, Zona 4
Guatemala City, Guatemala
Phone: (502) 2-316-513
(Fax: same as phone number)

Federation of Private Businesses of
Central America and Panama
Apartado 539-1002
Barrio Francisco Peralta
Avenida 8, Entre Calle 33 y 35
San José, Costa Rica
Phone: (506) 53-9815
Fax: (506) 25-2025

Foreign Investment Promotion
Council
Apartado 21291
Avenida Abraham Lincoln
Edificio Alico, 2 Piso
Santo Domingo, Dominican
Republic
Phone: (809) 532-3281
Fax: (809) 533-7029

Foundation for Investments and
   Development of Exports
2 Nivel, Centro Commercial Maya
Boulevard Morazan, Apartado
   Postal 2029
Tegucigalpa, D.C., Honduras
Phone: (504) 3-2-9345
Fax: (504) 3-1-1808

Haitian Investment and Export
   Promotion Center
John Brown Avenue
P.O. Box 1621
Port-au-Prince, Haiti
Phone: (509) 1-2-6381
Fax: (509) 1-2-8005

Honduran Council of Private
   Enterprise
Edificio la Plazuela, 1er Piso
Barrio La Plazuela, Honduras
Phone: (504) 3-7-4371
Fax: (504) 3-7-4339

Jamaica Promotion (Jampro)
35 Trafalgar Road
Kingston 5, Jamaica
Phone: (809) 929-7190
Fax: (809) 924-9650

Joint Agribusiness Consulting and
   Coinvestment Council, Inc.
Alberto Laranquent 16
Ensdanche Naco
Apartado Postal 388-9
Santo Domingo, Dominican
   Republic
Phone: (809) 541-6644
Fax: (809) 451-4565

National Association for the
   Economic Development of
   Panama
Apartado Postal 503

Panama 9A, Panama
Phone: (507) 63-5878
Fax: (507) 64-9280

National Association of Private
   Enterprise
Apartado Postal 1207
Almeda Roosevelt y 55 Avenida
   Sur, #2827
San Salvador, El Salvador
Phone: (503) 24-1236
Fax: (503) 23-8932

National Council of Private
   Enterprise
Apartado 1276
Zona 1, Calle Aquilino de la
   Guardia No. 19
Panama 1, Republic of Panama
Phone: (507) 63-51-97
Fax: (507) 6-4-2384

Panama Promotion Group
Apartado Postal 55-1297
Estafeta de Paitilla
Panama City, Panama
Phone: (507) 64-3000
Fax: (507) 64-2815

Superior Council of Private
   Enterprise
Apartado 5430
Managua, Nicaragua
Phone: (505) 2-2-7130
Fax: (505) 2-2-7136

Salvadoran Foundation for
   Economic and Social
   Development (FUSADES)
Edificio la Centroamericana
Apartado Postal 01-278
San Salvador, El Salvador
Phone: (503) 2-3-2738
Fax: (503) 2-3-4723

Appendix H
New York Offices of Latin American Banks

Argentina

Banco de Galicia & Buenos Aires
300 Park Avenue, 20th Floor
New York, NY 10022
Phone: (212) 906-3700
Fax: (212) 906-3777
Attn: M. Sempe; staff, 2

Banco de la Nación
299 Park Avenue, 2nd Floor
New York, NY 10071
Phone: (212) 303-0600
Fax: (212) 303-0805
Attn: Jorge L. Volpini; staff, 85

Banco de la Provincia de Buenos
  Aires
650 Fifth Avenue, 30th Floor
New York, NY 10019
Phone: (212) 397-7650
Fax: (212) 397-7676
Attn: O. Salvestrini; staff, 30

Banco Quilmes
366 Madison Avenue, Suite 1052
New York, NY 10017
Phone: (212) 867-3460
Fax: (212) 867-4193
Attn: J. G. Franco; staff, 3

Banco Rio de la Plata
650 Fifth Avenue, 29th Floor
New York, NY 10019

Phone: (212) 974-6800
Fax: (212) 974-6828
Attn: Bernardo Lanardonne; staff,
  25

Brazil

Banco Bamerindus do Brasil
10 East 50th Street, 28th Floor
New York, NY 10022
Phone: (212) 478-5700
Fax: (212) 888-5878
Attn: Anthony Pain; staff, 40

Banco Bandeirantes
280 Park Avenue, 38th Floor
New York, NY 10017
Phone: (212) 972-7455
Fax: (212) 949-9158
Attn: R. L. Paladini; staff, 5

Banco Bradesco
450 Park Avenue, 32nd Floor
New York, NY 10022
Phone: (212) 688-9855
Fax: (212) 754-4032
Attn: J. J. de Faria; staff, 30

Banco do Brasil
550 Fifth Avenue
New York, NY 10036
Phone: (212) 626-7000
Fax: (212) 626-7045
Attn: R. M. Franco; staff, 208

Banco de Crédito Nacional
499 Park Avenue
New York, NY 10022
Phone: (212) 980-8383
Fax: (212) 755-0626
Attn: C. V. Barison; staff, 28

Banco Económico
499 Park Avenue, 20th Floor
New York, NY 10022
Phone: (212) 758-3700
Fax: (212) 758-3881
Attn: J. R. D. de Azevedo; staff, 27

Banco do Estado do Parana
125 West 55th Street, Suite 900
New York, NY 10019
Phone: (212) 956-0011
Fax: (212) 956-0506
Attn: Marcos Gomes; staff, 8

Banco do Estado do Rio Grande
  do Sul
500 Fifth Avenue, Suite 1238
New York, NY 10110
Phone: (212) 827-0390
Fax: (212) 869-0844
Attn: C. R. Becker; staff, 3

Banco do Estado do Rio de Janeiro
55 East 59th Street, 18th Floor
New York, NY 10022
Phone: (212) 759-7878
Fax: (212) 759-7288
Attn: A. J. E. Cavour; staff, 6

Banco do Estado de São Paulo
153 East 53rd Street
New York, NY 10022
Phone: (212) 888-9550
Fax: (212) 371-1034
Attn: L. L. Marangoni; staff, 51

Banco Itau
540 Madison Avenue
New York, NY 10022
Phone: (212) 486-1280
Fax: (212) 888-9342
Attn: L. A. Serra; staff, 23

Banco Mercantil de São Paulo
450 Park Avenue, 14th Floor
New York, NY 10583
Phone: (212) 888-0030
Fax: (212) 888-4631
Attn: C. N. Ryan; staff, 12

Banco Nacional
645 Fifth Avenue
New York, NY 10022
Phone: (212) 935-6920
Fax: (212) 593-2611
Attn: Edson F. da Silva; staff, 16

Banco Real
680 Fifth Avenue, 3rd Floor
New York, NY 10019
Phone: (212) 489-0100
Fax: (212) 307-5627
Attn: H. M. de Carvalho; staff, 67

Banco Safra
Safra National Bank of New York
1114 Avenue of the Americas
New York, NY 10036
Phone: (212) 382-9200
Fax: (212) 768-8972
Attn: J. Cho; staff, 35

Unibanco
555 Madison Avenue
New York, NY 10022
Phone: (212) 832-1700
Fax: (212) 754-4872
Attn: R. F. Lima; staff, 30

Chile

Banco Central de Chile
200 Liberty Street, Suite 5127
New York, NY 10048
Phone: (212) 432-0680
Fax: (212) 423-0747
Attn: F. Kreis; staff, 3

Banco de Chile
124 East 55th Street
New York, NY 10022
Phone: (212) 758-0909

Fax: (212) 593-9770
Attn: Hernan Donoso; staff, 25

Banco Santiago
375 Park Avenue, Suite 2605
New York, NY 10152
Phone: (212) 826-0550
Fax: (212) 826-1218
Attn: J. A. Valenzuela; staff, 2

Banco Sud Americano
200 Liberty Street, Suite 8947
New York, NY 10048
Phone: (212) 938-5896
Fax: (212) 938-5985
Attn: J. N. Myers; staff, 2

Colombia

Banco de Bogotá Trust
375 Park Avenue
New York, NY 10152
Phone: (212) 826-0250
Fax: (212) 715-4313
Attn: Richard Backus; staff, 59

Banco Popular Dominicano
BPD International
4186 Broadway
New York, NY 10033
Phone: (212) 581-4430
Fax: (212) 581-4520
Attn: L. A. Canela; staff, 43

Mexico

Banamex
767 Fifth Avenue
New York, NY 10153
Phone: (212) 751-5090
Fax: (212) 303-1489
Attn: C. Sotomayor; staff, 100

Banca Serfin
88 Pine Street, 26th Floor
New York, NY 10005
Phone: (212) 574-9500
Fax: (212) 344-0727
Attn: J. de la Torre; staff, 60

Banco Internacional
45 Broadway, 16th Floor
New York, NY 10006
Phone: (212) 480-0111
Fax: (212) 635-2086
Attn: M. Guillermin; staff, 65

Bancomer
115 East 54th Street
New York, NY 10022
Phone: (212) 759-7600
Fax: (212) 832-8459
Attn: C. Harrison Smith; staff, 88

Banco Mexicano Somex
235 Fifth Avenue
New York, NY 10016
Phone: (212) 679-8000
Fax: (212) 951-2085
Attn: C. Peralta; staff, 65

Multibanco Comermex
1 Exchange Plaza, 16th Floor
New York, NY 10006
Phone: (212) 701-0100
Fax: (212) 422-3559
Attn: R. Rivera; staff, 38

Nacional Financiera
450 Park Avenue, Suite 401
New York, NY 10022
Phone: (212) 753-8030
Fax: (212) 753-8033
Attn: Hector F. Aizcorbe; staff, 6

Panama

Banco Latinoamericano de
  Exportaciónes
750 Lexington Avenue, 26th Floor
New York, NY 10022
Phone: (212) 754-2600
Fax: (212) 754-2606
Attn: Daniel A. Casal; staff, 7

Uruguay

Banco de la Republica Oriental
  del Uruguay

1270 Avenue of the Americas,
Suite 30F
Phone: (212) 307-9600
Fax: (212) 307-6786
Attn: W. Calcagno; staff, 14

Venezuela

Banco Consolidado
220 East 51st Street
New York, NY 10022
Phone: (212) 980-1770
Fax: (212) 644-9809
Attn: R. Santandreu; staff, 45

Banco de la Guaira
Venezuelan American Banking
Corporation
55 East 59th Street
New York, NY 10022
Phone: (212) 888-9400
Fax: (212) 838-9629
Attn: R. M. Lanza; staff, 9

Banco Industrial de Venezuela
400 Park Avenue
New York, NY 10022
Phone: (212) 688-2200
Fax: 832-1588
Attn: Ana Drossos; staff, 60

Banco Interamericano
630 Fifth Avenue, 31st Floor
New York, NY 10111
Phone: (212) 459-0310
Fax: (212) 459-0315
Attn: Ian de Andrade; staff, 2

Banco Mercantil
410 Park Avenue, 16th Floor
New York, NY 10022
Phone: (212) 838-4455
Fax: (212) 374-1711
Attn: F. R. Fernandez; staff, 14

Banco Union
609 Fifth Avenue, 2nd Floor
New York, NY 10017
Phone: (212) 735-1500
Fax: (212) 735-1551
Attn: A. J. Gonzalez; staff, 31

Banco de Venezuela
500 Park Avenue
New York, NY 10022
Phone: (212) 980-0350
Fax: (212) 593-3948
Attn: G. Franceschi; staff, 30

Source: *The Banker.*

Appendix I
Key Contacts for Doing Business in Mexico

Mexican Contacts in Mexico

For Customs Information

Dirección General de Aduanas
Secretaria de Hacienda y Credito
  Publico
20 de Noviembre No. 195
6 Piso, C.P. 06090
Mexico 1, DF, Mexico
Phone: (011) (52) 585-0525

For Business Information:

Confederación de Camaras
Nacionales de Comercio
Servicios y Tourismo
Balderas 144, 2 y 3 Pisos
Apartado 113 Bis
Centro Cuauhtemoc
06079 Mexico, DF, Mexico
Phone: (011) (52) 709-1559

Camara Nacional de Comercio
  de la Ciudad de Mexico Paseo
  de la Reforma 42
Apartado 32005
Mexico 1, DF, Mexico
Telex: 1777318 CCNCME

American Contacts in Mexico

U.S. Embassy
Paseo de la Reforma 305
06500 Mexico, DF, Mexico
Phone: (011) (905) 211-0042

U.S. Trade Center
Liverpool 31
06600 Mexico, DF, Mexico
Phone: (011) (905) 591-0155

John D. Perkins, Minister
  Counselor for Commercial
  Affairs
U.S. Consulate General
Foreign Commercial Service
Progreso 175
44100 Guadalajara, Jalisco, Mexico

Mexican Contacts in the United States

Mexican Embassy
2829 16th Street, NW
Washington, DC 20009
Phone: (202) 234-6000

Consulate General of Mexico
8 East 41st Street
New York, NY 10017
Phone: (212) 689-0456

Consulate General of Mexico
125 Paseo de la Plaza
Los Angeles, CA 90012
Phone: (213) 624-3261

Trade Commission of Mexico

225 North Michigan Avenue, Suite
708
Illinois Center
Chicago, IL 60601
Phone: (312) 856-0316

2777 Stemmons Freeway, Suite
1622
Dallas, TX 75207
Phone: (214) 688-4095

8484 Wilshire Boulevard, Suite 740
Beverly Hills, CA 90211
Phone: (213) 655-6421

229 Peachtree Street, NE
Cain Tower Building, Suite 917

Atlanta, GA 30343
Phone: (404) 522-5373

100 Biscayne Boulevard, Suite 1601
Miami, FL 33132
Phone: (305) 372-9929

150 East 58th Street, 17th Floor
New York, NY 10155
Phone: (212) 826-2916

Mexican-American Chambers of Commerce

Mexican Chamber of Commerce of
the County of Los Angeles
125 Paseo de la Plaza, Room 404
Los Angeles, CA 90012
Phone: (213) 688-7330

Mexican Chamber of Commerce of
the United States
730 Fifth Avenue, 9th Floor
New York, NY 10019
Phone: (212) 333-8728

U.S.–Mexican Chamber of
Commerce
1900 L Street, NW, Suite 612
Washington, DC 20036
Phone: (202) 296-5198

Appendix J

Foreign Trade Organizations in the United States

U.S. Trade Promotion Organizations

American Association of Exporters
and Importers
11 West 42nd Street
New York, NY 10036
Phone: (212) 944-2230

Federation of International Trade
  Associations
1851 Alexander Bell Drive
Reston, VA 22091
Phone: (703) 391-6108

National Council on International
  Trade and Documentation
350 Broadway, Suite 205
New York, NY 10013
Phone: (212) 925-1400

United States Council for
  International Business
1212 Avenue of the Americas
New York, NY 10036
Phone: (212) 354-4480

World Trade Centers Association
  (WTCA)

One World Trade Center, 55th
  Floor
New York, NY 10048
Phone: (212) 313-4600

Foreign Government Trade Offices

Argentina Trade Office
900 Third Avenue, 4th Floor
New York, NY 10022
Phone: (212) 759-6477

Argentina Trade Office
Two Illinois Center, Suite 1408
233 North Michigan Avenue
Chicago, IL 60601
Phone: (312) 565-2466

Argentina Trade Office
2000 Post Oak Boulevard, Suite
  1840
Houston, TX 77056
Phone: (713) 871-8890

Argentina Trade Office
3580 Wilshire Boulevard, Suite
  1412
Los Angeles, CA 90010
Phone: (213) 623-3230

Argentina Trade Office
Royal Bank Center, Suite 803
Hato Rey, Puerto Rico 00917
Phone: (809) 756-6100

Brazilian Government Trade
Bureau
551 Fifth Avenue, Suite 201
New York, NY 10176
Phone: (212) 916-3200

British Trade and Investment
Office
845 Third Avenue
New York, NY 10022
Phone: (212) 745-0495

Canadian Commercial Corporation
Embassy of Canada
501 Pennsylvania Avenue, NW
Washington, DC 20001
Phone: (202) 682-1740

Colombian Export Promotion
Agency
259 Park Avenue
New York, NY 10177
Phone: (212) 972-7474

Colombian Export Promotion
Agency
One Biscayne Tower, Suite 2570
2 South Biscayne Boulevard
Miami, FL 33131
Phone: (305) 374-3144

Colombian Government Trade
Bureau
Embassy Commercial Section
1701 Pennsylvania Avenue, NW,
Suite 560
Washington, DC 20006
Phone: (202) 463-6679

Invest-in-France
610 Fifth Avenue, Suite 301
New York, NY 10020
Phone: (212) 757-9340

Netherlands Foreign Investment
Agency
One Rockefeller Center, 11th Floor
New York, NY 10020
Phone: (212) 246-1434

Foreign Chambers of Commerce

Argentine-American Chamber of
Commerce
10 Rockefeller Plaza, Suite 1001
New York, NY 10020
Phone: (212) 698-2238

Brazilian-American Chamber of
Commerce
80 South 8th Street, 18th Floor
Miami, FL 33130
Phone: (305) 579-9030

Colombian-American Chamber of
Commerce
150 Nassau Street, Suite 2015
New York, NY 10038
Phone: (212) 233-7776

Latin American Manufacturing
Association
419 New Jersey Avenue, SE
Washington, DC 20003
Phone: (202) 546-3803

North American–Chilean Chamber
of Commerce
220 East 81st Street
New York, NY 10028
Phone: (212) 288-5691

Puerto Rico Chamber of
Commerce of the United States
212 West 79th Street, 2nd Floor
New York, NY 10024
Phone: (212) 724-4731

Trinidad and Tobago Chamber of
   Commerce of the United States
c/o Trintoc Services, Ltd.
400 Madison Avenue, Room 803
New York, NY 10017
Phone: (212) 759-3388

Venezuelan-American Association
   of the United States
115 Broadway, Room 1110
New York, NY 10006
Phone: (212) 233-7776

Appendix K

U.S. Department of Commerce Trade Development Officers

Industry Organization	Phone Number*
Central office	377-1461
Aerospace	377-8228
Automotive	377-0823
Chemicals and allied products	377-0128
Consumer goods	377-0337
Computer and business equipment	377-0572
Energy	377-1466
Export trading companies	377-5131
Forest products and domestic construction	377-0384
General industrial machinery	377-5455
Instrumentation	377-5466
Medical services	377-0550
Major projects and international construction	377-5225
Metals, minerals, and commodities	377-0575
Microelectronics and instrumentation	377-2587
Service industries	377-3575
Special industrial machinery	377-0302
Telecommunications	377-4466
Textiles	377-5078
Trade information analysis	377-1316
Export statistics and trade data (foreign)	377-4211
Export statistics and trade data (domestic)	377-4211

*All in area code 202.

Appendix L

Cities and States Participating in Eximbank's City-State Agency Cooperation Program

Cities	Programs
Dianne Allen, Manager Columbus Economic Development Program 99 North Front Street Columbus, OH 43215 Phone: (614) 645-8172	Counseling, loan packaging, referral service for Eximbank/ FCIA*
Marian Zorn, Director City Economic Office Room 2008, City Hall Los Angeles, CA 90012 Phone: (213) 485-6154	Complete range of financial assistance for Eximbank/FCIA, including funding capabilities
Rosie Roediger, Executive Director Tucson Local Development Corp. P.O. Box 27210 Tucson, AZ 85726-5413 Phone: (602) 791-4444	WCGP** packaging and funding location

States	Programs
Irene L. Fisher, Director California Export Finance Office 107 South Broadway, Suite 8039 Los Angeles, CA 90012 Phone: (213) 620-2433	Financial advice, FCIA* umbrella policy, and pre- and post-shipment loans guarantee packaging
Marie V. Torres, Director Export Finance Program Maryland Industrial Development Financing Authority World Trade Center, 7th Floor 401 East Pratt Street Baltimore, MD 21202-3042 Phone: (301) 333-8189	Trade finance structuring, WCGP** packaging location, and FCIA umbrella policy
Mark Chin, Associate Massachusetts Industrial Finance Agency 400 Atlantic Avenue Boston, MA 02110 Phone: (617) 451-2477	WCGP packaging location
Harry H. Weinberg, President Nevada State Development Corp. 350 South Center, Suite 310 Reno, NV 89501 Phone: (702) 323-3625	Counseling, loan packaging, and referral service for Eximbank/FCIA
Barry Watkins, Finance Manager Xport Trading Co. Port of NY/NJ One World Trade Center, 63E New York, NY 10048 Phone: (212) 466-4107/3248	Trade finance structuring, WCGP packaging, and FCIA umbrella policy

Tim Durgan, Export Finance
  Coordinator
Michigan Export Development
  Authority
4th Floor, Ottawa Towers North
Lansing, MI 48909
Phone: (517) 373-1054
	Trade finance structuring, WCGP packaging, and FCIA umbrella policy

States	Programs
H. Scott Plummer, Finance Program Specialist North Carolina Department of Economic and Community Development 430 North Salisbury Street Raleigh, NC 27611 Phone: (919) 733-2829	WCGP packaging and FCIA umbrella policy
David G. Wantland, Director Oklahoma Department of Commerce Export Finance Program 6601 Broadway, P.O. Box 26980 Oklahoma City, OK 73126-0980 Phone: (405) 841-5199	Trade finance structuring, WCGP packaging, FCIA umbrella policy, and foreign accounts receivable financing
Owen Kane, Marketing Staff Specialist Pennsylvania Department of Commerce Office of International Development 486 Forum Building Harrisburg, PA 17120 Phone: (717) 787-7190	WCGP packaging location
Ed Sosa, Export Finance Coordinator Texas Department of Commerce Finance Division P.O. Box 12728 Austin, TX 78711 Phone: (512) 320-9662	Ten-city network for WCGP packaging and FCIA umbrella policy
James E. Herrin, Trade Executive Division of Business and Economic Development 324 South State Street, Suite 200 Salt Lake City, UT 84111 Phone: (801) 538-8731	WCGP packaging location

States	Programs

Kenneth Keach, President
Export Assistance Center of
  Washington
2001 6th Avenue, Suite 1700
Seattle, WA 98121
Phone: (206) 464-7123
	Trade finance structuring and
	  WCGP packaging

* FCIA = Federal Credit Insurance Association.
** WCGP = Working Capital Guarantee Program.

Index